THE CALL OF THE TRIBE

THE
CALL
OF THE
TRIBE

MARIO VARGAS LLOSA

TRANSLATED FROM THE SPANISH BY
JOHN KING

FARRAR, STRAUS AND GIROUX
NEW YORK

•

Farrar, Straus and Giroux
120 Broadway, New York 10271

Library of Congress Control Number: 2022945777
ISBN: 978-0-374-11805-1

Designed by Abby Kagan

Our books may be purchased in bulk for promotional, educational, or business
use. Please contact your local bookseller or the Macmillan Corporate and
Premium Sales Department at 1-800-221-7945, extension 5442, or by email at
MacmillanSpecialMarkets@macmillan.com.

www.fsgbooks.com
www.twitter.com/fsgbooks • www.facebook.com/fsgbooks

1   3   5   7   9   10   8   6   4   2

For Gerardo Bongiovanni,
promoter of liberal ideas and loyal friend

CONTENTS

THE CALL OF THE TRIBE

THE CALL OF THE TRIBE

I would never have written this book had I not read Edmund Wilson's *To the Finland Station* more than twenty years ago. This fascinating study traces the evolution of the idea of socialism from the moment when the French historian Jules Michelet, intrigued by a quotation, started to learn Italian to read Giambattista Vico, up to the arrival of Lenin at the Finland Station in Saint Petersburg, on April 16, 1917, to lead the Russian Revolution. I then had the idea for a book that would do for liberalism what the American critic had done for socialism: an essay that, starting in the small Scottish town of Kirkcaldy with the birth of Adam Smith in 1723, would trace the evolution of liberal ideas through their main exponents and the historical and social events that caused them to spread throughout the world. Although it is quite different from Edmund Wilson's book, this was the early inspiration for *The Call of the Tribe*.

It might not seem so, but this is an autobiographical work. It describes my own intellectual and political history, the journey from the Marxism and Sartrean existentialism of my youth to the liberalism of my mature years, a route that took me through a reappraisal of democracy helped by my readings of writers such as Albert Camus, George Orwell, and Arthur

Koestler. I was being drawn to liberalism by certain political events and, above all, by the ideas of the seven authors to whom I dedicate these pages: Adam Smith, José Ortega y Gasset, Friedrich August von Hayek, Karl Popper, Raymond Aron, Isaiah Berlin, and Jean-François Revel.

I discovered politics when I was twelve, in October 1948, when a military coup in Peru led by General Manuel Apolinario Odría overthrew president José Luis Bustamante y Rivero, a relative of my mother's family. I think that it was during Odría's eight-year reign that I developed a hatred for dictators of any stripe, one of the few invariable constants in my political outlook. But I only became aware of the social dimension, that Peru was a country weighed down by injustice, where a minority of privileged people exploited the vast majority in abusive fashion, when, in 1952, I read *Out of the Night* by Jan Valtin in my final year of school. This book led me to go against the wishes of my family, who wanted me to attend the Catholic University—then the place where wealthy young Peruvians studied—as I applied to San Marcos University, a public, popular university, not cowed by the military dictatorship, where, I was sure, I would be able to join the Communist Party. The party had almost been eradicated by Odría's repressive measures when I entered San Marcos in 1953 to study literature and law, its leaders imprisoned, killed, or forced into exile; and it was trying to reconstitute itself as the Cahuide Group that I belonged to for a year.

It was there that I received my first lessons in Marxism, in clandestine study groups, where we read José Carlos Mariátegui, Georges Politzer, Marx, Engels, and Lenin, and we had intense discussions about socialist realism and "left-wing" communism, branded by Lenin as "an infantile disorder." The great admiration I felt for Sartre, who I read devotedly, inured me against dogma—we Peruvian communists at that time were, in the words of Salvador Garmendia, "few but very sectarian"—and in my reading group I adhered to Sartre's theory that upheld historical materialism and class struggle but not dialectical materialism, which caused my comrade Félix Arias Schreiber to label me in one of our discussions as "subhuman."

I left the Cahuide Group at the end of 1954 but I remained, I believe, a socialist, at least in my readings, an interest that took on fresh impetus with the struggle of Fidel Castro and his *barbudos* in the Sierra Maestra and the triumph of the Cuban Revolution in the final days of 1958. For my generation, and not just in Latin America, what happened in Cuba was decisive, an ideological watershed. Many people, as I did, saw Fidel's epic achievement as a heroic and generous adventure, of idealistic fighters who wanted to end the corrupt dictatorship of the Batista regime, and also as a means of establishing a nonsectarian socialism that would allow for criticism, diversity, and even dissidence. Many of us believed this, which explains why, in its early years, the Cuban Revolution had such great support the world over.

In November 1962 I was in Mexico, sent by Radiodiffusion-Télévision Française, where I worked as a journalist, to cover an exhibition that France had organized in Chapultepec Park, when the Cuban missile crisis erupted. I was sent to cover this event and was on the last flight by Cubana Airlines to leave Mexico before the blockade. Cuba was in a state of general mobilization, fearing an imminent invasion by U.S. marines. It was an impressive sight. Along the Malecón, small antiaircraft guns called *bocachicas* were operated by young men, almost boys, who put up with the low-level flights of U.S. Sabre jets without firing at them, and radio and television gave instructions to the people as to what to do when the bombing started. What they were living through brought to mind the emotion and enthusiasm of a free and hopeful people described in Orwell's *Homage to Catalonia*, when he reached Barcelona as a volunteer at the beginning of the Spanish Civil War. Profoundly moved by what seemed to me to be the personification of socialism in freedom, I joined a long queue to donate blood. Thanks to my old companion at the University of Madrid, Ambrosio Fornet, and the Peruvian Hilda Gadea, who had met Che Guevara in Guatemala during the Jacobo Arbenz regime and had married and had a daughter with him in Mexico, I spent time with a number of writers connected to Casa de las Américas and its president, Haydée Santamaría, whom I met briefly. When I left, some weeks later, young people were singing in the streets of Havana, "Nikita/mariquita/lo que se da/no se quita" ("Nikita, you little poof, what's given can't be taken back") because the Soviet leader had accepted Kennedy's ultimatum and withdrawn the missiles from the island. Only afterward did it become known that in this secret agreement John F. Kennedy had promised Khrushchev that in return for the removal of the weapons, the United States would refrain from invading Cuba and would withdraw its Jupiter missiles based in Turkey.

My support for the Cuban Revolution lasted for most of the sixties. I traveled five times to Cuba as a member of the International Council of Writers affiliated with Casa de Las Américas and I defended the revolution in manifestos, articles, and public acts, both in France, where I was living, and in Latin America, where I traveled quite regularly. In those years I took up my Marxist readings again, not only the classics but also work by writers identified with the Communist Party, or close to it, like György Lukács, Antonio Gramsci,

Lucien Goldmann, Frantz Fanon, Régis Debray, Che Guevara, and even the ultraorthodox Louis Althusser, professor at the École Normale, who later became insane and killed his wife. However, I remember that, during my years in Paris, once a week I would stealthily buy a copy of the paper deplored by the left, *Le Figaro*, to read the column by Raymond Aron, whose penetrating analyses of current events made me uneasy but also captivated me.

Several events at the end of the sixties began to distance me from Marxism. There was the creation of the UMAP camps in Cuba, where, behind the euphemistic term, Military Units to Aid Production, there lay the reality of concentration camps where counterrevolutionaries were kept with homosexuals and common criminals. My visit to the U.S.S.R. in 1968, when I was invited to a commemoration related to Pushkin, left me with a bad taste in my mouth. I discovered there that, had I been a Russian, I would have been a dissident in that country (that is, a pariah) or I would have been rotting in the Gulag. That made me feel somewhat traumatized. Sartre, Simone de Beauvoir, Merleau-Ponty, and the journal *Les Temps Modernes* had convinced me that, despite everything that was wrong with the U.S.S.R., it represented progress and the future, a country where, as Paul Éluard put it in a poem that I knew by heart, "there are no prostitutes or thieves or priests." But there was poverty, drunks sprawled in the street, and a widespread apathy; one felt everywhere a collective claustrophobia due to the lack of information about what was happening inside the country and in the rest of the world. One just had to look around to realize that although class divisions based on money might have disappeared, in the U.S.S.R. the inequalities were enormous and were exclusively related to power. I asked a talkative Russian, "Who are the most privileged people here?"

He replied, "Submissive writers. They have dachas for their holidays and they can travel abroad. That puts them way above ordinary men and women. You can't ask for more!" Could I defend this model of society, as I had been doing, knowing now that it would have been unlivable for me? And my disappointment with Sartre was another important factor, the day I read in *Le Monde* an interview with Madeleine Chapsal where he stated that African writers should give up literature and dedicate themselves first and foremost to revolution and to creating a country where literature might then become possible. He also declared that, faced with a child dying of hunger, "*La Nausée* ne fait pas le poids" ("*Nausea* has no weight"). I felt I had been knifed in the back. How could he say that, this man who had made us believe that writing was a form of action, that words were acts, that writing influenced history? Now it turned out that literature was just a luxury that could only be allowed in countries that had achieved socialism. At that time I began to read Camus again and to agree with him, realizing that he had been right in his famous polemic with Sartre over the Soviet concentration camps. His idea that assassinations and terror began when morality became divorced from politics was as plain as could be. I later charted this evolution in my thinking in a short book that brought together articles on both writers that I had written in the sixties: *Entre Sartre y Camus (Between Sartre and Camus).**

My break with Cuba, and, to some extent with socialism, came as a result of the then very famous (though now almost no one remembers it) Padilla affair. The poet Heberto Padilla, an active participant in the Cuban Revolution—he became

---

* Mario Vargas Llosa, *Entre Sartre y Camus*, Ediciones Huracán, San Juan, Puerto Rico, 1981.

vice minister of Foreign Trade—began to make some criticism of the cultural politics of the regime in 1970. He was first virulently attacked by the official press and then jailed, with the absurd accusation that he was a CIA agent. Indignant at this news, five friends who knew him—Juan and Luis Goytisolo, Hans Magnus Enzensberger, Josep María Castellet, and I—drafted a letter of protest in my apartment in Barcelona, which was signed by many writers throughout the world, including Sartre, Simone de Beauvoir, Susan Sontag, Alberto Moravia, and Carlos Fuentes, all protesting this outrage. Fidel Castro replied in person, accusing us of serving imperialism and stating that we would not step on Cuban soil again for "an indefinite and infinite period of time" (that is, for all eternity).

Despite the campaign of abuse that I received as a result of this manifesto, it lifted a great weight from me; I would now no longer have to feign an adherence that I did not feel to what was happening in Cuba. However, it took me a few years to break with socialism and reassess the meaning of democracy. It was a period of uncertainty and reappraisal during which I slowly began to understand that the "formal freedoms" of so-called bourgeois democracy were not a mere appearance that covered up the exploitation of the poor by the rich, but rather the boundary between human rights, freedom of expression, and political diversity and an authoritarian and repressive system in which, in the name of the one truth represented by the Communist Party and its leaders, all forms of criticism could be silenced, dogmatic orders could be imposed, and dissidents could be buried in concentration camps or even "disappeared." With all its imperfections, which were many, democracy at least replaced arbitrary action with laws and allowed free elections and independent parties and unions.

Opting for liberalism was above all an intellectual process that took a number of years. I was greatly helped by living in Britain at the time, teaching at the University of London in the late sixties and, later, witnessing firsthand the eleven years of the government of Margaret Thatcher. She belonged to the Conservative Party but she was guided as a politician by convictions and above all, an instinct, that were profoundly liberal; she was very similar to Ronald Reagan in this respect. When she assumed office in 1979, Britain was a country in decline, where Labour (and also Tory) reforms had been running out of steam, mired in increasingly statist and collectivist routines, although public freedoms, elections, and freedom of expression were all respected. But the state had grown everywhere with the nationalization of industries and with policies, such as in housing, for example, that made citizens ever more dependent on state benefits. Democratic socialism had made the country of the industrial revolution lethargic, as it now languished in monotonous mediocrity.

The government of Margaret Thatcher (1979–1990) was a revolution, conducted within strict legal boundaries. State enterprises were privatized and British companies stopped receiving subsidies and were forced to modernize and compete in a free market, while council houses, which governments up until then had rented out to people with low incomes—thus maintaining electoral clientelism—were sold to their tenants, in line with a policy that sought to turn Britain into a country of property owners. Its borders were opened to international competition while obsolete industries, such as coal, were closed down to allow for the renovation and modernization of the country.

All these economic reforms, of course, led to strikes and

social mobilization, like the miners' strike that lasted two years, during which Margaret Thatcher showed a courage and a conviction that Britain had not seen since the days of Winston Churchill. These reforms, which, in a few years, made the country the most dynamic society in Europe, were accompanied by a defense of democratic culture, and an affirmation of the moral and material superiority of liberal democracy over authoritarian, corrupt, and economically bankrupt socialism that resonated across the world. These policies coincided with those being implemented in the United States under president Ronald Reagan. At last there were leaders at the head of Western democracies who had no inferiority complex with regard to communism, who highlighted achievements in human rights, equal opportunities, and respect for individuals and their ideas, in contrast to the despotism and economic failure of the communist countries. While Ronald Reagan was an extraordinary disseminator of liberal theories that he doubtless understood in a rather general way, Mrs. Thatcher was more precise and ideological. She has no qualms about saying that she consulted Friedrich von Hayek and that she read Karl Popper, whom she considered to be the most important contemporary philosopher of freedom. I read both men in those years and from that time *The Road to Serfdom* and *The Open Society and Its Enemies* became fundamental texts for me.

Although on economic and political issues Ronald Reagan and Margaret Thatcher had an unequivocally liberal outlook, on many social and moral issues they defended conservative and even reactionary positions—neither of them would have accepted gay marriage, abortion, the legalization of drugs or euthanasia, which seemed to me to be legitimate and necessary reforms—and on these matters, of course, I disagreed with them. But taking everything into account, I am convinced that both made a great contribution to the culture of freedom. And in any event, they helped me to become a liberal.

I had the good fortune, through my old friend the historian Hugh Thomas, to meet Mrs. Thatcher in person. Thomas was an adviser to the British government on Spanish and Latin American affairs and he organized a dinner of intellectuals in his house in Ladbroke Grove to pit Mrs. Thatcher against the tigers. (The left, was, of course, the most vehement enemy of the Thatcher revolution.) She was seated next to Isaiah Berlin, whom she spoke to the entire evening with the utmost respect. Also present were the novelists V. S. Naipaul and Anthony Powell; the poets Al Alvarez, Stephen Spender, and Philip Larkin; the critic and short story writer V. S. Pritchett; the playwright Tom Stoppard; the historian J. H. Plumb, from Cambridge; Anthony Quinton, the president of Trinity College, Oxford; and someone else whose name escapes me. She asked me where I lived and when I replied Montpelier Walk she reminded me that I was a neighbor of Arthur Koestler, whom she had clearly read. The conversation was a test that the intellectuals set the prime minister. The delicacy and good form of British courtesy scarcely disguised deep-seated aggression. The host, Hugh Thomas, opened fire by asking Mrs. Thatcher if the opinion of historians interested her and helped her in any way when it came to government concerns. She answered the questions clearly, without being intimidated or putting on airs, with conviction for the most part, but, at times, expressing her doubts. At the end of the dinner, after she had left, Isaiah Berlin summed up very well, I think, the opinion of most of those present: "Nothing to be ashamed of." And yes, I thought, quite a bit to be proud of to have a leader with such mettle, culture, and convictions. Margaret Thatcher was going to travel to Berlin in the coming days, where she would visit for the first time the wall of shame erected by the Soviets to stop the increasing number of citizens fleeing from East Germany to West Germany. There she would deliver one of her most important speeches against authoritarianism and in defense of democracy.

I also met Ronald Reagan in person, but at a very large dinner at the White House, having been invited by Selwa Roosevelt, the then chief of protocol. She introduced me to the president and in the briefest of conversations I only managed to ask him why, since the United States had writers like Faulkner, Hemingway, or Dos Passos, he always referred to Louis L'Amour as his favorite novelist. "Well," he told me, "he was very good at describing something very American, cowboy life in the old West." He did not convince me here, of course.

Both were great statespersons, the most important of their day, and both contributed in a decisive way to the collapse and disintegration of the U.S.S.R., the greatest enemy of democratic culture. But neither of them were charismatic leaders, like Hitler, Mussolini, Perón, or Fidel Castro, who appealed to the "spirit of the tribe" in their speeches. This is the term given by Karl Popper to the irrationality of the primitive human being that nests in the most secret recesses of all civilized people, for we have never completely overcome that yearning for the traditional world—the tribe—when men and women were still an inseparable part of the collective, subordinate to the all-powerful sorcerer or chief who made every decision for them, where they felt safe, free of responsibilities, submissive, like animals in a pack or herd, like human beings in gangs or soccer crowds, lethargic in the midst of those who spoke the same language, worshipped the same gods, and hated outsiders, people different from them, whom they could blame for all the calamities that befell the tribe. The "tribal spirit," a source of nationalism, has, along with religious fanaticism, been responsible for the largest massacres in the history of humanity. In civilized countries, like Great Britain, the call of the tribe could be seen in those big spectacles, like soccer matches or the open-air pop concerts that the Beatles or the Rolling Stones gave in the sixties, in which the individual disappeared, swallowed up by the mass, finding a momentary escape, which was both healthy and cathartic, from the daily drudgery of being citizens. But in certain countries, and not just in the third world, this "call of the tribe," which democratic and liberal culture—ultimately, rationality—had sought to free us from, had reappeared from time to time in the guise of dreadful charismatic leaders, under whom citizens revert to being a mass in thrall to a caudillo. This is the substratum of nationalism that I had detested from a very early age, intuiting that it was the antithesis of culture, democracy, and rationality. That is why I had been a man of the left and a communist in my early years; but, in recent times, nothing has illustrated the return to the "tribe" better than communism, under which sovereign responsible individuals regress to being part of a mass submissive to the dictates of a leader, a sort of religious holy man, the bearer of irrefutable sacred truths, which revived the worst forms of demagogy and chauvinism.

In those years I read and reread many of the thinkers to whom I have dedicated these pages. And many others who might also have figured, like Ludwig von Mises, Milton Friedman, the Argentine Juan Bautista Alberdi, and the Venezuelan Carlos Rangel, these last two truly exceptional cases of liberalism on the continent of Latin America. At that time

I also made a trip to Edinburgh to lay flowers at the grave of Adam Smith, and to Kirkcaldy to see the house where he wrote *The Wealth of Nations,* where I discovered that all that was left of the house was a crumbling wall and a plaque.

It was in those years that my political convictions were shaped and I have defended them in articles and books since that time. It was these convictions that led me, in Peru in 1987, to oppose the nationalization of the finance system proposed by president Alan García in his first term of office (1985–1990) and to found the Freedom Movement and stand as presidential candidate for the Democratic Front in 1990 with a program that proposed a radical transformation of society in Peru, to turn it into a liberal democracy. I should say, in passing, that although my friends and I were beaten at the ballot box, many of the ideas that we outlined in that long campaign of almost three years, which are in this book, did not disappear but have gained ground in ever broader sectors of society and are now part of the political agenda in Peru.

Conservatism and liberalism are different things, as Hayek argued in a famous essay. Which does not mean that there are not points of convergence and shared values between liberals and conservatives just as there are between democratic socialism—social democracy—and liberalism. Remember, for example, that the great economic and social transformation of New Zealand was initiated by a Labour government and its finance minister Roger Douglas, and was supported and extended by Ruth Richardson, the finance minister of a Conservative government (1984–1993). We should not, therefore, think of liberalism as just another ideology, one of those secular acts of faith that are so prone to irrationality and dogmatic truths, just like all religions, from the primitive magical-religious forms to the most modern. Among liberals, as the figures in this book illustrate, there are often more disagreements than agreements. Liberalism is a doctrine that does not have answers to everything, as Marxism purports to do, and it has a place for divergence and criticism around a small but unequivocal core set of convictions. For example, that freedom is the supreme value, it is not divisible or fragmentary, but rather indivisible, and must be evident in every sphere—be it economic, political, social, or cultural—in a genuinely democratic society. Not understanding this fact is what led to the failure of all the regimes that, in the sixties and seventies, tried to stimulate economic freedom but were despotic, generally military dictatorships. These ignorant people thought that a market policy could be successful under repressive and dictatorial regimes. But many democratic initiatives also failed in Latin America, because they respected political freedoms but did not believe in economic freedom—the free market—which is what brings material development and progress.

Liberalism is not dogmatic; it knows that reality is complex and that often ideas and political programs must adapt to this reality if they wish to be successful, instead of trying to bind it to rigid forms that often lead to failure and political violence. Liberalism has also generated its own "infantile disorder," sectarianism, as can be seen in certain economists who are bewitched by the market as a panacea capable of resolving all social problems. These people in particular should be reminded of the example of Adan Smith himself, the father of liberalism, who, in certain circumstances, even allowed privileges like subsidies and controls to remain in place for a time should their removal cause more harm than good in the short term. This tolerance shown by Smith to his opponents is perhaps the most admirable of all the traits of liberal doctrine: accepting that this doctrine might be wrong and its opponent might be right. A liberal government should deal with social and historical reality in a flexible manner, not believing that all societies can be contained within a single theoretical framework, for this is a counterproductive attitude that leads to failure and frustration.

We liberals are not anarchists and we do not wish to do away with the state. Quite the reverse, we want a strong and efficient state, which does not mean a large state involved in doing things that civil society can do better under a system of free competition. The state must guarantee freedom, public order, the respect for law, and equal opportunities.

Equality before the law and equality of opportunities do not mean equality of income, something that no liberal would propose. For that would be possible only in a society run by an authoritarian government that would "equalize" all citizens economically through an oppressive system, doing away with different individual capacities, imagination, inventiveness, concentration, diligence, ambition, work ethic, and leadership. This would imply the disappearance of the individual, subsumed into the tribe.

So it is right that, beginning from a more or less similar point, individuals would have different incomes according to how much or how little they contribute to the benefits of society as a whole. It would be stupid to ignore that people are intelligent and obtuse, diligent and lazy, inventive and unadventurous and slow-witted, studious and indolent, and so on. And it would be unjust, in the name of "equality," that everyone should receive the same wage despite their different aptitudes and merits. Societies that have tried this have hampered individual initiative, subsuming these individuals into an anodyne mass where a lack of competition demotivates them and stifles their creativity.

But there is also no doubt that in very unequal societies, such as those in the third world, the children of the most prosperous families enjoy infinitely greater opportunities to be successful in life than those of poor families. For that reason, "equal opportunity" is a profoundly liberal concept, despite the small bands of dogmatic, intolerant, and often racist economists—there are many in Peru, all Fujimoristas—who abuse the term.

That is why it is so important for liberalism to offer young people a high-quality education system that allows each generation a common starting point from which legitimate differences in salary can later emerge based on the talent, the effort, and the service that each individual offers to the community. It is in the world of education—secondary, technical, and university education—where we find the greatest injustice in terms of privilege, where some young people receive a very high level of education while others are condemned to a rudimentary or inefficient system that can only offer them a limited future, failure, or mere survival. This is not a utopia but something that France, for example, achieved in the past with free public education, which was often at a higher level than private education and was accessible to all. The crisis in education suffered in France recently has seen a decline in standards but this is not true of Scandinavian countries, or Switzerland, or Asian countries like Japan and Singapore, which guarantee equal opportunities in the field of education—secondary and higher—without this being detrimental in any way, quite the reverse, to their democratic way of life and their economic prosperity.

Equal opportunity in the field of education does not mean having to ban private education in favor of public education. Not at all: it is important that both exist and compete because there is nothing like competition to advance higher standards and progress. The idea of competition between educational establishments was an idea of a liberal economist, Milton Friedman. The "school vouchers" program he proposed has had excellent results in countries where it has been applied, like Sweden, giving parents a very active participation in the improvement of the education system. The "school voucher" that the state gives to parents allows them to choose the best schools for their children, thus giving greater state aid to the institutions that attract, because of their quality, the largest number of applications for places.

We should bear in mind that, in our age of great technological and scientific change, education is ever more costly—if one wishes it to be of the highest level—and that means that civil society has as much responsibility as the state in maintaining the highest academic standards in schools, colleges, and universities. It is not fair that children from wealthy families are exempt from paying for their education just as it would not be fair for a young person to be excluded, for economic reasons, from having access to the best institutions if they have the necessary talent and desire. So alongside "school vouchers," a system of grants and aid is fundamental to achieving equal opportunities in education.

A minimal state is generally more efficient than a large state: this is one of the firmest convictions of liberal doctrine. The more the state grows and takes on greater influence in the life of nations, the more the freedoms of its citizens are diminished. The decentralization of power is a liberal principle that allows the whole of society greater control over different social and political institutions. Apart from defense, justice, and public order, where the state has primacy (not a monopoly), the ideal is for citizens to have the greatest participation possible in stimulating the remaining social and economic activities through a system of free competition.

Liberalism, more than any other political outlook, has been traduced and slandered throughout history, first by conservatism—think of the papal encyclicals and the pronouncements of the Catholic Church against it, which still persist despite the existence of so many liberal believers—and later by socialism and communism, which, in the modern era, have presented "neoliberalism" as the spearhead of imperialism and the most shameless forms of colonialism and capitalism. The truth of history gives the lie to these calumnies. From its very beginnings, liberal doctrine has given expression to the most advanced forms of democratic culture, and in free societies has given the greatest impulse to human rights, freedom of expression, the rights of sexual, religious, and political minorities, the defense of the environment and the participation of ordinary citizens in public life. In other words, it has given us the greatest protection from the inextinguishable "call of the tribe." This book seeks to be a small contribution to this indispensable task.

MADRID, AUGUST 2017

ADAM SMITH (1723–1790)

We know almost nothing about the childhood and early years of Adam Smith save that he was born one day in 1723, in Kirkcaldy, a Scottish trading town located some ten miles north of Edinburgh, where he spent much of his life and at least six of the ten years that it took him to write his magnum opus: *An Inquiry into the Nature and Causes of the Wealth of Nations* (1776). He did not know his father, a lawyer and customs inspector who died before he was born, and he always loved his mother, Margaret Douglas, with a great passion. There is no proof to the story that he was abducted by gypsies at the age of three and rescued a few hours later. He was a sickly, rather plain child, and before he was known for his wisdom he was known for being extraordinarily absentminded. One day the driver of the coach coming from London discovered on the outskirts of Kirkcaldy a solitary figure walking in the middle of the countryside far from the town. He stopped the coach to ask Mr. Smith where he was going; disconcerted, Adam Smith acknowledged that he had been so lost in his thoughts that he had not noticed how far he had strayed. And one Sunday he appeared with his strange swaying gait—like a camel's—still in his dressing gown, in Dunfermline, some fifteen miles from

Kirkcaldy, staring into space and talking to himself. Years later the residents of Edinburgh would get used to him wandering around the Old Town, at odd hours, lost to the world, his lips moving silently, that solitary, somewhat hypochondriacal old man who everyone called the wise man. There are dozens of similar stories from throughout his life.

He went to school on Hill Street, near his house, between 1731 and 1737 and he must have been a good student of Latin and Greek because when he matriculated at Glasgow University, at age fourteen, he was exempted from the first year, which was dedicated to the classics. He described his three years in Glasgow in a letter quoted by his biographer Nicholas Phillipson as, "by far the most useful, and, therefore, as by far the happiest and most honourable period of my life."* He discovered Newton's physics, and Euclidian geometry, and was taught by a professor of moral philosophy, Francis Hutcheson, an eminent figure of the Scottish Enlightenment, who would have a great influence on his intellectual development. After spending three years at the University of Glasgow, he was awarded a scholarship to Oxford, where he studied from 1740 to 1746, at Balliol College. We know almost nothing about the life he led during those six years. His biographies surmise that he must have been quite lonely because the political and cultural climate of the university was imbued with a most conservative and reactionary "Jacobitism," at odds with his own Presbyterian, Whig formation. We do know that he learned French by himself and read French literature with a passion, and that his favorite authors were Racine and Marivaux. But the most important thing that happened to him in those years

---

* Nicholas Phillipson, *Adam Smith: An Enlightened Life*, Yale University Press, London, 2010, p. 40.

in Oxford was that he became acquainted with the work of David Hume, another of the great figures of the Scottish Enlightenment, and perhaps even met the man himself. Twelve years older than Smith, Hume, who was held in high regard in intellectual circles, was nonetheless condemned by the university hierarchy for being an atheist. One of the few things that we know about Adam Smith in Oxford was that he was reprimanded by his college after he was discovered reading the *Treatise of Human Nature* (1739) by the influential Scottish philosopher who would later become his best friend. He praised him and Hutcheson in his *The Theory of Moral Sentiments* (1759).

There is still the mistaken idea making the rounds that Adam Smith was first and foremost an economist—he is called the "Father of Economics"—something that would have amazed him. He always thought of himself as a moralist and a philosopher. His interest in economic questions, as in other disciplines like astronomy—he wrote a "History of Astronomy" that was only published after his death—came as a consequence of his endeavors to develop a "science of human nature" and to explain how society functions. There is more news of him after he left Oxford and arrived in Edinburgh where, between 1748 and 1751, thanks to Lord Kames, another figure of the Scottish Enlightenment, he gave a series of public lectures that had a great impact and cemented his reputation. The texts of these talks have been lost but we know of them through the notes of two students who took a similar course with Smith a number of years later. The first course of lectures was on rhetoric and the way in which language and human communication had developed, an activity that Smith identifies not only as a need for survival but also as a form of propriety and congeniality, based on people's customs and common sense, that underpinned society and sociability. To demonstrate this he used examples from literature. In his opinion, clear, direct, and concise language best expresses emotions, feelings, and ideas and should be preferred to a baroque and pompous style (like that of the third Earl of Shaftesbury, he said) that was favored by a select minority and excluded the common man.

In another course of lectures, on jurisprudence, Smith sketched out some of the ideas that he would develop later, based on David Hume's thesis that property was "the mother of the civilizing process." This topic fascinated the leading Scottish intellectuals of the time. Lord Kames, for example, argued that the most prominent instinct in human beings was "the hoarding appetite" and, from that, private property and, to some extent society itself, had been born. In his book, *Historical Law-Tracts* (1758), Lord Kames maintained that the development of history was made up of four stages: (a) hunter-gatherer society; (b) nomadic-pastoral society; (c) agrarian society and, finally, (d) commercial society. The exchange of goods, within and outside the group, would have been the true driving force of civilization. Governments appeared when the members of the community became aware of the importance of private property and understood that this needed to be protected by laws and by authorities who would uphold these laws. These ideas greatly influenced Adam Smith, who adopted them and would, over time, develop and nuance them. Perhaps from his Edinburgh years he began to formulate the conviction—that he held throughout his life—that the worst enemy of property was the landed nobility, that rentier aristocracy who often brought down governments that limited its powers and that was always a threat to justice, social peace, and progress. Thanks to these lectures in Edinburgh, this young man was beginning to be seen as a part of that movement, the Scottish Enlightenment, that would revolutionize the ideas, values, and culture of the time.

From Edinburgh, Adam Smith moved to Glasgow, where he stayed for thirteen years—until 1764—briefly as professor of logic and metaphysics and then as professor of moral philosophy. We have more details of his life from this period. He lived with his mother and a cousin, Janet Douglas, who kept house for him throughout all the time he spent in Scotland. His was a life of stoic austerity, Presbyterian, with no alcohol and probably no sex—he never married and there were no known girlfriends and the rumors that circulated about his supposed romantic attachments all sound unreal—dedicated to teaching and research. His prestige as a teacher was so great that, among others, James Boswell, the future biographer of Samuel Johnson, enrolled at the University of Glasgow to attend his courses. According to the testimonies of his students he had a written script for his lectures but often departed from his notes to develop or look more closely at specific topics and he loathed his students taking notes while he was talking: "I hate scribblers." He also stood out as an administrator. He was tasked with organizing and running the library and acquiring books and with building sites for new disciplines and he was involved in the administration and finances of the university, eventually becoming dean of faculties and vice rector. In all these activities he received the same respect and praise as for his intellectual work.

In those years Glasgow enjoyed an extraordinary prosperity due to the opening of markets facilitated by the Act of Union with England and, in particular, to the tobacco trade, where boats based in Glasgow brought back tobacco from Virginia in the United States and distributed it throughout the

United Kingdom and the rest of Europe. According to Arthur Herman, in his study of the Scottish Enlightenment, it was at this time, and because of Glasgow's notable development, that Smith began to take an interest in the commercial operations of large companies. "Smith struck up a close relationship with John Glassford, who kept him informed of events in America and also took a keen interest in Smith's progress with his *Wealth of Nations*. Glasgow Provost Andrew Cochrane organized a Political Economy Club, whose members included Smith, Glassford, and another wealthy tobacco merchant, Richard Oswald. Cochrane even presided over a special session of the Glasgow town council on May 3, 1762, when Professor Smith was made an honorary burgess of the city."*

THE THEORY OF MORAL SENTIMENTS (1759)

The first book that Adam Smith published, *The Theory of Moral Sentiments* (1759), had been taking shape in his classes over the years and shows to what extent morality was central to his vocation.† In the theory he develops we find the ideas of his old teacher Francis Hutcheson, as well as those of David Hume, Rousseau's thoughts on inequality, and Bernard Mandeville's writings on morality. But in the book there is also a solid spine of his own ideas, a first approximation to the "science of humankind" that he had been dreaming of developing since his childhood.

Certain words are key to the understanding of this book—

---

* Arthur Herman, *The Scottish Enlightenment: The Scots' Invention of the Modern World*, Fourth Estate, London, 2001, p. 158.
† Adam Smith, *The Theory of Moral Sentiments*, Penguin Books, London and New York, 2009. All the following quotations are taken from this edition.

sympathy (in the sense of empathy), *imagination, propriety*, the *impartial spectator*—and a question that this voluminous inquiry sought to answer: How can human society exist, maintain stability, and progress over time instead of disintegrating under the pressure of rivalries, opposing interests, and the instincts and egotistical passions of humankind? What makes *sociability* possible, this glue that binds society despite the diverse people and characteristics that comprise this society?

Human beings get to know each other through imagination, and a natural sense of sympathy toward one's neighbor is what draws one individual to another, something that would never occur if human actions were exclusively governed by reason. This feeling of sympathy, and imagination, brings strangers together and establishes between them a link that breaks down mistrust and creates reciprocal bonds. The vision of man and society that permeates this book is positive and optimistic, for Adam Smith believes that, despite all the horrors that are committed, goodness—that is, moral sentiments—prevail over evil. A good example of this innate decency that characterizes most human beings appears in the final pages of the book. "To tell a man that he lies is, of all affronts, the most mortal . . . The man who had the misfortune to imagine that nobody believed a single word he said, would feel himself the outcast of human society, would dread the very thought of going into it, or of presenting himself before it, and could scarce fail, I think, to die of despair" (p. 397). Things have changed a great deal in the centuries since Adam Smith wrote these lines and from a moral point of view human beings in our era have been getting worse because it would be very difficult to imagine at this point in time many people dying of despair at being thought of as a liar. However, Smith was not naive: his analyses of moral conduct are very subtle and complex, always upheld by the conviction that, even in the most dire circumstances, decency prevails over indecency. "Nature, when she formed man for society, endowed him with an original desire to please and an original aversion to offend his brethren. She taught him to feel pleasure in their pleasurable, and pain in their unpleasurable regard" (p. 140).

Another key word in this study is *propriety*, not in the sense of possession but rather as a suitable, just, and careful— appropriate—attitude in terms of an individual's relationship to others.

It is a curious, versatile, ambiguous, and subtle book: at times it seems a treatise on good manners, at other times a psychological analysis of the feelings and emotions that human beings have for their neighbors, and occasionally a sociology manual. In effect, it is a study of human relations and the ways in which such relations allow a society to function and to develop a sense of basic solidarity, which prevents it from breaking up and disappearing. It is also a study of the moral sentiment that allows us to differentiate between good and evil, falsehood and authenticity, and truth and lies. This was the first book of Adam Smith's to explore the "science of humankind," a study that would occupy the rest of his life and that he would never manage to complete.

The reactions and attitudes that the book describes take account of poverty and wealth, social prejudices, the place of individuals in society but, in general, it concentrates on ordinary citizens, who represent normality. Usually he passes swiftly over those who avoid or transgress normality (those men-monsters who fascinated Georges Bataille). For that reason the society described in *The Theory of Moral Sentiments* seems at times somewhat idealized as being exemplary and decorous. Because life is not made up just of normal people, there are abnormal and exceptional people as well. But this analysis does not simply correspond to Adam Smith's outlook on society but also, above all, to his way of being. Although there are not copious testimonies about him, those that do exist coincide in painting him not only as an intellectual of the highest order but also as a good man, with healthy habits, modest, simple, austere, very correct, with occasional outbursts of bad temper, whose life was dedicated to study. He surprised everyone by his habit of losing himself in his own thoughts and cutting himself off from anything around him at any time. One of his friends in the Select Society, who he used to meet in the taverns of Edinburgh, tells of how, in the middle of a discussion on law or philosophy, everyone noticed that Adam Smith *had gone*: he was there, his eyes staring into space, quietly muttering something almost inaudible, in a private world, absent from all that surrounded him.

The Theory of Moral Sentiments focuses above all on men, but he does point out certain characteristics that, for him, differentiate women from men; for example, this subtle comment: "Humanity is the virtue of a woman, generosity of a man" (p. 222). A large part of the book analyzes the individual in isolation but, in the final chapters, before he reviews systems of moral philosophy—Plato, Aristotle, Zeno, the Stoics, Epicurus, Cicero—and contrasts them with his own, his analysis extends to the individual as part of the family, of the nation, and finally, of humanity. These chapters anticipate some of the great insights to be found in *The Wealth of Nations*. For example, his very clear stand against nationalism, the idea that, because of the affective bond that unites individuals to their country, then they must always agree with their nation's actions, whether right or wrong: "The love of our own nation often disposes us to view with the most malignant jealousy and envy the prosperity and aggrandisement of any other neighbouring nation" (p. 269). He calls this "the mean principle of national prejudice" (p. 270). In a subsequent paragraph, referring to England and France, he states that "for either of them to envy the internal happiness and prosperity of the other is surely . . . beneath the dignity of two such great nations" (p. 270). This rejection of a nationalist perspective as a superior and egotistical attitude that justifies arbitrary actions leads him to condemn the dogmatic nature of the "man of system" who "is often so enamoured with the supposed beauty of his own ideal plan of government" that "he seems to imagine that he can arrange the different members of a great society with as much ease as the hand arranges the different pieces upon a chess-board" (p. 275). He goes on to state that these pieces have no other "principle of motion" than the hand that guides them, and that "in the great chess-board of human society every single piece has a principle of motion of its own" (p. 275), very different from what the legislature might seek to impose in arbitrary fashion. This is the first time in history that someone has pointed out that society might have a motion of its own, derived from its internal organization, which must be respected in order not to cause anarchy or to have to resort to the most brutal repression to achieve it, something that he opposes, remembering "the divine maxim of Plato": "never to use violence to his country no more than to his parents" (p. 275).

But perhaps the most original part of *The Theory of Moral Sentiments* is the appearance in its pages of the *impartial spectator*, this judge or arbiter that we human beings carry within us, which takes an objective position on our behavior and judges it, approving or condemning what we do and say. This character is described in different ways throughout the book: "the great demigod within the breast," "his own conscience," "this judge within," "the great judge and arbiter of our conduct," "the great inmate," "those vice-gerents of God within us," etc. This identification of the impartial spectator with one's conscience is not completely accurate because it supposes that human beings govern their conscience while impartial spectators maintain a distance from the subject that they are part of, a position that allows them to give independent approval or condemnation to whatever they do, think, or say. Nor is this an exact projection of divinity in the individual because, as some of Adam Smith's most subtle analyses in the book reveal, impartial spectators are not always as neutral as God might be; they tend to soften toward their subject, showing bursts of favoritism, or else demonstrate an excessive severity toward their desires, feelings, and passions, and, in an equally subjective way, exaggerate their condemnation and disapproval. To some extent this impartial spectator of the lives of human beings is, as Professor D. D. Raphael points out in his book on Adam Smith, a forerunner of what a century later Sigmund Freud would call, in his description of the life of the unconscious, the *superego*.* This impartial spectator also has a raison d'être that will later appear as one of the pillars of liberal doctrine: individualism. If moral conduct depends to a great extent on the personality of every individual, this then is the basic cell of society, the starting point for all the different communities to which individuals might belong. But none of these communities can subsume or eradicate the individual, be they the family, work, religion, social class, or a political party.

Adam Smith wrote with elegance and precision and he was sensitive to good literature (in this work there is a very

* D. D. Raphael, *Adam Smith*, Past Masters, Oxford University Press, 1985, p. 6.

enthusiastic appreciation of Racine's *Phèdre*) and beauty, which he found not only in literary and artistic works but also in human actions and, of course, in nature and objects. A virtuous action, a generous gesture, an act of solidarity, he says, awakens a sense of beauty comparable to that elicited by a beautiful landscape, harmonious music, or a life governed by prudence, respect for one's neighbors, friendship, and irreproachable behavior. In his conclusion he observes that animate and inanimate objects can give us this taste for beauty.

The Theory of Moral Sentiments was Adam Smith's favorite book and he never imagined the revolution that *The Wealth of Nations* would cause in the world of ideas, politics, and economics. *The Theory of Moral Sentiments* received great praise from David Hume, Edmund Burke, and, in the rest of Europe, from intellectuals as prestigious as Kant and Voltaire. Voltaire was reported to have said after reading it, "We have nobody to compare with him, and I am embarrassed for my dear compatriots."

But there was something even more important: the prestige that he achieved allowed him to free himself from his university obligations, be offered a job that would guarantee his future, allow him to write without impediments, and make a much coveted journey to the most cultured spots in Europe. David Hume informed him in April 1759 that Charles Townshend, the stepfather of the young Duke of Buccleuch, who was still at Eton, was considering sending him to Glasgow to study with Smith. This did not happen but, some years later, Adam Smith received a very concrete proposal from Townshend: to tutor the young duke—the heir to a great fortune—and accompany him on a long study visit to Europe. The conditions could not be more advantageous: a salary of five hundred pounds and a pension of three hundred pounds (much more than his professorial income). Smith accepted, resigned from the University of Glasgow, and set off for London to meet the young man—he was eighteen—who would be his student for the next three years. There was an immediate bond of understanding and affection between the two that would last for the rest of their lives. The young aristocrat was attentive and hardworking, respectful, and amiable and always felt an enormous admiration and gratitude for the private tutor who accompanied him on his European tour between 1764 and 1766.

Smith and his disciple went first to Toulouse, where they stayed for eighteen months. There are indications that in Toulouse Smith began to take notes for *The Wealth of Nations*. The second city of France was still shaken by "l'affaire Calas," which resonated through much of Europe due to the fanaticism and cruelty that surrounded it. In 1761 the son of a protestant merchant, Jean Calas, was found dead in the city. Calas was accused of having murdered his son to prevent him from converting to Catholicism. The poor man was sentenced by the *Parlement*, broken at the wheel, hanged, and then burned in March 1762. This led to the famous campaign by Voltaire against the injustice committed, seeking a posthumous exoneration for the victim. His famous pamphlet on the subject, published in his *Traité sur la tolérance*, was one of the many books and pamphlets that Smith sent back to Scotland in the two years that he spent in France and Switzerland.

This was the only occasion that Adam Smith visited these countries and, thanks to the recommendations of the stepfather of the Duke of Buccleuch, of David Hume and others, he attended the fashionable salons in Paris, went to the theater and to concerts, and got to know the most famous intellectuals. There is also word of a lady who was taken by him and pursued him, while he did what he could to escape her. He visited Voltaire several times in Ferney, and in Paris he met philosophers and writers like D'Alembert, Turgot, Helvétius, Baron d'Holbach, Marmontel, and, above all, François Quesnay and the physiocrats, whose economic theories he would later strongly criticize in *The Wealth of Nations*. But he got on well with Quesnay in person when they had several what must have been lively and argumentative meetings; he once said that if Quesnay had been alive when his book appeared, he would have dedicated it to him. The stay in Europe had to be cut short because the Duke of Buccleuch became ill and a younger brother of the duke died, forcing them to move forward their return. In the middle of November 1766 they were back in England. Adam Smith would never leave Britain again.

WRITING *THE WEALTH OF NATIONS*

On his return from France, he stayed some six months in London, until May 1767. He delayed returning to Scotland to correct the third edition of *The Theory of Moral Sentiments* and he worked in the extraordinary library of the recently opened British Museum. He traveled to Kirkcaldy with four big chests of books and stayed there for six years, living with his mother and Janet Douglas. It was in this period that he made great progress with an ambitious book in which he wanted to test his theories on the systems that maintained natural and social order. From an early age he had been convinced that only reason—not religion—could understand these systems and explain them. He had set himself the task, now, to describe the organization of economic life and the progress in society.

His life was spartan and he concentrated on his research and on the drafts of the book. He went out infrequently, usually for long walks along the seashore. The story goes that he could sometimes be found, very out of breath, in villages miles from his home, lost in his own world until the sound of church bells or the bells of a flock of sheep brought him out of his reveries. In his free moments he became absorbed in botany, classifying the plants in his garden according to the nomenclature of the Swedish naturalist Carolus Linnaeus, whose studies had impressed him. One of his few journeys was to attend the birthday party of his former pupil the Duke of Buccleuch, who had married Elizabeth, the daughter of the Duke of Montagu. He stayed two months with them at their residence, Dalkeith Palace, on the outskirts of Edinburgh.

Although he had assembled in his splendid library in Kirkcaldy most of the economic and political material that he needed to consult, we can see from his letters, asking friends in Britain and in Europe to send him books or pamphlets or other information, just what a demanding and lengthy task it was to write *The Wealth of Nations*.

In the spring of 1773, he decided to leave Kirkcaldy and move to London, where he spent the next three years. That is where he finished his book. But before leaving, he decided to make a will. He made David Hume the executor of the will and he stipulated that Hume should be sent the manuscript of *The Wealth of Nations* if he died before completing it. He also stipulated that all his papers should be destroyed with the exception of his unpublished history of astronomy: his friend would decide whether it was worth publishing. It is thought that health issues prompted him to make his will, but the truth is that in the seventeen years that he had still to live, he never had physical complaints that much bothered him. And there has never been a persuasive explanation as to why he decided to burn his manuscripts.

Unlike his time in Kirkcaldy, where he was completely isolated, in London he had an intense social life. He met up with his friends for discussions in the two clubs where he was a member—the Royal Society and the Club—both of which enjoyed high intellectual and social status, and in the homes of wealthy and high-ranking people, where he met and engaged with politicians and influential intellectuals like Edmund Burke, Edward Gibbon, and Samuel Johnson. Generally he was popular with his interlocutors, who were amused by his inevitable idiosyncracies. One exception was Samuel Johnson, for it seems that in one discussion Smith, who was usually so good-humored, got so irritated that he swore at him. It is not surprising, therefore, that the famous lexicographer and literary critic wrote a cruel comment about him: that he was "as dull a dog as he had ever met with," who slobbered and "was a most disagreeable fellow after he had drank some wine."[*] Adam Smith has left a similarly disdainful and sarcastic account of the great British lexicographer, traveler, and critic.[†]

THE WEALTH OF NATIONS

The book was published on March 9, 1776, and the first edition of five hundred copies sold out in six months; Smith received three hundred pounds from his editors. Almost at the same time another masterpiece of Western culture appeared: Edward Gibbon's *Decline and Fall of the Roman Empire*. The second edition of *The Wealth of Nations* was published a couple

[*] Ian Simpson Ross, *The Life of Adam Smith*, Oxford University Press, Oxford, 1955, p. 251.
[†] Nicholas Phillipson, op. cit., pp. 210–211.

of years later, with some changes; the third edition, in 1784, included a number of corrections and additions. During Adam Smith's lifetime fourth and fifth editions appeared in 1786 and 1789, with new changes, along with translations of the book into French (there were three versions), German, Danish, and Italian.* In Spain, Carlos Martínez de Irujo translated the work into Spanish and it was published in 1791, but the book was denounced to the Tribunal of the Holy Office (the Inquisition) and banned the following year. Three years later, in 1794, a small compendium of the work was published in Valladolid, without the name of Smith on the cover.†

Remarkable for the variety of themes that it covers, a monument to the culture of its time, a testament to what knowledge in the fields of politics, economics, philosophy, and history signified in the last third of the eighteenth century, what is most notable and long-lasting about the book is the discovery of the free market as a motor for progress. A mechanism that no one invented, that humanity arrived at through commerce. This continuous exchange produced the division of labor and the appearance of the market, a distributive system of resources that—without their intending to do so or even knowing what they were doing—all members of society, be they sellers, buyers, or producers, contributed to, thus increasing general prosperity. It was a rare insight to be told that, while working to achieve their own desires and egotistical dreams, ordinary men and women contributed to the well-being of everyone. This "invisible hand" that pushes and

---

* Adam Smith, *An Inquiry into the Nature and Causes of the Wealth of Nations*, vols. 1 and 2, edited by R. H. Campbell, A. S. Skinner, and W. B. Todd, Oxford, Clarendon Press, 1976. All quotations are taken from this edition.
† Ian Simpson Ross, op. cit., p. 432.

guides workers and creators of wealth to cooperate with society was a revolutionary insight and, at the same time, the strongest defense of freedom in the economic arena. The free market presupposes the existence of private property, equality of citizens before the law, a rejection of privileges, and the division of labor. No one before Adam Smith had explained so precisely and lucidly this self-sufficient system that brings progress to nations and for which freedom is essential, or argued so eloquently that economic freedom upholds and drives all other freedoms.

Reading this oceanic book, which is divided into an infinitude of themes and subthemes, one gets the impression that not even Adam Smith himself was aware of the importance of his findings. It is disconcerting for many readers of *The Wealth of Nations* to discover that the motor of progress is not altruism or charity but rather egotism: "It is not from the benevolence of the butcher, the brewer, or the baker that we expect our dinner but from their regard to their own interest. We address ourselves not to their humanity but to their self-love and we never talk to them of our own necessities but of their advantages" (vol. 1, pp. 26–27).

John Maynard Keynes, a diligent though somewhat unruly follower of Adam Smith, joked that Smith maintained that capitalism was founded on the astonishing belief that the nastiest motives of the nastiest men somehow work for the benefit of all. However, like all the great social and political thinkers who followed him, including Marx, Keynes ended up accepting, with great reluctance, the discovery that Adam Smith sums up here: "He [the individual] generally, indeed, neither intends to promote the public interest, nor knows how much he is promoting it. By preferring the support of domestic to that of foreign industry, he intends only his own security; and by directing that industry in such a manner as its produce may be of the greatest value, he intends only his own gain, and he is in this, as in many other cases, led by an invisible hand to promote an end which was no part of his intention" (vol. 1, p. 456).

The system that Adam Smith describes is not *created*, it is spontaneous: it came about through practical necessities that began with barter among primitive peoples, continued with more developed forms of trade, the appearance of private property, laws, and courts, that's to say, the state, and above all from the division of labor, which sparked productivity. This spontaneous order, as Hayek would later call it, has freedom— freedoms—at its foundations: free trade, freedom to intervene in the market as a producer and consumer in conditions of equality under the rule of law, freedom to sign contracts, export and import, to enter into partnerships and to form companies, et cetera. The great enemies of the market are privileges, monopolies, subsidies, controls, and prohibitions. The spontaneity and naturalness of the system reduce as society progresses and creates legal structures to regulate the market. But so long as these structures allow for freedom in large part, then the system will be efficient and produce positive results.

It is true that the market is cold because it rewards success and punishes failure in an implacable way. But Adam Smith was not the cerebral inhumane being that those who attack his liberalism would like to depict. Quite the reverse, he was acutely sensitive to the horror of poverty and he believed in equal opportunities, though he would never use that expression. That is why he argued that, in order to fight against the ignorance and slow-wittedness in workers that might result from the mechanical nature of their work, education was indispensable and should be financed, for those who could not afford it, by the state or civil society. He also favored competition in education and defended a system that offered both private and public education.

Adam Smith would have been surprised that, in the future, his theories would be accused, by enemies of liberalism and of private enterprise, of lacking sensitivity and solidarity; he was sure that his study favored the poor and would help to eradicate poverty: "No society can surely be flourishing and happy, of which the far greater part of the members are poor and miserable" (vol. 1, p. 96), he argued. His opinion of rich people of his time was often severe: "In every different branch (of business) the oppression of the poor must establish the monopoly of the rich, who, by engrossing the whole trade to themselves, will be able to make very large profits" (vol. 1, p. 112). Monopoly distorts supply and demand by giving a manufacturer or merchant the power to alter prices for profit; when competition is eliminated, the quality of the product goes down while trade is not a service but rather a means of exploiting the buyer. The great beneficiaries of the theories of Adam Smith are the consumers, the whole of society, more than the producers, a minority that, of course, have the right to benefit from the service that they providing, often with great talent and daring, but for this there must be equative competition, without favoritism, and which, of course, respects private property.

According to Adam Smith, "The property which every man has in his own labour, as it is the original foundation of all other property, so it is the most sacred and inviolable. The patrimony of a poor man lies in the strength and dexterity of his hands; and to hinder him from employing this strength and dexterity in what manner he thinks proper without injury to his neighbour, is a plain violation of this most sacred property. It is a manifest encroachment upon the just liberty both of the workman and of those who might be disposed to employ him" (vol. 1, p. 138).

The book sets out by explaining that "the division of labour" has increased productivity most markedly in the manufacture of goods. He uses the famous example of pins and the eighteen specialized tasks that combine to produce them; the division of labor led to the production of machines that have greatly alleviated the burden of workers. And it is these very workers who, he states, were often those who invented the machines themselves.

Civilization is born from the need of human beings to turn to others to satisfy their needs. The division of labor is limited by the size of the market. It is obvious that in a small village a farmworker must also be a painter, a builder, and a plumber. The growth of cities was a step forward that allowed people to specialize in different areas.

The Wealth of Nations explains the origins and the function of money in primitive societies that slowly became trading societies. At a certain point in historical evolution barter gave way to commodities that would act as an intermediary for buying and selling: commodities included cattle, seashells, dried cod, hides or dressed leather, and, finally, metals. Money would become the universal instrument of commerce. At the beginning, coins had the quantity of metal that they were supposed to have. Later, "the avarice and injustice of princes and sovereign states, abusing the confidence of their subjects, have by degrees diminished the real quantity of metal which had been originally contained in their coins" (vol. 1, p. 43). This enabled them to swindle their creditors.

The price of commodities, according to Adam Smith, was

measured by the quantity of labor involved in making them.* In terms of price one must distinguish between the "real price" and the "nominal price." The latter is fixed by the market according to the quantity of metals used in making the products. Although Smith declares his arguments to be "scientific," they reveal a great sensitivity. He argues that well-paid workers produce more and that their prosperity guarantees social peace. At the same time he describes the magnitude of poverty in countries like India and China where women kill their children because they cannot feed them, and in the Highlands of Scotland where some mothers had twenty children, only two of whom survived.

The minute descriptions of economic matters are combined with historical accounts and sociological analyses that are sometimes so detailed that they overwhelm the reader. But from time to time innovative ideas occur. For example, in chapter 10 of the first volume he gives five reasons to explain why certain employments are more profitable than others: "First, the agreeableness or disagreeableness of the employments themselves; secondly, the easiness and cheapness, or the difficulty and expense of learning them; thirdly, the constancy or inconstancy of employment in them; fourthly, the small or great trust which must be reposed in those who exercise them; and, fifthly, the probability or improbability of success in them" (vol. 1, pp. 116–117).

The inequalities caused by labor practices in Europe lead

---

* This idea, which was adopted by Marx, has been criticized by the liberal economists of the so-called Austrian School like Mises and Hayek. These economists argue that "value" is not an objective thing, as Smith and Marx believed, that is, there is no "real" value determined by the amount of labor required for each product but something subjective, created by the preferences of people in the market. Among liberal economists this is an area of intense debate.

him to severely criticize all restrictions on freedom of contracts as well as "the Statutes of Apprenticeship" that required that an apprentice should work up to seven years with a master before qualifying to work. Any restraint on liberty—for example, the residence laws that prevented a worker from seeking work outside his parish—generates injustice and hampers the creation of employment. Adam Smith insists that the privileges enjoyed by the guilds should be abolished: "People of the same trade seldom meet together, even for merriment and diversion, but the conversation ends in a conspiracy against the public, or in some contrivance to raise prices" (vol. 1, p. 144).

Economic analyses alternate with historical accounts such as the development of the price of wheat in the thirteenth, fourteenth, fifteenth, and sixteenth centuries in Scotland and England in comparison with Holland and Geneva, or on the effect that the discovery of gold and silver mines in Peru had on the trading of metals in the world.

Without the division of labor and the accumulation of capital, there would have been no development in productive forces. Capital is partly fixed and partly circulating; the first comprises machines, lands, and sites where the enterprise is established and the latter is the money spent on wages, taxes, and investments. The wealth of a nation is the sum total of all this capital. Stability is an essential condition for development because, when it does not exist, people take their capital out of circulation and hide it.

He goes on to explain the productive process, the appearance of banks, as credit allowed isolated individuals (businessmen or artisans) to set up their enterprises. This helps a social class to grow and take shape. Banks help merchants to convert circulating capital into fixed capital, giving them promissory notes that allowed the banks to spend and move their money around and then return it with an interest that in those days was 8 percent. He shows how companies evaded the ban on exceeding certain limits in order to extend the credit that they received, and he tells the story of a Scottish bank that failed because it issued promissory notes to a large number of traders who were irresponsible and were purely and simply swindlers.

Time and again he criticizes state intervention and the waste and unnecessary expenses incurred by "kings and ministers," which impoverished the whole of society. Perhaps the most important point he makes is his praise of a society where the state is small and functional, for it allows citizens to work and increase wealth, which benefits the whole of society. The ideal citizen, for Smith, is hardworking, austere, prudent, and never wastes his fortune on extravagant purchases. The employer must always set an example for his employees: "If his employer is attentive and parsimonious, the workman is very likely to be so too, but if the master is dissolute and disorderly, the servant, who shapes his work according to the pattern which his master prescribes to him, will shape his life, too, according to the example which he sets him" (vol. 2, p. 612). This entire chapter shows Smith's mistrust toward the state as a potential enemy of the hardworking law-abiding citizen.

The following chapter is dedicated to stock lent at interest. Smith ruled out banning these transactions as some churches— including the Catholic Church—requested, because, he says, if they are properly observed, then they have a useful function in increasing the greater circulation of capital. This is not the case of the borrower who squanders the loan on amusements and nonprofitable activities. But if the interest is not exorbitant and the money of the loan is put to good use, then it has a valuable function in the market. He quotes the case of countries that, in order to combat usury, prohibit bank loans, which just has the effect not of eliminating them but of making them clandestine and illegal.

Adam Smith shows how capitalism, without setting out to do so, undermines nationalism, with capital moving across national borders when profitable investments are not available in its own countries. The reason has an overwhelming logic. When capital in one country has saturated its productive investments, it is obliged to look outside; it does the same by importing what is necessary into its own country to guarantee consumption or to stimulate internal trade. It can also be driven to serve countries that lack capital. This, Smith says, might not directly benefit the country supplying the capital, but it does so indirectly by demonstrating this country to be more advanced in its development and progress. In short, international capitalism is a natural enemy of nationalism.

The main commercial activity takes place between the city and the country and entails the exchange of primary products for manufactured products. The city obtains all its wealth and subsistence from the country. If institutions had not frustrated the natural inclinations of human beings, cities would not have grown larger than the agricultural production of the land where they are located could sustain. The original destiny of men and women was the cultivation of the land. But the relationship between landowners and tenants who paid to rent the land and work it has distorted this reality. The tenants have no incentive to invest in improvements and for that reason agriculture does not develop. Smith criticizes the "right of primogeniture," which favors the oldest child to the detriment of the other children and he condemns slave labor both for moral and economic reasons because it is the most nonproductive work since slaves have no incentives at all to work hard.

The Wealth of Nations explains the birth of European cities as being based on commerce, or rather on merchants. Merchants were "despised" by the "lords" in England who, as in Spain and France, considered commerce a base activity. Kings allowed the formation of cities because of their antagonism with the "lords" and to receive tributes from merchants. Thanks to cities, local and foreign trade increased and manufacturing developed, which strengthened the cities. However, the countryside has continued to be the main provider of primary materials for factories.

Commerce and factories contributed to the development of the countryside by creating markets for agricultural products. Smith makes a curious distinction between a daring merchant, whose profession predisposes him to taking risks, and the timid landowner, who hesitates a great deal before making investments. The merchant, therefore, is the real pioneer of progress.

Commerce and factories gradually introduced order and good governance in society. He severely criticizes landowners for the way they treat their tenants and spend their money on ostentatious and frivolous concerns, unlike merchants and factory owners who invest in new projects motivated by competition. The landowner, by contrast, tends to become a rentier.

The growth of cities entails the growth of the middle classes, through trade and industry, and with it the growth of civilization, that is, liberty and legality. This process transforms society: trade and industry become the main sources of wealth and play their part in the modernization of agriculture and the disappearance of the feudal system. In such an extensive work, it is only natural that there are contradictions. Adam Smith is a supporter of free trade but he also accepts the establishment of tariffs and prohibitions if it can be certain that such measures would increase employment or if total freedom of imports threatens to ruin businessmen and manufacturers who cannot compete with imported products. Some pages later, this theory is contradicted because it is shown that freedom of external trade is the most efficient and beneficial system for countries despite the fact that nationalist prejudices might argue the contrary. It is false to say that it is good for a country to have its neighbors poor; that is only the case if there are wars between them. From a commercial point of view, having rich neighbors means prosperous markets for their own exports.

He then makes a curious observation, that there are more drunks in countries that are not major producers of alcoholic drinks. He gives the example of Spain, Italy, and France, all major wine producers, where, he argues, alcoholism is less extensive than in Central and Eastern Europe. And no less surprising is his statement that any tariff, however small, that does not spark the interest of smugglers has no great commercial effect.

The chapters dedicated to the colonies are very significant. He begins with a historical exposition: colonies were a natural expansion of the population in Greece and then in Rome until, stimulated by the adventures of Marco Polo in Asia, Portuguese and Spaniards went in search of gold in the Indies. Columbus reached Santo Domingo and believed that he had arrived at Marco Polo's Cipango. According to Adam Smith, human greed, the lust for gold, explains the rest of the discoveries and the conquest of the two Americas, north and south. But, he adds, this search for gold and silver mines was frustrating because neither metal compensated for the investment that their extraction required. Not even the richest mines in Peru (he is referring to those in Potosí) enriched the Spanish Crown.

All of Adam Smith's sympathy goes toward the British colonies in North America, the future United States. He explains that they have profited much more than Spanish and Portuguese colonies because Britain gave them greater freedom to produce and to trade, unlike the rigid control that Lisbon and Madrid imposed on their colonies. And once again he stresses that restrictions on trade are "a crime against humanity." He forecasts that the United States will be an enormously prosperous country because of the great expanses of its land and because of the impressive freedoms that these northern colonies enjoy. He also criticizes the very idea of colonialism, which he attributes to greedy adventurers, and he points out the brutality with which, from time immemorial, slaves have been treated. He emphasizes that state interventionism is an infallible recipe for economic failure because it stifles free competition.

Colonialism is immoral and it is also economically negative because it implies the practice of a monopoly that only benefits a small minority and harms both the colonizing country and the rest of the world. The entire chapter is a reasoned appeal to promote liberty as the best political, moral, and economic instrument to ensure progress in society.

As it seemed unlikely that Britain would part with its American possessions, Smith proposes a federation in which the old colonies would have the same rights as the metropolis.

Perhaps the most outrageous restriction is the law that penalizes with a fine and imprisonment anyone seeking to encourage artisans in the wool trade to move to another town or country, for this, says Adam Smith, is a flagrant violation of Britain's much vaunted freedoms.

He criticizes (albeit respectfully) Quesnay and the French physiocrats for arguing that only land produces wealth and for considering manufacturers and merchants as "unproductive." He shows how artisans, industrialists, and merchants are as progressive as agricultural workers. What diminishes their role in the creation of wealth are the impediments and interferences in the mercantile system. He offers many examples to prove that free trade is just and brings prosperity. He cites innumerable historical cases—like those of China, Indostan, Greece, and Rome—to illustrate how increased freedom had led to greater development in countries and how less freedom had led to further backwardness.

From economics, Adam Smith returns to history, to that moment when humanity was divided between societies of hunters and agriculturalists and later between merchants and manufacturers and he analyzes these societies in relation to the power that they had to protect themselves or to attack their neighbors. In hunting peoples, all the members of the community were warriors and supported themselves. In agricultural societies, militias emerged and, later on, armies. In each case the costs increase. Until, finally, the state finances the defense of society. An army will always be superior to a militia (although the history of revolutions contradicts this theory). And the costs incurred in maintaining an army always increase as arms and ammunition become more expensive, especially after the invention of firearms. Adam Smith examines the risks to freedom that a standing army entails.

The analysis then shifts to the law. He explains how the need for judges was born and he asserts that it is a consequence of private property. Judges emerged to defend the rich against "the indignation of the poor" (vol. 2, p. 710). Then society pays for people charged to administer justice. In more primitive societies, the people who sought justice paid the judges or offered them gifts and later the state took on this obligation. To feel safe about one's rights is fundamental to the existence of a free society. But judges have been corruptible and the administration of justice declined when judges, who received payment according to the number of words and pages that they had to deliver in their pronouncements, increased their income by inflating their statements.

Adam Smith is interesting on how the clergy maintain their position. And his idea is that when there are many different churches in a society, there will be less fanaticism and a greater spirit of tolerance. Adam Smith was far from being a fanatical believer because he talks very objectively about Catholics and Protestants alike. Some thought him an atheist, like his friend David Hume. Despite a natural sympathy for Presbyterianism and the Scottish Church, which educated him, he shows no bias and only refers to objective facts. In this, once again, one can see his serene and open nature; while not an atheist, he was probably an agnostic who kept up the appearance of being a believer because he saw that religion was one of those institutions that made living together easier and to some degree instilled moral order in society.

He talks of the sources of income that maintain the sovereign or the government, that is, taxes, offering some arguments that we would now call social democratic. Following Lord Kames and Montesquieu in this regard, he believes that taxes should help to "equalize" incomes, charging more to the rich than to the poor and avoiding any excessive or unjust taxes that might invite evasion. He is strongly critical of tax collectors who suck taxpayers dry.

He considers the tithes paid to the Church as purely negative because they do not benefit in any way the landowner or the tenant or the sovereign but only the Church itself (this shows what a lukewarm believer Adam Smith was).

A detailed discussion of the reasons for taxes, the types of taxes, and how they are collected in Britain and other countries illustrates clearly his belief that "there is no art which one government sooner learns from another than that of draining money from the pockets of the people" (vol. 2, p. 861). Since there must be taxes, then one must try to make sure that these are not unjust and do not weigh more heavily on the poor than on the rich since, otherwise, they might lead to evasion and contraband. And he gives the example of people who break the law because they are so weighed down by tax burdens.

He studies how countries take on debts to meet their budgetary requirements or to finance wars, the ways in which these debts are paid, and their impact on economic life. He concludes that once nations get used to taking on debts, it is almost impossible for them to pay the enormous obligations that these incur. And he is very critical of states who artificially pay their debts by devaluing their currency, thereby generally paying only a small part of the debts that they took on.

This brief synthesis gives only a remote idea of the ambition and enormity of *The Wealth of Nations*, of the variety of themes aired in its pages, and of how, although economic preoccupations prevail, philosophy, history, and sociology are all included. Adam Smith's ideas first spread across the British Isles, then through Europe and America, and, gradually, throughout the rest of the world. To some extent, by the nineteenth century they were influential across almost the entire Western world. However, many of these ideas, which were born in the eighteenth century, refer to a social reality that has changed enormously compared to today. But it is no exaggeration to say that these changes have been due in great part to the insights and ideas that became known for the first time in this seminal book.

ADAM SMITH'S FINAL YEARS

The repercussions of the publication of *The Wealth of Nations* were enormous but slow in developing and it does not seem that Adam Smith was anxious about the impact of his book. His correspondence shows that he responded quickly to friends, intellectuals, and political figures who commented on the work, praising or criticizing it and asking for clarifications, but he never foresaw the ways in which his ideas would spread throughout the entire world and would influence the course of economic life in the West in the following decades. He had already doubtless begun to map out in his mind, in his house in Kirkcaldy, what he considered would be his third and decisive study on the workings of society—dealing with jurisprudence—a book that he never managed to complete. But he was writing another study, on the imitative arts, when, according to his own confession, he had to interrupt it. And he would never finish it.

The illness of his best friend, David Hume, which began to manifest itself from 1775 with intense discomfort in the bladder and stomach—it was a cancerous tumor—and became a real torture over a number of months, affected him greatly. The following year, in January, Hume wrote his will naming Adam Smith as his literary executor and leaving him a two-hundred-pound inheritance. He also instructed him to publish his short autobiographical work, *My Own Life*, and to decide if and when to publish his polemical essay "Dialogues Concerning Natural Religion," written years earlier and which he had just revised, in which he defended his atheism and severely criticized established religions, in particular Christianity. The opinions of Hume's friends who knew the work were divided, but most of them, including Adam Smith, thought that, given the prevailing climate, it would be imprudent to bring out a book that would probably be banned by the Crown. Smith made a special visit to Edinburgh to visit Hume, who died on August 25, 1777, and did indeed begin to work on the edition of *My Own Life*, adding in some of Hume's letters and a text that he himself wrote in praise of his friend. This provoked a minor scandal because, on the subject of education, he allowed himself to make some criticism of religious institutions and, especially, of Oxford University, a place that brought back so many bad memories to him.

In 1778, thanks to the influence of his old pupil, the Duke of Buccleuch, and other important friends, Adam Smith was named commissioner or chief of customs in Edinburgh, a job that, on a minor scale, the father that he never knew once held in Kirkcaldy. Over the three years that he worked in this post he earned some eight thousand pounds, a small fortune, that allowed him to live out his final years very comfortably. But his biographers point out that he was always a generous man, who helped his friends and spent most of his income on charitable works. For that reason he left very little after his death. He moved his mother and his cousin Janet Douglas to an elegant home, Panmure House, in the Canongate, an aristocratic suburb in Edinburgh. In these final years he had an intense social life. Not that he was a negligent administrator, far from it. All accounts agree that he was a precise and responsible customs commissioner, who went to his office every day except Friday, his day off, attended all the commissioners' meetings, constantly wrote reports, and made suggestions for improving the service. It is something of a paradox that the greatest defender of free trade that the world has seen ended his days in a job whose very existence negated his most cherished ideas.

It is quite understandable that, with such strict obligations, he never had the time to write the volume on jurisprudence with which he thought to complete his research on social development. Only once in those years did he ask for several months' leave—in 1787, from January to July—most of which he spent revising the fifth edition of *The Wealth of Nations*, which was published with many corrections and additions. Every week he would invite to his house in the Canongate— where he had taken his nine-year-old nephew, David Douglas, his future heir, to live with him—his intellectual friends, among them the young Walter Scott, who wrote about the meetings. He also met these philosophers, writers, and men of culture in the Royal Society of Edinburgh, which he had helped to organize, and the Oyster Club, which he had also founded.

In May 1784 his mother died, at ninety years old. Adam Smith, who adored her and had lived almost all his life close to her, wrote of the loneliness and abandonment that he would feel for the rest of his life without the person who "certainly loved me more than any other person ever did or ever will love me."*

In 1787 he received a tribute from his alma mater: the University of Glasgow elected him rector. The following year Janet Douglas, who had dedicated her life to looking after him, died. The news also deeply affected him.

Like Hume, Adam Smith began to have problems in the lower abdomen from the beginning of 1790. He had always suffered from constipation and in those four months of leave he underwent a small surgical intervention that did not solve

* Letter to his editor, quoted in Nicholas Phillipson, op. cit., p. 262.

the problem but made it worse, blighting the final months of his life. The story goes, from the mouth of his friend Henry Mackenzie, that on the night of July 16, 1790, at a gathering in his house in Canongate, he said goodbye to the friends who were visiting him with the following words: "I love your company, gentlemen, but I believe I must leave you to go to another world." No sooner said than done: he died the following morning. He is buried in Edinburgh, in the neighborhood where he lived, in the Canongate Kirkyard; a simple headstone recalls that he was the author of *The Theory of Moral Sentiments* and *The Wealth of Nations*.

JOSÉ ORTEGA Y GASSET (1883–1955)

José Ortega y Gasset was one of the most intelligent and elegant liberal philosophers of the twentieth century, though various circumstances—the Spanish Civil War, the forty years of Franco's dictatorship and the rise of Marxist and revolutionary theories in the second half of the twentieth century in Europe and Latin America—have caused this thought to be discarded, unjustly, among the old junk in the loft or, worse still, to be misconstrued and held up as an example of conservative thought.

Although he never managed to synthesize his philosophy into an organic body of ideas, in the innumerable essays, articles, lectures, and notes that comprise his vast work, he developed an indisputably liberal discourse, in a Spanish context where such ideas were unusual—he would have said *radical*, one of his favorite words—in being just as critical of the dogmatic extremism of the left as of the authoritarian, nationalist, and Catholic conservatism of the right. Much of this thought is still relevant and very topical today in light of the bankruptcy of Marxism and its parasitic doctrines and the ways in which certain strands of liberalism have become overinterested in purely economic theories.

There is no better example of this than *The Revolt of the*

Masses, published as a book in 1930, though many of the arguments had been rehearsed in articles and essays two or three years earlier. This often happened with Ortega; rather than producing fully rounded studies from the outset, he developed his work through lectures and short texts, written for newspapers and journals, that he later brought together into books. Before this magisterial essay, Ortega y Gasset had reflected on topics that would, in subsequent years, become very relevant in Spain and Europe, such as the reemergence of nationalism and, in the field of art and literature, what he would call, most appositely, "dehumanization."

INDEPENDENCE MOVEMENTS AND DECADENCE

He was born in Madrid on May 9, 1883, the son of the journalist and writer José Ortega Munilla and Dolores Gasset Chinchilla, whose father was the owner of the liberal newspaper *El Imparcial*. He was educated by Jesuits at school and in the University of Deusto but graduated from the Universidad Central de Madrid, where he also completed his doctorate. In 1905 he traveled to Germany, first to Leipzig, then to Nuremberg, Munich, Cologne, and Berlin, although he lived and studied for the most part in Marburg, where he stayed until 1907. He was appointed to a professorship in metaphysics in Madrid in 1911; a grant took him back to Germany, to Marburg. He returned to Spain to take up his professorship and he became most active on the lecture circuit and in writing articles. His professed aim was to "Europeanize Spain" and take it out of its isolation—both cultural and political—and this caused him to debate with another prominent thinker, older than him, Miguel de Unamuno, who, among the many idiotic statements that he was prone to make, held that the objective should be to "Hispanicize Europe."

In 1923, Ortega published his first book, *España invertebrada. Bosquejo de algunos pensamientos históricos* (*Invertebrate Spain*), which brought together two series of articles previously published in the Madrid newspaper *El Sol*, on the problem of Catalan and Basque separatism.

Ortega always had an instinct for perceiving the great political and cultural events of his time before the wider public did, like "the dehumanization of art" and "the revolt of the masses," two phenomena that would characterize Western culture at the height of his intellectual career. He was also very accurate in warning that the independence movements in Catalonia and the Basque Country, two important regions in Spain, would in the future be one of the most important problems that his country would have to struggle with. A problem that, a century on, is still unresolved and which, from time to time, threatens the democratic stability and the economic progress of modern Spain.

The book *Invertebrate Spain* had an immediate success—it was the first of his works to reach a very wide readership—and went through several editions in the months and years following its initial publication.

For Ortega, Catalan and Basque separatism is "the greatest ill present in our Spain."* But he does not see these centrifugal tendencies as a deep and popular movement, with historical roots, but rather as two examples of the long and slow disintegration of Spain going back centuries, or more precisely when

---

* José Ortega y Gasset, *España invertebrada y otros ensayos*, Alianza Editorial, Madrid, 2014, p. 153. All the quotations are from this edition.

it stopped being "an active and dynamic reality" and became a society without ambitions or dreams, living "a passive and static existence like a pile of stones along a roadside" (p. 69).

In this book Ortega gave his famous definition of a nation as "a suggestive project for a life in common," complementary to that of Renan, whom he quotes enthusiastically, who argues that "a nation is a daily plebiscite" (p. 65).

Ortega does not believe in nationalist doctrines; he is convinced that they are mere pretexts used to express the disillusionment felt in all the regions of Spain (which now, "rather than a nation is a set of watertight compartments" [p. 91]), caused by the decline that had fractured the integration of all the regions around Castile, when they shared a great project that gave Spain its preeminence in the world, its imperial power, and its greatness. This project was not conquest but "colonization": "It is evident to me that this is the only truly great thing that Spain has achieved" (p. 138). And, for him, colonization was not the work of the monarchy or the nobility, but of "the people," the anonymous people of Spain, the ordinary, heroic men who, in difficult and often terrible conditions, entered an unknown world to win lands, peoples, and wealth for God, the empire, and an idea of Spain that then flourished and spread throughout the nation, keeping it both unified and alive. All that is now very much in the past; since that time Spain has both declined and become "invertebrate," leading to a sense of "particularism" that affects the entire country: Catalan and Basque nationalism are the most visible symbols of this general disease. And, he adds dramatically, "It is worse to be a disease than to have a disease" (p. 100).

This toxic ailment that Spain carries from its distant past is manifest in the present in the intellectual and political poverty of its nobility, the mediocrity and ignorance of its politicians, and the isolation of its men of science. His criticism of the state of affairs in the country is very severe and it is in this context that Ortega analyzes the separatist movements in Catalonia and the Basque Country: "Nationalist theories, political programmes of regionalism and the utterances of their supporters lack interest and are, in large part, a contrivance. But in these historical movements, generated by the masses, what is said is a mere pretext, a superficial, transitory and fictitious premise which has merely a symbolic value as a conventional and almost always incongruent expression of deep, ineffable and obscure emotions that operate in the subsoil of the collective soul" (p. 60).

There is a lot of truth in what Ortega says. In the years of the Franco dictatorship, with its harsh suppression of all forms of "particularism" in the regions of Spain, the Catalan and Basque independence movements seemed to die out save for sporadic acts of terrorism by ETA (the extremist Basque organization). I lived in Barcelona for five years, from the early to mid-seventies, and during that time the activities of intellectuals and the political vanguards were focused—despite the repression—on the reestablishment of democracy. Independence movements languished, confined to minuscule traditionalist and marginal sectors. However, following the restoration of democracy and the creation of the state of autonomies, which led to the transfer of important administrative, political, and, above all, educational responsibilities to the regional communities, the nationalist sectors in power in both Catalonia and the Basque Country began an active campaign of spreading their ideology, mixed with historical falsifications, and undertook a determined policy of expanding the Catalan and Basque languages at the expense of Spanish, all of which bore fruit over time, reviving the theme of independence until it became the greatest threat to Spanish democracy. Ortega y Gasset was prophetic.

THE DEHUMANIZATION OF ART

In 1925, three years after the publication of *Invertebrate Spain*, another important book by Ortega was published, another collection of essays that had previously appeared in the press: *La deshumanización del arte y otros ensayos de estética (The Dehumanization of Art and Other Essays on Art, Culture and Literature)*.

It opens with a bold statement: the masses hate new art because they do not understand it. The reason is obvious; romantic art, which dazzled the nineteenth century, and also naturalism, were accessible to all through their impassioned representation of sentimental life and its mawkish effusions, or its clinical treatment of social problems, but the new movements in music, painting, theater, and literature, which did not seek to show life as it is but rather to create an "other" life, require laborious intellectual effort—a change of perspective and of the very definition of art itself—that the "great philistine herd" is not prepared to make. Therefore there is an irreparable separation—a chasm—between the new art, its cultivators and defenders, and the rest of society.

According to Ortega, what most people appreciated in the romantic and naturalist art of the past was their least artistic aspects, the depiction of real life in operas, paintings, plays, and novels, the description of family travails, the passions of love, historical facts, social problems, everything that made up daily existence in which spectators, listeners, and readers thought they recognized their own experiences. But the artists of our time do not want their art to appear as an illustration of "real life"; to the contrary, they seek to create a life that is distinct from real life, dissociated from lived experience, forged from beginning to end by art through exclusively artistic techniques such as metaphor. This, Ortega observes, is what Debussy has done in music ("Debussy dehumanized music and for that reason the new era of sonorous art begins with him" [p. 77]),* Mallarmé in poetry ("Mallarmé's verse annuls all human resonance and presents us with figures so extraterrestrial that merely to contemplate them is pure delight" [p. 79]), Pirandello in theater with his *Six Characters in Search of an Author* ("Traditional theatre expects us to interpret its characters as real people and their exaggerated gestures as the expressions of a 'human' drama. Here, by contrast, our interest is aroused by characters as characters themselves; that is, as ideas or pure patterns" [pp. 85–86]). In literature, he cites Joyce, Proust, and Gómez de la Serna. And in painting he sees the expressionist and cubist movements as equivalent ("From painting things they now paint ideas: artists have blinded themselves to the outside world and turned their gaze towards internal and subjective landscapes" [p. 85]), because they avoid representing reality as we experience it, creating instead a pure and exclusively invented reality.

Ortega points out that, despite the variations and different movements, this new art shares certain characteristics: dehumanization, avoiding living forms, considering art as a game, injecting an essential irony, avoiding insincerity, and recognizing that the new artistic objects lack transcendence. This is an unpretentious art that, unlike its predecessor, does not have political or social objectives since it knows that art does not operate in these areas, nor, in general, does it engage with

* José Ortega y Gasset, *La dehumanización del arte y otros ensayos de estética*, with an introduction by Valeriano Bozal, Austral, Barcelona, 2016. The page references for the quotations are from this edition.

practical concerns, for it has lost its gravity and wants to entertain and make its spectators laugh, returning them to the innocence of childhood.

In this essay, Ortega pointed out, most perceptively, a direction in modern culture that, with momentary deviations, would, in subsequent decades, gain force throughout the Western world, above all in certain genres like painting, revolutionizing and negating tradition in unusually extreme ways. The third world would also soon be affected, so that, in a few years, the entire planet would embrace the concept of art as spectacle. The trend that Ortega outlined accelerated in the decades following the publication of his book. In this climate of increasing confusion and banality, under the label of "art," some of the most puerile experiments and the greatest confidence tricks in the history of culture began to emerge. In the conclusion to his essay, Ortega stated that because what led him to write was "exclusively the pleasure in trying to understand," he did so "predisposed towards benevolence": "From these youthful works I have tried to extract their intention, which is playful, and I have not been concerned with their finished product. Who knows what will come out of this nascent style?" (p. 99). Ortega could never have imagined that the "new art" that he welcomed so enthusiastically would come to produce artifacts so exquisitely celebrated—and valued in millions of dollars—as the colored photographs of Andy Warhol, the cut-up sharks preserved in formaldehyde or the diamond skulls by Damien Hirst, or the multicolored circus balls of Jeff Koons.

THE REVOLT OF THE MASSES

The Revolt of the Masses is structured around a brilliant intuition: that the primacy of elites has ended and the masses, now liberated from their domination, are having a decisive impact on today's society, turning upside down civil and cultural values and social conventions. Written at a time when communism and fascism were on the rise, along with union organization, nationalism, and the first manifestations of mass-consumption popular culture, Ortega's intuition was correct and he defined, before anyone else, one of the key features of modern society.

He was also correct to base his criticism of this phenomenon on the defense of the individual, whose sovereignty is being threatened—and has in many ways already been destroyed—by this uncontainable irruption of the crowd—the masses—into modern life. The concept of the "mass" for Ortega has nothing to do with social class and is opposed to the Marxist definition of the term. The "mass" that Ortega refers to embraces men and women across different social classes, who have been subsumed across the board into a collective entity by abdicating their sovereign individuality and taking on a collective identity, becoming just a "part of the tribe." The mass, in Ortega's book, is a group of individuals who have become deindividualized, who have stopped being freethinking human entities and have dissolved into an amalgam that thinks and acts for them, more through conditioned reflexes—emotions, instincts, passions—than through reason. These are the masses that, at the time of writing, were forming around Benito Mussolini in Italy and in later years would flock to Hitler in Germany or to venerate Stalin, "the little father of the people," in Russia. Communism and fascism, Ortega writes, are "two clear examples of substantial regression," typical examples of the transformation of the individual into the "mass-man." But in his definition of "massification," Ortega y Gasset does not just include the regimented multitudes that form around political bosses and supreme leaders in totalitarian regimes. For him, the masses are also a new reality in democratic countries where the individual becomes increasingly absorbed by different collectives that now play leading roles in public life, a phenomenon that he sees as a return to primitivism (the "call of the tribe") and to certain forms of barbarity under the guise of modernity.

This frightening vision of the growing hegemony of collectivism in the life of nations is that of a liberal thinker who sees the disappearance of the individual into the collective as a historical setback and a very grave threat to democratic civilization.

Published on the eve of the Second World War, the book also makes an early and surprising defense of a unified Europe in which the nations of the old continent, without completely losing their traditions and cultures, would meld into a community. "Europe will be the ultra-nation," he declares. It is only through this union, for Ortega, that there is possible salvation for a continent that has lost the historical leadership role that it held in the past—which is now in decline—while, around it, Russia and the United States seem bent on taking over this leadership. Ortega's audacious proposal in favor of a European Union that would only begin to take shape half a century later is one of the most prescient parts of the work, and proof of the visionary insight that its author sometimes achieved.

The essay also sets out another pure liberal principle. Part of Europe's decline is due to the enormous growth of the state, whose suffocating bureaucratic and interventionist networks have "jugulated" the initiatives and creativity of its citizens.

Ortega points out that one of the effects of this eruption of the masses into political and social life has been, in the cultural field, the cheapening and vulgarization of culture, the replacement of genuine artistic production by caricatures or stereotyped and mechanical forms, and by a wave of bad taste, vulgarity, and stupidity.

Ortega was an elitist with respect to culture, but his elitism was not at odds with his democratic convictions because it focused on the creation of cultural goods and how they matched up to a demanding scale of values. When it came to their dissemination and consumption, his position was democratic and universalist: culture should be accessible to everyone. Put simply, Ortega believed that great artists and the best thinkers—those who had renewed tradition and had established new models and forms, introducing new ways of understanding life and its artistic depiction—should set the aesthetic and intellectual standards of cultural life. And were this not the case and were the aesthetic and intellectual values for the whole of society to be established by the average taste of the masses—ordinary men and women—then this would lead to a brutal impoverishment of cultural life and nothing less than the suffocation of creativity. Ortega's cultural elitism is inseparable from his cosmopolitanism, from his conviction that true culture has no regional and much less national borders, that it is a universal patrimony. In this respect, his thinking is profoundly anti-nationalist.

In his defense of liberalism, Ortega insists that in a democratic society the state should be secular. ("History is the reality of man. There is no other" [p. 54].*) and that there is a deep incompatibility between liberal thought and dogmatic Catholic thought, which he terms anti-modern (p. 153). History is

* José Ortega y Gasset, *La rebelión de las masas*, introduction by Julián Marías, commemorative edition, Austral collection, Madrid, Espasa Calpe, 2005. All the quotations are taken from this edition.

not written, it has not been mapped out in advance, by an almighty deity. It is the work of humans alone and, for that reason, "Everything, everything is possible in history, both triumphant and indefinite progress and periodic regression" (pp. 131–132).

The very least that one can say about his arguments and assertions in the book is that Ortega demonstrated a great independence of spirit and a sense of conviction that were capable of withstanding the dominant intellectual and political pressures of his day. These were, let us not forget, times in which the intellectual class believed less and less in democracy, which suffered abuse equally from both extremes, the fascist right and the communist left, and these intellectuals often gave in to the temptation of joining one of the two factions, with a marked preference for communism.

However, Ortega y Gasset's liberalism, while genuine, is partial. His defense of individuals and their sovereign rights, of a small, secular state that stimulates rather than suffocates individual liberty, of a plurality of opinions and criticisms, does not include a defense of economic freedom and the free market. Ortega treats this aspect of social life with a mistrust bordering on disdain, about which, at times, he reveals an ignorance that is surprising in an intellectual who was so curious and open toward all disciplines. This is doubtless a generational limitation. Without exception, like the Latin American liberals of their time, Spanish liberals who were more or less Ortega's contemporaries, like Ramón Pérez de Ayala and Gregorio Marañón, with whom he would form the Agrupación al Servicio de la República (Association at the Service of the Republic) in February 1931, were liberals in political, ethical, civic, and cultural terms, but not in economic terms. Their defense of civil society, democracy, and political freedom ignored a key part of liberal doctrine, which had been set out by Adam Smith: that without economic freedom and without firm legal guarantees for private property and for contracts, political democracy and public freedoms are always compromised. Despite being a freethinker, who had distanced himself from the Catholic education he had received in a Jesuit school and university, there were always echoes in his thought of the disdain or at least the inveterate mistrust of Catholic morality toward finance, business, economic success, and capitalism, as if these social endeavors reflected the most base, materialistic aspects of human beings, at odds with their spiritual and intellectual capacities. No doubt this is the source of his disparaging remarks, scattered throughout *The Revolt of the Masses*, about the United States, "the paradise of the masses" (p. 164), a country that Ortega views through a lens of cultural superiority, as having, by its rapid growth in quantitative terms, sacrificed its "qualities," thus creating a superficial culture. From this premise he puts forward one of the few nonsensical ideas in the book: that the United States, by itself, will be unable to achieve the scientific development that can be found in Europe. And with the rise of the "mass-man," Ortega sees this science to be in jeopardy.

This is one of the weakest aspects of *The Revolt of the Masses*. One of the consequences of the primacy of the mass-man in the life of nations, he says, is the lack of interest that a society beset by primitivism and vulgarity shows for the general principles of culture, that is, for the very foundations of civilization. At a time when the collective holds sway, pure science takes second place and the attention of the masses is centered on technology, on the marvels and wonders that this subproduct of science has produced, for, without it, luxury automobiles with their sleek lines or painkillers that take away headaches would not be possible. Ortega compares the deification of consumer products made by technology with primitive African villagers' bedazzlement at the objects of modern industrial production that they regard, like fruit and animals, as merely the products of nature. For science to exist, Ortega argues, it must be developed from a long-established civilization. And for that reason, he believes that, however powerful it might be, the United States will never surpass the purely technological phase that it has reached. "What a mess we'd be in if we thought that if Europe were to disappear the North Americans could *continue* science!" This is one of the flawed predictions in a book full of prophecies that are now realities.

In *The Revolt of the Masses* Ortega criticizes nationalism as a typical phenomenon of the growing hegemony of the collective over the individual. He argues that the idea that a nation is built on communities defined by race, religion, or language is a myth and inclines more toward Renan's formulation: a nation is a "daily plebiscite" whose members reaffirm each day, through their behavior and adherence to laws and institutions, their desire to form a "unity of destiny" (the phrase is Ortega's). This idea of a nation is flexible, modern, and chimes with his conviction that Europe will soon form a supranational union in which European nations will come together in pluralist unity, something that seemed a utopian fantasy in that context of belligerent nationalisms that a few years later would plunge Europe into the slaughterhouse of the Second World War.

The "Epilogue for the British," a critique of pacifism, was written in 1937, seven years after the first edition of *The Revolt of the Masses*, at the height of the Spanish Civil War. It criticizes the stereotypical views that foreign countries have of what is happening within a society. Ortega offers as an example the case of British intellectuals who, "sitting comfortably in their offices or their clubs," sign texts stating that communists who in Spain coerce writers to sign manifestos or to speak on the radio to support their interests, are "defenders of liberty." From all this he argues that foreign public opinion is, in certain cases, "a bellicose intervention" in the internal affairs of a country, something that could have "chemical" (lethal) effects on its future. This theory is untenable, of course: to accept it would be to justify supressing freedom of expression and opinion on the grounds of national security. Ortega does not recognize that it is normal for outsiders to have a better understanding of what is happening inside dictatorial regimes, because censorship prevents those suffering under dictatorship from being fully aware of the situation in which they are living. (I remember that, in 1958, in the lodgings in Dr. Castelo Street where I was living in Madrid, we listened every night to the news bulletins of Radio Paris, to find out everything that the censored press in Spain was hiding or distorting.)

In effect this strange declaration reflects the anxiety and despair that Ortega suffered in a civil war in which he felt that European intellectuals embellished the Republic for ideological reasons, without taking into account the abuses and antidemocratic excesses that had also been committed in its midst. For this reason, Ortega could not and did not want to choose between the warring parties, above all after he reached the conclusion that the struggle was not so much between the democratic Republic and fascism, but between fascism and the communists, an alternative that Ortega equally rejected. However it is true that, without making it public, through his correspondence and the testimonies of people close to him, it seems evident that he came to believe, at a certain moment, that Franco and the "nationalists" represented the lesser evil. This did not imply any sympathy for fascism, of course, but rather a desperate choice. It was a mistake for which he would be mercilessly reproached by posterity and that would contribute to the so-called progressive intellectual sectors distancing themselves from his work. What is true is that there is no lesser of two evils when it comes to choosing between two totalitarian systems—it is like choosing between AIDS and terminal cancer—something that Ortega himself was able to confirm when he returned to Spain, in 1945, at the end of the Second World War, thinking that after the Allied victory over fascism, it would be possible to do something for the democratization of his country from within. He could not do much, except live in internal exile, in a sort of limbo, unable to take up his university post again, under constant surveillance and, at the same time, running the risk of seeing his work misconstrued by Falangists, who wanted to appropriate it, in a permanent state of frustration and anxiety. For that reason, the last ten years of his life were extremely unsettled, and he took frequent trips to Portugal.

ORTEGA Y GASSET AND THE REPUBLIC

Ortega y Gasset celebrated the advent of the Republic as the beginning of an era of civic and cultural progress for Spain. In the first republican elections he stood as a candidate for the Constituent Assembly and was elected as a deputy for the province of León. In December 1931, the Revista de Occidente publishing house in Madrid brought out his *Rectificación de la República (Artículos y discursos)* ("Rectification of the Republic: Articles and Speeches"), which shows his enthusiasm for the new regime. It had already been in power for a year and Ortega offers some criticisms and observations, but from a supportive position. His interventions in the Constituent Assembly and his articles in the press in this first year of the Republic appear in his name and also on behalf of his "small group," the Agrupación al Servicio de la República. Though this was not such a small group. According to Shlomo Ben-Ami, within two weeks of its founding, the Agrupación had some fifteen thousand members, mainly students, teachers, and intellectuals.* Ortega dissolved the Agrupación in October 1932, arguing that the Republic was already "sufficiently consolidated."†

The book also contains the lecture that Ortega gave on December 6, 1931, in the Cinema de la Ópera in Madrid, in which, in a closely argued text, he proposed the creation of a great national Republican party to defend the new regime and suggested some corrections to its current policies. The idea of being at the forefront of a great political force came to nothing because of the more extreme positions and the violent confrontations that emerged in the Republic in the following years, which cooled the enthusiasm for the new system in democrats such as Ortega, who finally expressed his disillusionment in his emblematic article, "Not like this, not like this!"

His idea of the brand-new Republic was somewhat naive and idealist—"to make a Republic that is robust, fecund and generous"‡—but he is unequivocal in his rejection of the monarchy. He accuses it of having become "a source of fundamental disorder" and of serving the "conservative classes" whose "absenteeism" he sharply criticizes, along with taking their

* Shlomo Ben-Ami, *The Origins of the Second Republic in Spain*, Oxford University Press, Oxford, 1978, p. 44.
† Rockwell Gray, *José Ortega y Gasset. El imperativo de la modernidad*, Espasa Calpe, Madrid, 1994, p. 250.
‡ José Ortega y Gasset, *Rectificación de la República (Artículos y discursos)*, Revista de Occidente, Madrid, 1931, p. 63.

money out of the country and showing no interest at all in the fate of Spain at a time when a new nation is being built. He states that he is not a Catholic and explains that his liberal and democratic ideas make him a republican: "I have come to the Republic, like many others, moved by the enthusiastic hope that, finally, after many centuries, it would allow our people, our national spontaneity, to correct its own fortune, to regulate itself, as any healthy organisation does; to reshape its impulses in complete freedom without violence from anyone, so that in our society every individual and every group are authentically who they are without their heartfelt reality being deformed by pressure or favour" (p. 156).

His ideas on the new republic were very general and rhetorical—he declares himself in favor of separatism and against federalism—and, in any event, he did not in any way foresee the violence that the uncontrolled extremism of the right and the left would bring to the country, a violence that would reduce the number of citizens who, like him, hoped that the new regime would bring about economic progress, serenity and stability, freedom, and a civilized coexistence between political forces. Ortega confesses his ignorance of economics; yet an instinct makes him see that economics is an absolutely essential issue that will determine the success or failure of the new regime. This is why he recommends that a body of economists be set up to advise the government on political economy, even contracting specialists from abroad if within Spain there are not the necessary financial experts.

THE COURTESY OF THE PHILOSOPHER

Reading Ortega is always a joy, an aesthetic pleasure, because of the beauty and fluency of his style, which is clear, expressive, intelligent, and cultured, with an inexhaustible vocabulary, laced with irony, and accessible to any reader. Because of this accessibility, some argue that he is not a philosopher, but merely a man of letters and a journalist. I would be delighted if this were the case because, were the premise on which this exclusion is based to be true, then philosophy would be super- fluous and literature and journalism would amply fulfill its function.

It is true that his writing could sometimes be affected as when he wrote *rigoroso* instead of the standard term *riguroso* and that, when it comes to the two rules that he established for intellectuals—to oppose and to seduce—his flirtatiousness and vanity led him at times to neglect the first obligation in favor of the latter. But these occasional weaknesses are more than compensated by the vigor and grace that his talent was able to inject into ideas that, in his essays, seem like the living, unpredictable characters of Balzac's La Comédie humaine, which so entranced him in his youth.

What helped to humanize his thought was his commitment to realism, which, as in the great tradition of Spanish art and literature, was inseparable from his intellectual commitment. Neither philosophy in particular, nor culture in general, should be a mere exercise in rhetorical acrobatics, the narcissistic gym- nastics of a select few. For this "elitist," the mission of culture could not be more democratic: to immerse itself in, and take nourishment from, everyday life. Long before French existen- tialists developed their theory about the intellectuals' "com- mitment" to their time and society, Ortega had made this conviction his own and put it into practice in everything he wrote. This does not mean that he wrote about everything; for example, he is reproached for not having openly declared his views on the outcome of the civil war and the Franco dictatorship. But I have already explained the complex reasons for this silence.

One of his most famous phrases was "Clarity is the courtesy of the philosopher," a maxim that he always adhered to when it came to writing. And I do not think that this effort to be accessible, inspired by Goethe's desire always to "move from obscurity to clarity," which he called a "Luciferian desire," impoverished his thinking, reducing him to the role of a mere popularizer. Quite the reverse, one of his great merits is to have been able to bring the great issues of philosophy, history, and culture in general to a nonspecialist public, to ordinary readers, in a way that enabled them to understand and feel concerned about these issues, without trivializing or betraying their complexities. This led him to journalism, of course, and to public lectures where he spoke to vast, heterogeneous audiences, convinced as he was that ideas confined to the classroom or to professional enclaves, far removed from the agora, simply withered. He firmly believed that philosophy helps human beings to live, to resolve their problems, and to deal lucidly with the world that surrounds them and should not therefore be the exclusive property of philosophers but should reach ordinary people.

This obsessive urge to make himself understood by all his readers is one of the most important lessons that he has bequeathed us, an example of his democratic and liberal vocation that is of luminous importance in these times when, increasingly, in different spheres of culture, ordinary language has been displaced by jargon or specialized, hermetic dialects that do not express complexity and scientific depth but are rather a mask for verbose conjuring and trickery. Whether we agree or disagree with his ideas and his claims, one thing is always evident about Ortega: he plays no tricks; the transparency of his writing prevents this from happening.

His Luciferian desire for clarity did not prevent him from being bold and offering, before anyone else, an interpretation of the dominant trends of his age in social life and in art that appeared fanciful but that history has since proved right. In *The Revolt of the Masses*, he warned, most accurately, that in the twentieth century, unlike what had happened before, the decisive factor in social and political evolution would no longer be the elites but rather the anonymous popular sectors, workers, peasants, the unemployed, soldiers, students, collectives of every stripe, whose intervention in history—peaceful or violent—would revolutionize society in the future and make a clean break with the past. And in *The Dehumanization of Art* (1925), he described, with a wealth of detail and great accuracy, the progressive divorce—driven by the extraordinary revolution in form introduced by vanguard movements in music, painting, and literature—between modern art and the general public, a phenomenon without precedent in the history of civilization. These are two important, but by no means unique, examples of the lucidity with which Ortega analyzed his "circumstance" and perceived, ahead of his time, the trends and the power lines of the immediate future. His work is laced with notable predictions and accurate intuitions.

What was he, politically speaking? A freethinker, an atheist (or, at least, an agnostic), a civilist, a cosmopolitan, a European, an opponent of nationalism and of all ideological dogmatism, a democrat: his favorite word was always *radical*. Analysis and thought should always go to the root of problems and never remain on the margins or on the surface. However, in politics, to some extent, he was at times far from the radicalism that he preached. He was, through his open nature and his tolerance for other people's ideas and positions, a liberal. But a liberal limited by his lack of understanding of economics, a gap that led him at times, when he proposed solutions to problems such as centralism, *caciquismo*, or poverty, to call for state intervention and arbitrary controls, totally at odds with the individual and civil liberty that he defended with such conviction and strong arguments.

Furthermore he was one of the few Spanish intellectuals of his time to take an interest in Latin America. He went to Argentina for the first time in 1916 and stayed for almost six months. And he returned on two occasions, in 1928 when he also visited Chile, and he lived in Argentina from 1939 to 1942 in voluntary exile. His lectures and university classes in Buenos Aires and his contributions to the newspaper *La Nación* earned him great prestige and he was a close friend of many Argentine writers, like Victoria Ocampo; it is said that it was he who suggested the name *Sur* for the famous journal that she edited, with the help of Jorge Luis Borges. His essays on Argentine history and culture provoked passionate debate and, in some nationalist sectors, hostility toward him, which doubtless contributed to his decision to return to Europe in 1942.

ORTEGA AND THE SPANISH CIVIL WAR

The failure of the Republic and the bloodbath of the Spanish Civil War had a traumatic effect on the political ideals of Ortega y Gasset. He had supported and put a lot of faith in the Republic at its outset but the disorder and crimes that ensued scared him. Then the Franco rebellion and the extreme polarization that accelerated the war trapped him in a sort of ideological catacomb. In his view, liberal democracy "is the political model that has expressed the highest form of coexistence" and that has shown a spirit of tolerance unprecedented in history because liberalism is "the right that the majority concedes to the minority," "the decision to coexist with the enemy."* Was such a position possible in the midst of a civil war? What he defended—an enlightened, free, European, civil society, based on coexistence and legality—turned out to be unrealistic in a Europe shaken by the symmetrical advance of totalitarian regimes that crushed in their path the very foundations of the civilization that he envisaged for Spain. Ortega never got over the collapse of those dreams.

When one frequents the work of a writer for as long as I have done with Ortega, albeit in small daily doses, one becomes so familiar with him—I mean with his persona—that after reading and rereading him so many times, I feel that I am on intimate terms with him, and have been present at one of those literary gatherings with his friends which, as Julián Marías and other disciples have described them, were usually dazzling. He must have been an extraordinary conversationalist, communicator, and teacher. Reading his best essays one can listen to Ortega, his dramatic silences, the sibilant lash of an unusual adjective, the labyrinthine sentence that suddenly closes, rounding out an argument with the rhetorical insolence of a matador. Quite a show.

In recent years Ortega has been much maligned by the left, accusing him, as Gregorio Morán has done in *El maestro en el erial: Ortega y Gasset y la cultura del franquismo*,† of having been a discreet accomplice of the nationalists during the civil war. This assertion is based on very flimsy arguments like two of

---

* *La rebelión de las masas*, op. cit., p. 130.
† Gregorio Morán, *El maestro en el erial: Ortega y Gasset y la cultura del franquismo*, Tusquets Editores, Barcelona, 1998.

his sons fighting with the rebels, his friendship and correspondence with several Franco diplomats, or his eagerness to publish in *The Times* of London, with the help of a representative of the nationalists in Great Britain, a text in which he criticized European intellectuals for having sided with the Republic without much understanding of the problems in Spain. There also seems no substance to the rumor, to the gossip, that at one point, through an intermediary, Ortega offered to write Franco's speeches. How ridiculous. There has never been any reliable proof of this story put forward, and in his correspondence there is not the slightest indication that it might have any validity. The truth is, and Morán's book gives ample examples of this, that if Ortega had wanted to be part of the Franco regime, a regime that both attacked or silenced him and made frequent attempts to bribe him, he would have been greeted with open arms. It would have been enough for him to make a public declaration of support. He never did so.

The fact that he continued to receive the pension that was owed him as a university professor after he retired—a man of modest means, he had earned this pension through working for many years—should also not be used as an argument to discredit him. But of course, it might have been better if he had never gone back to Spain or had died in exile or had firmly and unequivocally opposed the regime. For then, all the confusion about who he was, what he believed in, and what he supported would have been avoided and it would be very easy today to present him as a politically correct figure. But Ortega's true "circumstance" was not to side with either group when the civil war broke out; the option he chose was seen as untenable in the conflict—and before the conflict, if truth be told, because of the upheavals, killings, and political polarization that occurred during the Republic—and left him in no-man's-land. Despite this and recognizing how vulnerable and isolated his position was, he remained true to it until his death. This stance was impractical in the context of violent splits in society and a belligerent Manichaeism that did not allow for nuance and moderation, but it was not dishonest. The civil, republican, democratic, plural regime that he had defended in 1930 and 1931, in the Agrupación al Servicio de la República, in parliament, and in the press, was nothing like what was established in Spain after the fall of the monarchy. Nor was a fascist uprising the answer and, for that reason, he did not take a public position during the war in favor of either side and, subsequently, he did not support the victorious regime.

When Ortega returned to Spain in 1945, he did so convinced that the end of the World War would lead to a transformation of the Franco dictatorship. He was wrong and he paid a heavy price for this mistake. He lived in Spain, with long escapes to Portugal, in an in-between world, vilified on the one hand by the ultraconservative sectors of the regime who did not forgive him his secular views, and on the other hand forced to slip away from those who sought to reclaim him, use him, and turn him into a proto-ideologue of the Falange. These attempts reached ridiculous extremes with a week of spiritual exercises organized by the Arts Faculty of the Universidad Complutense in Madrid for "the conversion of Ortega y Gasset," and the systematic campaigns led from the pulpits to persuade the philosopher to emulate his colleague Manuel García Morente, who was indeed visited by the holy spirit and returned to the Catholic fold. Despite his timorous nature, which some critics reproached him for, he resisted the immense pressure he was put under—not just by official circles but also by people who respected him and whom he respected—and he did not write a single line that went against these ideas.

This led the regime, on the eve of Ortega's death, to give the grotesque order to the Spanish press, released by Franco's information minister, Arias Salgado: "Faced with the possible contingency of the death of don José Ortega y Gasset, the newspaper will give the news with a headline covering no more than two columns and the inclusion, if so desired, of a single eulogy, which will not leave out his political and religious errors, and which will not, at any point, use the term 'maestro.'"

Ortega's errors were not those of a coward or an opportunist; at worst they were the mistakes of a naive man who was determined to offer a moderate, civil, and reformist alternative in times when this had not the remotest chance of becoming a reality in Spain. His lack of enthusiasm or his doubts should not be flung in his face as an accusation. They reveal the dramatic destiny of an intellectual who was viscerally and rationally allergic to extremes, intolerance, absolute truths, nationalisms, and all dogmas, whether religious or political. Of a thinker who, for that reason, seemed behind the times, a relic at a moment when democratic coexistence was evaporating in the fierce conflict of the civil war and, later, in the long night of totalitarianism. It was not just Ortega but also the democratic and liberal position that was dazed and destroyed by the hecatomb of the civil war. But what of the present? Are the ideas of Ortega y Gasset, disdained by both fascists and Marxists, not in many ways now a living, very up-to-date reality in the plural, free, and emphatic Spain of today? Instead of erasing him, contemporary history has endorsed Ortega y Gasset as the most brilliant and coherent thinker that Spain has bequeathed to secular and democratic culture in its entire history. And also as the best writer.

Contemporary liberal thought has much to benefit from

the ideas of Ortega y Gasset. Above all, to rediscover that—contrary to what people determined to reduce liberalism to an economic formula of free markets, fair rules, low tariffs, controlled public spending, and privatization of companies suppose—liberalism is above all an attitude toward life and society based on tolerance and respect, a love for culture, a desire to coexist with others and a firm defense of freedom as a supreme value. A freedom that is, at the same time, the driving force of material progress, of science, arts, and letters, and of a civilization that has produced sovereign individuals, with their independence, their rights, and their responsibilities that are always held in balance with those of other individuals, protected by a legal system that guarantees coexistence within diversity. Economic freedom is a key element of liberal doctrine but certainly not the only one. We must regret, of course, that many liberals of Ortega's generation were ignorant of this fact. But it is no less serious an error to reduce liberalism to an economic policy of the market functioning with minimal state intervention. Is not the failure of so many attempts to liberalize the economy in Latin America, Africa, and Europe itself over recent decades a clear proof that economic formulas by themselves can fail spectacularly if they are not supported by a body of ideas that justify them and make them acceptable to public opinion? Liberal doctrine is a culture in the broadest sense of the term, and Ortega's essays reflect this in stimulating and lucid ways on every page.

If he had been French, Ortega would today be as widely known and read as Sartre, whose existential philosophy of "man in his situation" he anticipated and expressed more elegantly in his concept of man and his circumstances. If he had been British, he would be another Bertrand Russell, like him a great thinker and a notable communicator of his ideas. But he was only a Spaniard, when the culture of Cervantes, Quevedo, and Góngora wandered in the basement (the image is his) of what were considered the great modern cultures. Now things have changed and the doors of this exclusive club have opened up to the vigorous language that he enriched and renewed as much as Jorge Luis Borges and Octavio Paz. It is time for today's culture finally to know José Ortega y Gasset and give him the recognition he deserves.

FRIEDRICH AUGUST VON HAYEK (1899–1992)

I f I had to name the three modern thinkers to whom I owe the most, politically speaking, I would not hesitate for a second: Karl Popper, Friedrich August von Hayek, and Isaiah Berlin. I began to read the three of them in the 1970s and 1980s when I was emerging from the illusions and sophisms of socialism and was searching, among the philosophies of freedom, for the one that had exposed most clearly the errors of constructivism (the phrase is Hayek's) and had put forward the most radical ideas as to how to achieve, in democracy, what collectivism and statism had promised without ever bringing about: a system capable of harmonizing the contradictory values of equality and liberty, social justice and prosperity.

Among these thinkers, perhaps none has gone as far or in such depth as Friedrich von Hayek, the old master born almost with the century (1899) into a well-off family in Vienna, the capital of the then Austro-Hungarian Empire. An apathetic student but voracious reader, a walker and mountain climber from his youth through to old age, his first passion, influenced by his father, when still a child, was botany: he set up a herbarium and tried to write a short monograph on an orchid (*Orchis condigera*) that he never managed to see. Curious and wide-ranging, in his youth he was interested in paleontology, the theory of evolution, and theater. It was only years later, when he was serving as a young artillery officer on the Italian front during the First World War, that he discovered his passion for economics, and for psychology, after reading a book by Carl Menger, *Principles of Economics* (1871). This reading would dispel the socialist follies of his youth and turn him into a defender of individualism, private enterprise, and the market. Although he chose to study economics, he never lost interest in psychology and years later wrote a curious essay in this field called *The Sensory Order.**

From his studies at the University of Vienna, where he graduated with a doctorate in law in 1921, he would always remember Carl Menger who, he says, was the first to conceive of the idea that would later become one of the pillars of his economic and political theory: the spontaneous evolution of institutions. In his home country, as a recent graduate, he worked for almost five years with another great liberal thinker, Ludwig von Mises, and was a member of his famous *Privatseminar*. He said of him that he was someone "from whom I have probably learned more than from any other man."† Between March 1923 and May 1924, he was in New York. He went on his own, with very little money, and lived on sixty dollars a month for those fifteen months in which he let his beard grow, worked as an assistant to Jeremiah Jenks, a professor at New York University, and read tirelessly in the New York Public Library. His poverty was so extreme that, he would later admit, he had only two pairs of socks, both with

* F. A. von Hayek, *The Sensory Order*, the University of Chicago Press, Chicago, 1952.
† In *Hayek on Hayek: An Autobiographical Essay*, edited by Stephen Kresge and Leif Wenar, the University of Chicago Press, Chicago, p. 68.

holes in them, which he put on over each other to keep out the cold.

Returning to Vienna he married for the first time, in 1926; his first wife was Hella Berta Maria von Fritsch, with whom he would have two children: Christine Maria Felicitas (born in 1929) and Laurence Joseph Heinrich (born in 1934). Before leaving for New York, he fell in love with a distant cousin, Helene Bitterlich, but she left him and became engaged to someone else while he was in New York. He would revive this old sentimental relationship years later.

In 1931 he was invited to London to give a lecture at the London School of Economics where, the following year, he became professor of economic science and statistics, a post he held until the end of 1949. At first his students found it difficult to follow his halting English with its Germanic inflection, but once they made the effort they were fascinated by his classes. He met Karl Popper in London in 1935 and they became close friends as well as sharing many philosophical ideas and views on society; Hayek dedicated his book *Studies in Philosophy, Politics and Economics* (1967) to Popper. Popper, who was always grateful for the help that Hayek gave him in finding a publisher for *The Open Society and Its Enemies* (1945) and in securing a lectureship at the London School of Economics, had, some years earlier, dedicated to Hayek his *Conjectures and Refutations* (1963). Hayek became a British national in 1938. He would later teach at the Universities of Chicago (1950–1962), Freiburg (1961–1969), and Salzburg (1969–1977). He was a true citizen of the world. He died a brilliant ninety-two-year-old in 1992, in Freiburg, Germany.

Destiny offered Hayek the greatest reward that an intellectual can have: to see how contemporary history—or, at least, the governments of Ronald Reagan in the United States and

Margaret Thatcher in the United Kingdom—confirmed many of his ideas and discredited the ideas of his adversaries, among them the famous John Maynard Keynes (1883–1946). Of all his ideas, the best-known, and today so widely accepted that it has almost become a commonplace, is one that he developed in his short paper (which later became a book), *The Road to Serfdom* (1946): that centralized planning of the economy inevitably undermines the bases of democracy, and that fascism and communism were therefore two expressions of the same phenomenon of totalitarianism. By the same token, all regimes, even those appearing to be free, would be contaminated by the virus of totalitarianism if they sought to control the functioning of the market.

HAYEK AND KEYNES

The famous polemic between Hayek and Keynes that is so often spoken about was never very equitable, although they had a brief but intense intellectual exchange in 1931, following Hayek's very strong criticism of Keynes's *A Treatise on Money* in *Economica*, the journal of the London School of Economics. But as Robert Skidelsky has argued in a persuasive essay on the polemic, "Hayek versus Keynes,"* despite their differences, there was an important point of convergence between the two that is clearer now than it was then, when almost all the influential figures in the spheres of economics and politics shared Keynes's ideas. Hayek's radical critique, therefore, had only

* Robert Skidelsky, "Hayek versus Keynes" in Edward Feser, ed., *The Cambridge Companion to Hayek*, Cambridge University Press, Cambridge, pp. 82–111. The quotations from Keynes are taken from this article. There is another, more recent book on this topic, Thomas Hoeber, *Hayek vs Keynes: A Battle of Ideas*, Reaktion Books, London, 2017.

minority appeal; it was a seemingly useless and transient concern, a quixotic struggle of a man firmly at odds with the dominant culture of his time. But they were both liberals, although Keynes believed that some state intervention in the economy could better protect capitalism, while Hayek rejected this idea. According to Skidelsky, employing the famous distinction that Isaiah Berlin made between foxes and hedgehogs in his essay on Tolstoy, Hayek is the hedgehog (who has one great defining idea) while Keynes is the fox (who knows a number of things). Both had come to economics via philosophy and both believed in the subjective element in intellectual endeavors, which could never be reduced to a purely scientific focus. Neither was an ardent democrat and they both declared themselves admirers of Hume, Burke, and Mandeville. And they both thought that Western civilization was "precarious," though they differed as to how to save it. Although they knew each other and treated each other with respect, they were not friends and corresponded infrequently. Keynes read *The Road to Serfdom* when he attended the Bretton Woods Conference in 1944; on June 28 of that year he wrote to Hayek thanking him for having written a "grand book." "We all have the greatest reason to be grateful to you for saying so well what needs so much to be said," he added. "Morally and philosophically I find myself in agreement with virtually the whole of it, and not only in agreement with it, but in a deeply moved agreement." But later on he outlines his criticisms. "You admit here and there that there is a question of knowing where to draw the line (with planning). But you give us no guidance whatever as to where to draw it . . . It is true that you and I would probably draw it in different places. I should guess that, according to my ideas, you greatly underestimate the practicability of the middle course . . ." On this point, Keynes was clearly right. Hayek loathed middle courses and tepid waters; he was a man of extremes, which meant that along with his great achievements he committed at times huge mistakes. But there is no doubt that, despite their differences, he always had a great respect for Keynes. And he made this sentiment known to Keynes's widow, Lydia Lopokova, when Keynes died in 1946: "(Your husband is) the only great man I knew and for whom I always felt a limitless admiration."*

The interventionist theories of the brilliant John Maynard Keynes, according to which the state could and should regulate economic growth and ensure full employment by making up for the shortcomings and correcting the excesses of laissez-faire systems became, over the years (and probably going further than Keynes himself would have wished) an incontrovertible axiom of socialists, social democrats, conservatives, and even of supposed liberals in the old and new world. And this was the state of affairs when Hayek brought to the attention of a wide audience his synthesis of what he had been arguing in academic and specialist works since the 1930s when, along with Ludwig von Mises, he began reclaiming and bringing up-to-date the classic liberalism of Adam Smith.

Although *The Road to Serfdom* obtained widespread distribution in Great Britain and the United States, where the popular *Reader's Digest* published an abridged version of the book, it was banned in Germany by the occupying powers, which did not wish to upset the U.S.S.R. His ideas, therefore, only had resonance in marginal academic and political circles and, for example, the country where the book was written,

---

* Alan Ebenstein, *Friedrich Hayek: A Biography*, Palgrave, New York, 2001, p. 344.

Great Britain, set out, in those years, on its road toward labor populism and the welfare state, that is, toward inflation and decline, a course that would only be interrupted, decades later, by the formidable (but alas, truncated) libertarian advances made by Margaret Thatcher. Instead of earning him the respect of his economist colleagues, *The Road to Serfdom* had the opposite effect, although this mistrust would begin to disappear in the following years, especially when he won the Nobel Prize for Economics in 1974.

Like Mises, like Popper, like Berlin, Hayek cannot be pigeonholed within a single discipline, economics, because his ideas are as innovative in economics as they are in the fields of philosophy, law, sociology, politics, psychology, science, history, and ethics. In all of these he displayed an originality and radicalism that is matchless among modern thinkers. And he always maintained a scrupulous respect for the classic liberal tradition and rigorous forms of academic research. But his works are imbued with polemical fervor, irreverence against established norms, an intellectual creativity that could be expressed through cold and rigid analysis, and often with explosive ideas, as in 1950 when he proposed that West Germany should become integrated with the United States and that other European countries should follow this lead (he was thinking mainly about Scandinavian countries). Or take his no less polemical idea of competing currencies, to privatize and open to the market the printing of money, an idea that the government of Margaret Thatcher was on the verge of proposing to the European Union through her chancellor of the exchequer, Nigel Lawson, as Thatcher reveals in her memoirs.* He could

* Margaret Thatcher, *The Downing Street Years*, HarperCollins, London, 1995, p. 715.

defend, in the name of individual freedom, things that disgusted him, like the right to be homosexual without being persecuted or discriminated against and, at the same time, he could be pragmatic, intervening in the U.S. gun debate by suggesting that only people of a certain proven intellectual and moral standing should be allowed to buy guns freely.

But some of his convictions are difficult for an authentic democrat to share, as when he argues that a dictatorship that practices liberal economics is preferable to a democracy that does not do so. In this vein he went so far, on two occasions, as asserting that under the Pinochet military dictatorship there was more freedom than under the populist democratic and socialist-leaning government of Salvador Allende, which brought on a justified storm of criticism, even from his admirers.*

From the 1960s, after the publication of *The Constitution of Liberty*, he began to suffer from periods of depression that paralyzed his intellectual work for a time. These bouts of depression became more acute in his later years, above all when the ailments of old age prevented him from working.

In April 1947, invited by Hayek, thirty-nine eminent thinkers, including Karl Popper, Milton Friedman, George Stigler, Ludwig von Mises, Lionel Robbins, and Maurice Allais, along with other prestigious economists and researchers from the United States and Europe, met in Vevey in Switzerland, on the banks of Lake Geneva, for ten days of debates and presentations. This was the origin of the Mont Pelerin Society,

---

* He made the statement in *The Times* newspaper, August 3, 1978. ("More recently I have not been able to find a single person even in much maligned Chile who did not agree that personal freedom was much greater under Pinochet that it had been under Allende.") And he repeated the statement in the Chilean newspaper *El Mercurio* on April 12, 1981.

whose aims were to modernize and defend classic liberalism; Hayek became the first president of the society. It would have a long-term influence on intellectual and political life.

At the end of 1949, he went through a personal drama that would affect his relationship with some of his friends, including his closest friend, his colleague at the London School of Economics, Lionel Robbins. It happened when Hayek left his first wife, Hella, and obtained a divorce in Arkansas, where he had moved because of the divorce laws in that state. He would then get married to the distant cousin who was the love of his early years, Helene Bitterlich. This split upset several of his friends, including Robbins, who broke off their friendship and any form of relationship with Hayek for many years; they would only be reconciled some eleven years later, according to Alan Ebenstein, at the wedding of Hayek's son, Larry.

His magnum opus is *The Constitution of Liberty* (1960), which was further enriched by the three thick volumes of *Law, Legislation and Liberty* (1973–1979) published in the seventies. In these books we find explained, with a conceptual lucidity based on an encyclopedic knowledge of praxis, what the market is, this almost infinite system of relations among people in a society, and between societies, which allows them to communicate reciprocally their needs and aspirations, to satisfy them and to organize production and resources around those needs. Nobody, not even Mises, has explained better than Hayek the benefits to society, in all areas, of this system of exchanges that nobody invented, that was born and perfected by chance, above all by that historical accident called liberty.

When do we witness the birth of the socialist idea to organize society according to a predetermined plan that would end the exploitation of the poor by the rich and replace class struggle with a supposed universal brotherhood? It is born at the same time as the idea that we should explore social questions with the same scientific method used to study nature, something that Hayek always considered a sly way of justifying "constructivism," that is, planning, the enemy of liberty. This idea predates the "scientific socialism" of Marx and Engels, which was a product of the nineteenth century, the century of great ideological constructions, those intellectual creations that sought to establish a perfect society or, in the words of the time, "to bring heaven to earth." In a book published for the first time in 1952, which brings together articles from different periods, all questioning whether scientific methods can be valid when dealing with social questions, Hayek demonstrates that "socialist planning" has its true origins in Saint-Simonianism and that this doctrine is the most evident and unequivocal precursor to Marxist-Leninist socialism and its obsession with planning.*

The essays that Hayek dedicates to Count Henri de Saint-Simon, to Auguste Comte, to Barthélemy-Prosper Enfantin, and, in passing, to Charles Fourier, Victor Considerant, and Pierre-Joseph Proudhon—that is, to the Saint-Simonians and the Fourierists and other movements and sects formed by ideologues that were in conflict with one another but which all sought to reconstruct society root and branch according to predetermined intellectual models—paint a lively mural of furious-paced lives, daring ideological fantasies, and novelesque adventures united by the conviction that human reality can be built like a work of engineering (we remember that Stalin wanted writers to be "engineers of human souls"). Saint-

* F. A. von Hayek, *The Counter-Revolution of Science: Studies on the Abuse of Reason.* I am quoting from the second edition, Liberty Fund, Indianapolis, 1979.

Simonianism eliminates everything that could be the cause of division and inequality among people: private property, the market, competition, and, in the final instance, liberty, that is the source of inequalities, abuse, and exploitation in the capitalist system. Science and order would thus replace anarchy and greed in the field of economics. Productive life would be under the watch of a central bank through which the state would wield its benevolent authority, sustained by the competence of its engineers, businessmen, and experts, the intellectual heroes of the moment, especially if they were graduates of the École Polytechnique, which the Saint-Simonians considered to be a factory turning out geniuses. Somewhat later, Marx and Engels dismissed rather disdainfully what they would call this "utopian socialism." Hayek shows that the arrogant delirium of refashioning society, transforming it from perfectible to perfect in accordance with a model that functions like a machine that Marxist socialism would make its own, derives unequivocally from the Saint-Simonian dream through which the intrepid count believed that human beings would achieve true freedom for the first time.

It is only ignorant people and enemies of the market who look to caricature truth so that they can dismiss it, who consider that the market is just a system of free exchanges. The entire work of Hayek is a prodigious scientific and intellectual attempt to show that the freedom to produce and to trade is worth nothing—as the former Soviet Union, the former socialist republics of Central Europe, and the mercantilist democracies of Latin America have shown—without a strict and efficient legal order that guarantees private property, respect for contracts, and an honest and capable judicial system independent of political power. Without these basic requisites, the market economy is mere rhetoric behind which the demands and the corrupt practices of a privileged minority continue at the expense of society, what we liberals call "mercantilism."

Those who through naivete or bad faith use the difficulties faced by Russia and some of its old satellite countries in moving from totalitarianism to a form of market-oriented democracy as examples of the failure of liberalism, have not read Hayek, or have read him badly. For no one has been more insistent in pointing out that liberalism is not about liberalizing prices and opening up borders to international competition, but rather about the integral reform of a society, privatizing and decentralizing it at every level, and about transferring to civil society—to the initiative of sovereign individuals— essential economic decisions. And about the existence of a consensus over ground rules that favor the consumer over the producer, the producer over the bureaucrat, the individual over the state, and flesh-and-blood men and women in the here and now over that abstract concept that totalitarians use to justify their excesses: the future of humanity.

Individualism is a central factor in liberal philosophy and, of course, in Hayek's thought. Needless to say, individualism does not mean the romantic vision whereby all the great events in history as well as the definitive advances in the scientific, cultural, and social fields are the products of the feats of exceptional individuals, of heroes. More simply it means that individual people are not merely the epiphenomena of the collectives to which they belong, which mold them the way that machines produce industrial products. Individuals enjoy sovereignty and although part of what they are can be explained by the environment in which they are born and brought up, they have consciousness and an ability to take initiatives that can detach them from the herd and allow them to act freely, according to their vocation and talent, and, often, they can leave their mark on the surroundings in which they live. Individual ambition is the force that energizes the market economy and makes progress possible. For that reason the Keynesian formulas of entrusting the state to guide and direct economic life, through planning, seems to him to dull that "ambition" and produces deep distortions in the functioning of the market.

This concept derives from the idea of liberty that is at the heart of liberal doctrine. Human destinies are not written, they are not mapped out as fate. Individuals and societies can transcend geographical, social, and cultural conditions and change the order of things through their acts, opting for certain decisions and rejecting others. For this reason, because they always enjoy this margin of freedom, they are responsible for their own destiny. Hayek describes all this admirably in an essay that shows the similarities between two thinkers whom one might think would be very different: "Comte and Hegel."*

For Hayek, respect for the law is inseparable from his faith in the free market, but he always distinguished—and he explained this in great detail in the three volumes of *Law, Legislation and Liberty*—between law and legislation: *kosmos*, the spontaneous legal order, and *taxis*, legality imposed by power. The first is the form of natural law, created and shaped by custom and tradition, in response to the need to create an order to resolve disputes and avoid chaos and violence in the heart of society. The second is justice that is planned and sanctioned rationally by parliaments and courts, which, at times, can fracture and distort natural law and can be very harmful in the legal realm, as in the case of economic planning that, in Hayek's worldview, is always a threat against liberty.

* F. A. von Hayek, ibid., pp. 367–400.

The great enemy is constructivism, the fatal desire—Hayek's last book is entitled *Fatal Conceit* (1989)—to organize the life of the community from any center of power, replacing the institutions that have emerged without premeditation or control (common law, the *kosmos*) with artificial structures designed to achieve objectives like "rationalizing" production, "redistributing" wealth, imposing egalitarianism, and standardizing the whole of society into an ideology, a culture, or a religion.

Hayek's ferocious criticism of constructivism does not stop at the collectivism of Marxists or the welfare state of socialists and social democrats or at what Christian Democrats call the "principle of substitution" or at the degenerate form of capitalism we call mercantilism—the mafioso alliances between political power and influential business leaders that prostitute the market by distributing handouts, monopolies, and benefits. His criticism does not stop anywhere, if truth be told. It does not even stop at the system that he had defended so robustly and influentially: democracy. In his later years above all, the indomitable Hayek began to examine democracy in a very critical manner, describing its deficiencies and distortions, one of which is mercantilism, the other the dictatorship of majorities over minorities. This topic led him to proclaim that he feared for the future of liberty in the world at the precise moment when, with the fall of the communist regimes, it seemed that the high point of democracy on the planet had been achieved.

To counterbalance the monopoly of power that majorities exert in open societies and to guarantee the participation of minorities in government and in decision making, Hayek imagined a complicated system—that he himself called a "utopia"—called *demarchy*. In it a legislative assembly, elected for terms of fifteen years from among citizens over forty-five years of age, would keep watch over fundamental rights. At the same time a parliament, much like those that exist in democratic countries, would look after current issues and concerns.

The only time I spoke to Hayek, in Lima in November 1979, during a conference called "Democracy and Market Economy," which was a gust of modernity and liberation in a country that had already suffered eleven years of military rule, I managed to say to him that, when reading him, I sometimes got the impression that some of his theories seemed to conjure up that ambitious will-o'-the-wisp: the revival, through liberalism, of the anarchist ideal of a world without coercion, of pure spontaneity, with a minimum of authority and a maximum of liberty, constructed entirely around the individual. He looked at me kindly and quoted a teasing remark by Bakunin for whom, naturally, he did not have the least sympathy.

And yet there was some similarity between the disheveled nineteenth-century prince with his adventurous life, who wanted to break all the chains that restricted the creative impulses of human beings, and the methodical and erudite professor with his peaceful life who, shortly before dying, remarked in an interview that every liberal should be an agitator. They shared the same mistrust of human reason that was arrogant enough to think itself capable of remodeling society without taking into account spontaneously created institutions and they also shared an excessive faith in that child of chance and necessity that is liberty, the most precious creature that the West has brought to civilization to offer a solution to its problems and to propel the human adventure toward new and risky achievements.

THE FATAL CONCEIT

The Fatal Conceit (1988), the last book that Hayek published, when he was eighty-nine years old, is one of the most important works of the twentieth century and also one of the most original and revolutionary. It is not an essay on economics but rather a philosophical and moral treatise written by a thinker with a solid economic formation, who, like Adam Smith and John Stuart Mill, his predecessors and mentors, never believed that the economy was capable of resolving all human problems on its own.

The central theme of the book is civilization and progress, what distinguishes humankind from other living beings that always remain the same, prisoners of their instincts or of their immovable biological makeup, unable to transform themselves.

In the autumn of his life, a long existence devoted to study, research, and teaching, Hayek explains in this book without notes, in a simple manner accessible to all reasonably cultured readers, his conception of how and why human beings, over thousands of years, have changed the conditions in which they lived and at the same time transformed themselves, until, in our time, they have achieved *civilization*, a word that on Hayek's lips means liberty, legality, individualism, private property, free market, human rights, coexistence, and peace. That nobody invented civilization, that it developed gradually and in a somewhat unexpected manner was an old idea of Hayek's: "But our civilisation is indeed largely an unintended and unforeseen outcome of our submitting to moral and legal rules which were never 'invented' with such a result in mind, but which grew because those societies which developed them piecemeal prevailed at every step over other groups which followed different rules, less conducive to the growth of civilisation."*

This process that has allowed human beings to leave behind the animal life of their ancestors—the life of the cave and the tribe—and reach the stars and our democratic systems was possible, according to Hayek, because of what he calls "the spontaneous order," which emerged, as its name suggests, in an unforeseen manner, not planned or directed. It was a movement of large social groups intent on changing their lives and who found certain ways or certain forms of relationship to improve their living conditions.

Typical examples of these "spontaneous orders" are language, private property, currency, trade, and the market. None of these was invented by a single person, community, or culture. They emerged naturally, in different places, as a consequence of specific conditions that the community responded to creatively, following intuition or instinct rather than intellectual reasoning, and then lived experience would either legitimize, change, or eliminate them, replacing them with something different.

These spontaneous orders, for Hayek, are pragmatic but also moral institutions because, thanks to them, it is not just material reality, our standard of living, that has evolved but also our customs, how we behave toward others, our notions of citizenship and ethics. In other words, thanks to the appearance of trade, of contracts, of legality, and of communication and dialogue, humans began to shed their barbarity, expelling the beast within and replacing it with a citizen, respectful and supportive of others equal to or different from

* F. A. von Hayek in *What's Past Is Prologue: A Commemorative Evening on the Occasion of Leonard Read's Seventieth Birthday*, the Foundation for Economic Education, New York, 1968, p. 38.

themselves. According to Hayek, the key factor in civilization is not reason or knowledge per se—which are always fragmentary, incomplete, and disperse—but rather that reason and knowledge should be subject to some degree to a tradition that has been distilled by lived experience.

Spontaneous orders are not always good, of course. In the long process of civilization, human beings have elected those institutions that contributed to real progress and have abandoned those that are detrimental to them. Lived experience was the great teacher and counselor when it came to selection. And religions also helped social groups to understand with greater clarity the positive and negative characteristics of institutions created by "spontaneous order." All this, of course, without taking into account the claim of all religions to express an ultimate and definitive truth, something that has caused and still causes much bloodshed in history. Hayek, who called himself an agnostic, unable to accept the anthropomorphism of God postulated by Christianity, judged the positive role of religions in strictly historic and social terms.

The great enemy of civilization is, for Hayek, constructivism or social engineering, which looks to develop intellectually an economic and political model and then implant it in reality, something that is only possible by force—violence that degenerates into dictatorship—and which has failed every time it has been attempted. For Hayek, intellectuals have been innate constructivists and, for that reason, great enemies of civilization. (There are some exceptions to this extremist creed, of course, beginning with Hayek himself.) They do not usually believe in the market, that impersonal system that orders individual initiatives and produces employment, wealth, opportunities, and, in the final instance, human progress. As the market is the product of liberty, intellectuals are often the great enemies of liberty. Intellectuals are convinced that simply by developing rationally a just and equal model of society, this can be *imposed* on society. This explains the success of Marxism among intellectuals. This belief seems to Hayek "an expression of an intellectual hubris, which is the opposite of that intellectual humility which is the essence of the true liberalism that regards with reverence those spontaneous social forces through which the individual creates things greater than he knows."* The practical effect of this belief is socialism (which Hayek identifies with economic planning and state intervention), and establishing socialism requires the abolition of freedom, private property, respect for contracts, the independence of the law, and limitations on free individual initiative. The result is productive inefficiency, corruption, and despotism.

Hayek's idea of civilization has been severely eroded since his death. Ideas that, for him, played such an important role in the life of free nations have deteriorated and in the modern world images now have the prominence that ideas once had. To some extent, screens have replaced books as the primary source of knowledge and information for what is called public opinion.

Furthermore, Hayek could not have imagined that corruption would be as extensive as it has become, reaching into the very heart of institutions which, as a result, have lost much of the authority they once had. One such example is the law, beset in many places by claims of widespread corruption through bribery or the influence of power.

This also has repercussions in public and private enter-

* F. A. von Hayek, "Opening Address," Mont Pelerin Society, April 1, 1947.

prises and in the functioning of the market, which has not only been affected by state interventionism but, often, by deals and contacts that favor certain firms or individuals through the political or economic power that they wield.

Public morality, which Hayek set so much store by, has also fractured everywhere due to the desire for profit, which takes precedence over values and leads many companies and individuals to play dirty, violating the rules that regulate free competition.

The great modern financial crisis has been a dramatic expression of the collapse of Hayek's ideas and values.

THE ROAD TO SERFDOM

The basic ideas contained in *The Road to Serfdom*, another great statement about freedom in the twentieth century, which was published in 1944, had been in Hayek's mind since 1933, to judge from an article he wrote in that year on the rise to power of Nazism in Germany. He argues that, despite their mutual loathing, there is a common denominator between communism and Nazism: collectivism. That is, their hatred of individualism and liberal thought based on respect for private property, the coexistence of different ideas and beliefs within democratic society, free trade, the market economy, and political freedom.

For Hayek, only individualism, private property, and market capitalism guarantee political freedom. The opposite leads in the short or in the long term to economic failure, dictatorship, and totalitarianism. The idea that there is a basic identity shared by communism, socialism, and fascism was revolutionary when Hayek sketched it out for the first time in 1933. He was wrong in not giving sufficient weight, in the case of Nazism, to its nationalism and racism, the delirious belief that the Aryan race was superior to other races and could thus exert brutal dominance over all others. This was substantially different from communist collectivism, which defended "proletarian internationalism" and did not encourage theoretical prejudices about a so-called Aryan racial superiority, nor did it discriminate against Jews as an inferior race or seek to exterminate them.

Hayek's critique of planning as being, firstly, an attempt at economic control of society doomed to failure and, secondly, a process that inevitably leads to the disappearance of freedoms and the establishment of a dictatorship, has a steely lucidity. Radically new, this critique was a logical development of his mistrust of the ability of great rational constructions to transform society and his defense of "spontaneous orders" like the free market and competition regimes, which, according to him, initiated the process of modernization in the West.

Hayek is very perceptive in pointing out how, in Western democracies, the idea of economic planning has, without its proponents understanding what the political consequences would be, sooner or later led to the reduction of freedom in all spheres, not just economic but also political, cultural, and individual. That is why the book is dedicated "to the socialists of all parties," that is, to those who, thinking that they are opposed to socialism, accept an interventionist economic policy that could, in the short or long term, destroy democracy. Hayek gives as an example the case of H. G. Wells, who declared himself a committed supporter of economic planning while at the same time writing a book on the rights of man. "The individual rights which Mr Wells hopes to preserve," Hayek admonishes, "would inevitably obstruct the planning he desires." His case is the opposite of that of Max Eastman, a former supporter of communism and the U.S.S.R. who, after visiting that country and seeing the distance between the collectivist utopia and reality, understood that "private property" gave man "an amount of free-and-equalness that Marx hoped to render infinite by abolishing this institution."*

One can nuance some of Hayek's arguments. The rule of law, which he defends with solid arguments, is a mild form of planning since it points social and economic activities in a certain direction and imposes limits on them. This type of planning—legislation—is indispensable on condition, of course, that it respects private property and free competition and reduces state intervention to the minimum required to guarantee the security of its citizens and their peaceful coexistence. This "indispensable minimum" varies from country to country and from era to era.

A topic that Hayek does not explore, in this or in any other of his essays—at least not in any extensive way given the importance of the topic today—is corruption. Corruption is one of the phenomena that most weakens the rule of law and, in general, the functioning of democracy and, of course, the functioning of the free market. The excessive growth of the state without doubt facilitates corruption, but in our time perhaps the main reason why it has increased to such an extent—in developed and underdeveloped, democratic and authoritarian, societies—is the collapse of moral values, be they religious or lay values, which in the past strengthened our adherence to the law but which are now so weak, and shared by so few, that they can offer no limits, but rather encourage greed to circumvent legal controls. The last financial crisis, which shook the United

* F. A. von Hayek, *The Collected Works of F. A. von Hayek, Vol. 2: The Road to Serfdom*. The Definitive Edition, ed. Bruce Caldwell, Routledge, 2014, pp. 121, 136.

States and Europe from 2008, came about to a large extent due to the desire for profit that led banks and companies to commit gross violations of the law. These violations hastened the collapse of different economies that became bankrupt and had to be rescued with public money, that is, the money of its victims. All this has done enormous damage to capitalism and the market economy and has given some vitality to what seemed to be a moribund collectivism. Here one should remember the old idea of the founders of liberal thought, like Adam Smith, that without solid moral convictions (which Smith thought were inseparable from religion), liberalism cannot function.

In *The Road to Serfdom* as in other books, Hayek uses the term *socialism* in a way that confuses it with *communism*: a concept that means collectivism, economic dirigisme or planning, the disappearance of freedoms and political pluralism, totalitarianism. Why did he never differentiate between Marxist-Leninist socialism and the democratic socialism espoused by, among others, the British Labour Party? The latter was something that he could observe up close because he lived in Britain for many years and wrote his book there during the Second World War.

The reason is simple and it is explained in *The Road to Serfdom*. He believed—it was one of his great errors—that the distinction between totalitarian and democratic socialism was an illusion, something provisional and mere surface, which, in practice would always become blurred in favor of totalitarianism. For Hayek, all socialism, by initiating economic planning and ending competition and private property, automatically sets up a mechanism that sooner or later, whether the planners intended this outcome or not, destroys political pluralism and liberties.

Was his reasoning flawed? If a government puts an end to

competition in the economic sphere and allows no other alternative in this field, then it will be obliged, sooner or later, to use force against its critics to impose its policies, as happened in the U.S.S.R. That is undeniable. But Hayek did not consider that an important number of socialists—precisely those who wanted to maintain freedoms and had distanced themselves from the communists—rejected economic planning and decided to respect the market, competition, and private enterprise, looking to achieve equality through redistribution, fiscal measures, and socially oriented institutions like medical insurance and benefits. This is the policy that Swedish socialists and, in general, most European social democratic parties pursued. It is true that in many Western countries this democratic socialism is no longer socialism in the traditional sense of the term and is much closer to liberalism than to Marxism. But the fact that Hayek does not mention this and lumps together all forms of socialism without differentiation in his severe critique of planning and planners leads to confusion, which might make him appear intolerant, which, if truth be told, he never was.

The book *Hayek on Hayek* (1994) is a good example of the diversity of opinions among liberals on economic matters, and that economic liberalism is incompatible with any form of dogmatism or sectarianism.

Hayek, Mises, and Friedman are considered liberal economists, as indeed they are. All this means is that there are more things that unite them than separate them. But their differences are important and Hayek was the one who expressed these differences the most, with his characteristic and often ferocious frankness.

He had a great deal of admiration for Ludwig von Mises (1881–1973), with whom he worked as a young man in Vienna soon after graduating. As I already mentioned, he said of Mises that he had learned more from him than from any other man, despite the fact that Mises was never his teacher. In 1921, Mises recommended him for a post in the Austrian government and for the following eight years they were very close. Hayek recognized that Mises was giving him jobs and responsibilities that he should have entrusted to more experienced people. Hayek also attended the famous seminar (*Privatseminar*) that Mises ran in his own office in Vienna twice a month from 1920. They met at seven in the evening in a spacious location that could accommodate between twenty and twenty-two people. They discussed economics, philosophy, sociology, logic, and "the epistemological problems of the sciences of human action." During the seminar, Mises usually served chocolate to those in attendance. Everyone came voluntarily, as his pupils, and they ended up becoming his friends. At ten they went to eat in an Italian restaurant and some would then argue till dawn in the Cafe Kustler.* Mises offered Hayek key support in setting up the Austrian Institute for Business Cycle Research, his brainchild, where Hayek's wife also worked.

Hayek points out that their differences became explicit in 1937, when he published an article titled "Economics and Knowledge," trying to persuade Mises that he was wrong to uphold that *market theory* was a priori. What was a priori, Hayek argues, was only "the logic of individual action." He adds that although Mises was very resentful of criticism by his pupils, he never mentioned Hayek's article, as if he had not been aware that it was a criticism of his own views.

He further argues that while he was as much an agnostic

* Alan Ebenstein tells this story in *Hayek: A Biography*. Palgrave, New York, 2001, p. 42.

as Mises, he believed that liberal thought would not have been possible just as an "intellectual insight" but rather as part of a "moral tradition" (he means a religious and doubtless Christian tradition).

He also accuses Mises of being a "utilitarian," a strict rationalist, "that implies we can arrange everything according to our pleasure."* He then insists that being a "strict rationalist" is as mistaken as being a socialist.

With regard to Milton Friedman (a few years younger than Hayek, he was born in 1912), Hayek remarked that they were in agreement "on almost everything except on monetary policy." And he reproaches him for being a "logical positivist" methodologically. He recognizes that Friedman has "this magnificent expository power." And he is sorry not to have written an in-depth critique of Friedman's *Essays in Positive Economics*, which he considers "a dangerous book." † Friedman responded with jibes of his own. In conversation with Hayek's biographer, Alan Ebenstein, he said that he was a great admirer of Hayek, "but not for his economics" and that although he thought that the *Road to Serfdom* was "one of the great books of our time," the theory of capital that Hayek develops in *Prices and Production* was "unreadable."‡

Is this not a persuasive proof that liberalism is a broad church with different currents of opinion, and also that liberals, however wise they might be, are also human, are susceptible to envy, irascibility, and vanity, just like the rest of humanity?

In *The Road to Serfdom*, Hayek emphasizes a topic that he

* Quotations from F. A. Hayek, *Hayek on Hayek: An Autobiographical Dialogue*, op. cit., pp. 72–73.
† Ibid., pp. 144–145.
‡ Alan Ebenstein, op. cit., p. 81.

will return to time and again, with further nuance and refinement, in many of his later studies: how, with the best intentions in the world, ignorance causes many democratic governments and political parties that believe that they are clearly anti-authoritarian to undermine the economic foundations that uphold open society. This interventionism in the economy seeks to be moderate, and obtain morally just results, curbing the excesses of the market, creating an equality of opportunities that gives the poor the same advantages as the rich, to prevent such excessive economic inequalities as might provoke civil unrest, and, above all, to ensure job and wage security for workers. In the name of this security, many countries have justified intervention in economic life that has eroded liberty and even on occasion destroyed it. According to Hayek, state intervention has its own dynamic that, once put in motion, cannot be stopped or reversed and forces planners to increase their intrusion into free markets until they eradicate them and put in their place a system in which the state ends up fixing the price of products, producing them, selling them, and even determining the number of workers that each industry can have. This is how freedom is eroded bit by bit until it disappears in the economic sphere. This disappearance, concludes Hayek, spells the beginning of the end for all other freedoms, the fateful road to authoritarianism. This happened in 1933, he argued, when Hitler came to power in Germany: democracy was to a great extent corroded by state intervention in economic life and all that was needed was the political coup de grâce.

Another factor that Hayek could not have considered in his tenacious fight against state intervention in the running of society and in the life of its citizens is terrorism. Although terrorism has existed from the earliest times, it has increased to such an extent in our day and age and has caused so many cataclysmic events, like those in New York, Paris, Madrid, London, Brussels, and Barcelona in recent years, that in modern societies there is now an increased feeling of insecurity and a fear of some new apocalypse unleashed by Islamic fundamentalism. This has caused public opinion to turn to the state, which it sees as the only institution that can save society from this danger and, as a result, to be less hostile toward accepting a "big" state and to be supportive, as an example of the state's willingness to protect its citizens, of state intervention in life in general, including the economy.

One of the most brilliant chapters in *The Road to Serfdom* is chapter 11, "The End of Truth." This is about politics and philosophy, not economics. It deals with the primordial function of lies and the ways in which these become truths in totalitarian regimes. It sets out an essential difference between dictatorial and totalitarian regimes. While the former are interested in the exercise of authoritarian power and nothing else (that often includes theft), the latter, while they might also steal, are interested in ideas that they consider absolute truths and, for that reason, go to extreme lengths to inculcate the public with them. How? By convincing them, through propaganda, that these ideas are their own ideas, ones that they have always held but dimly seen, and which now the regime will teach them to understand clearly. And through this irrefutable logic, any ideas that might be contrary to those they put forward to justify their policies will be erased, allowed no possible means of expression, censured in the media, eradicated from teaching curricula, condemned in university lecture theaters and in books, journals, newspapers, and radio and television channels. In this way, official "truth"—the truth of Marxist-Leninism, National Socialism, fascism, Maoism, jihadism—will become established, turned into something more important than a mere idea: it becomes a cultural climate, the air that is breathed in all disciplines and forms of knowledge, which permeates science, technology, arts and letters. Ideology and religion then become two sides of the same coin: knowledge becomes, like theology, an act of faith. For Hayek this is an inevitable consequence of planning. Planning can never limit itself to being a mere adjunct to economic policy; it is forced, through its internal dynamism, to propel itself forward, to control and shape all social activities, including the intellectual field, the realm of ideas. This leads not only to economic catastrophe but also to a deep perversion and distortion of truth: truth is no longer independent, a product of scientific or intellectual research, but rather something fabricated—in the majority of cases, a lie presented as a truth for political reasons, to control power— and then disseminated through all official organizations, thus permeating all disciplines, even the most abstract like mathematics or metaphysics. On this issue Hayek makes an incontrovertible observation: "In any society freedom of thought will probably be of direct significance only for a small minority. But this does not mean that anyone is competent, or ought to have power, to select those to whom this freedom is to be reserved. It certainly does not justify the presumption of any group of people to claim the right to determine what people ought to think or believe" (p. 203).

THE CONSTITUTION OF LIBERTY

Hayek's most important book, *The Constitution of Liberty*—to which we should also add his *Law, Legislation and Liberty* (1973–1979), which is something of a complementary text—is not easy to read. Hayek is rigorous and persuasive as an essayist but his intellectual genius lacked expressive grace and elegance, his style was dense and somewhat rigid and at times, as in this exceptional work, his exposition becomes entangled, which makes his ideas difficult to follow. (Doubtless one of the reasons is that his mother tongue was German and that many of his books, like *The Constitution of Liberty*, were written in English.) His arguments are often interrupted by asphyxiating footnotes that make one lose the thread of the main point. His very broad economic background often causes him to lapse into such extreme erudition that the general ideas become bogged down in minutiae, as often occurs with great scholars. Despite all this, the book is a masterpiece, one of the intellectual pillars of the twentieth century, indispensable for understanding the culture of freedom.

The effort it took him to write this book must have been enormous; so much so that, when he finished it, the accumulated tiredness and also, doubtless, the nervous tension around his giving up smoking, plunged him into a depression that lasted a year (1960–1961). Later, joking, he would say that he tried to get out of this mental state by smoking a pipe. But he only managed this later, when he substituted snuff for tobacco.

The Constitution of Liberty was intended to be, in the author's original plan, a study of the appearance of liberty—the beginning of civilization—in the life of the West and the ways in which this freedom was consolidated through traditions, customs, and laws until it permeated all manifestations of social life, the economy, politics, culture, religion, family, work, the sovereign individual, the public, and the private. The book analyzes all this, of course. But its main focus is developed in the second part of the book, entitled "Freedom in the Welfare State": how this freedom has diminished and how interventionism has increased in our time with the birth of the welfare state. Hayek almost always draws his examples from Great Britain, though he also makes frequent references to Germany and the United States. The book explores with a wealth of detail and with solid arguments how the responsibilities of the individual have been expropriated by increasing statism and collectivism, reducing his or her degree of freedom and increasing the capacity of the state in matters that are essentially the concern of private life. This increasing state control takes place in democratic countries in discreet fashion, sometimes invisibly and often with the consent of the individuals whose individual freedoms have been eroded, who see these "liberticide" measures as useful or justified from a moral point of view. Hayek analyzes in detail all the areas that have experienced this gradual increase of state power in contemporary life: employment, health, monetary policy, education, housing, agriculture, et cetera.

Social security and health provisions, services that were once private and are now, increasingly throughout the world, state benefits, are a typical proof of the ways in which, with the best of intentions, problems are sometimes created that are impossible to resolve; for example, the funding of these services is often beyond the reach of the governments themselves. And at times, measures such as progressive taxation, which are put in place to correct excessive inequalities and foster equal opportunities, can have counterproductive results, discouraging investment and entrepreneurial creativity, quashing competition, and opening the doors to economic controls that impoverish the nation and mire it in statist lethargy.

In another of the most lucid and brilliant chapters of the book, chapter 21, "The Monetary Framework," Hayek explores the negative phenomena of inflation and deflation (the first more damaging than the second) and the limited ways in which the state, in a free society, can control them through a central bank. And he explains that those who propose inflationary policies, arguing that they can achieve full employment, are always the people who want greater state control in economic life: "Those who wish to preserve freedom must recognise, however, that inflation is probably the most important factor in that vicious circle wherein one kind of government action makes more and more government control necessary."*

In *The Constitution of Liberty*, Hayek explains and defends inequality, refuting the old democratic belief according to which "all men are created equal." This does not in any way imply that Hayek is proposing any discriminatory treatment of human beings. Quite the opposite: he argues compellingly that all men are "equal before the law." But it is precisely this "equality before the law," that, for Hayek, highlights differences between human beings that stem from inequalities in terms of talent, ambition, capacity for work, inventiveness, imagination, education, and the like. All these differences, in a free society, mean that individual labor will offer different levels of production and output in society. If different levels of income correspond to this unequal contribution to production, this does not affect in any way the principle of equality before the law, it merely rewards the different contributions in an equitable and fair manner.

The inequality that derives from this system is also an important stimulus to the whole of society and to individuals within it because it establishes goals or records that can be emulated, stimulating self-improvement.

---

* F. A. von Hayek, *The Constitution of Liberty: The Definitive Edition*, University of Chicago Press, Chicago, 2011, p. 338.

Hayek refers to underdeveloped countries and argues that it is to their benefit that Western countries have been able to prosper and progress through their economic and social systems, for underdeveloped countries have a model to emulate and first world countries can also give them assistance in their struggle for progress. It would have been much worse if progress in the West had been limited and stifled through distributive and egalitarian justice, which would have kept them underdeveloped, forcing them to share out their wealth. Sharing out poverty does not bring wealth to anyone and only serves to universalize poverty. Liberty, says Hayek, is inseparable from a certain degree of inequality. Though one should emphasize that, to be ethically acceptable, this inequality should only reflect differences in talent and hard work and not be based in any way on privilege or forms of discrimination and injustice.

While Hayek in the main expresses his opinions and assertions on a range of topics with absolute conviction, this is not always the case. One such exception is the area of public education (chapter 24). In principle Hayek accepts the idea that there should be public education accessible to social sectors that, without it, would not have the necessary training to allow them to work, earn a living, be successful, and contribute to the common good. But he points out the difficulties in finding a system that guarantees equal opportunities through good public education without allowing the state to impose a single model of education or confusing the fair principle of equal opportunities with an equality that would arbitrarily homogenize the whole of society, thus impeding the free development of individuals in accordance with their own talents and endeavors. The ideal is that differences should not be determined by privilege but by the effort and creativity of each person in a system of free competition. Hayek describes the difficulties and contradictions in creating schools and institutes for an "intellectual elite" of gifted students that would not lead to unjustifiable privileges and cause, inadvertently, class distinction at an early age, but he does not come up with a solution to this dilemma.

And something similar occurs when he discusses scientific research and scientific institutions and researchers created or subsidized by the state. He merely states that it is fundamental that there should be no single criterion imposed on this work but rather that researchers should be guaranteed their freedom, which would allow for different and contradictory ideological persuasions. With some limits, of course, as, for example, that "tolerance should not include the advocacy of intolerance." He adds that he believes for this reason that communist lecturers should not be given university posts— something that is not compatible with the freedom of the market that Hayek defended—but that if they are employed, their teaching and their ideas should be respected.

"WHY I AM NOT A CONSERVATIVE"

As a postscript to *The Constitution of Liberty*, there is an essay titled "Why I Am Not a Conservative," which he had delivered as a lecture in 1957 on the tenth anniversary of the Mont Pelerin Society. In it Hayek explains the difference between a liberal and a conservative, something that is essential in our day and age when the left often looks to confuse the two positions. It is a seminal text in which he defines the ideological, moral, and civic attitudes, which, despite sharing many things, mark liberalism as essentially different from conservatism. And he explores the ways in which, despite being at opposite extremes, conservatives and socialists, who consider themselves incompatible enemies, do in fact coincide on many issues.

A conservative, Hayek says, does not offer any alternative to the direction in which the world is traveling, while for a liberal what is essential is *what we are moving toward.*

A conservative attitude, says Hayek, is dictated by fear of change and the unknown and by a natural tendency toward "authority" and a lack of understanding of economic forces. It tends not to object to coercion and arbitrary power, which it can justify if it thinks that the use of violence is for the "right purposes." This opens up an unbridgeable gulf between conservatives and liberals, for whom "neither moral nor religious ideals are proper objects of coercion" while socialists and conservatives have no such limits.* Furthermore conservatives tend to blame "democracy" for all the ills of society. And unlike liberals, who are convinced of the power of ideas to transform history, conservatives, "bound by the stock of ideas inherited at a given time," see the very idea of change and reform as a threat to their social ideals. That is why conservatives are often obscurantist, that's to say, reactionary, on political issues. They are also often nationalists and do not understand that the ideas that are changing civilization know no borders and are equally valid in different cultures and geographical locations. A conservative finds it difficult to understand the difference between nationalism and patriotism; for them, both are identical. Not so for liberals. Patriotism for liberals is a beneficial feeling, one of solidarity and love for the country in which they are born, for their ancestors, for the language they speak, for their shared history, something that is perfectly

---

* All the quotations from "Why I Am Not a Conservative" are taken from F. A. von Hayek, *The Constitution of Liberty: The Definitive Edition*, pp. 517–533.

healthy and legitimate, while nationalism is a negative passion, a pernicious affirmation and defense of one's own *against* the outsider, as if the national were a value in itself, something superior, an idea that is the source of racism, discrimination, and closed thinking.

Liberals and conservatives share a certain mistrust of reason and rationality; liberals are conscious that "we do not have all the answers" and we do not know if the answers are always the right ones and even if we can find all the answers to the questions that we pose about so many things in so many different fields. Conservatives usually are very firm about everything, which prevents them from doubting themselves. And for Hayek—like Karl Popper on this issue—constant doubt and self-criticism are essential for the advancement of learning in all fields of knowledge.

Liberals are often "skeptics," who accept as provisional even those truths that they hold most dear. This skepticism about themselves is what allows them to be tolerant and conciliatory to the convictions and beliefs of others, even though they may be very different from their own. This spirit of openness, the ability to change and overcome one's own convictions, is rare and often inconceivable for people who, like so many conservatives, believe that they have arrived at absolute truths, invulnerable to any questioning or criticism.

Conservatives usually identify with a religion while many liberals are agnostic. But that does not mean that liberals are enemies of religion. Many are practicing believers, as was Adam Smith, the father of liberalism. They simply believe that spiritual matters and earthly matters are different spheres and that it is necessary to keep this reciprocal independence because when both become mixed in a single entity, violence often breaks out, as the history of religions shows and which we have seen confirmed in recent times by the outbreak of Islamic extremism and its collective murders. For this reason, unlike conservatives, who believe that the true religion could be imposed on the pagans, by force if necessary, liberals tend not to favor one religion over another in economic and social terms and, above all, they reject the notion that any religion can give itself the right to impose itself on others by force. In the book *Hayek on Hayek: An Autobiographical Dialogue* (1994), edited by Stephen Kresge and Leif Wenar, there is an interview, probably from the last years of his life, where Hayek says that he has discovered "recently" that he feels more attracted to Buddhism than to the "monotheistic religions of the West" because they are "frightfully intolerant." And he finds it "admirable" that in Japan people can be both Shinto and Buddhist.*

Hayek recognizes that the word *liberal* means different things in our day and age—in the United States, for example, it has changed its meaning to that of "radical," or even "socialist"—but that nobody has found a term to replace it. And he adds, humorously, that the term *Whig*, although quite precise, would seem excessively anachronistic, even though its meaning is clear when it is used by intellectuals like himself. Indeed Hayek was a man who, throughout his entire work, has contributed in a decisive fashion to give liberalism a very clear content and very precise boundaries.

* *Hayek on Hayek*, op. cit., p. 42.

SIR KARL POPPER (1902–1994)

A TWENTIETH-CENTURY LIFE

Without Hitler and the Nazis Karl Popper would never have written that key book of modern democratic and liberal thought, *The Open Society and Its Enemies*, and probably his life would have been confined to that of an obscure professor of philosophy of science in his native Vienna. Very little was known of his childhood and early years—his autobiography, *Unended Quest* (1976), an exclusively intellectual testimony, is almost completely silent about this period—before the publication of Malachi Haim Hacohen's *Karl Popper: The Formative Years, 1902–1945* (2000), an exhaustive account of that stage in his life in the dazzling setting of the capital of the Austro-Hungarian Empire. Vienna at the end of the nineteenth and the beginning of the twentieth centuries was a cosmopolitan multicultural and multiracial city, with an effervescent literary and cultural life and a critical spirit that fueled intense intellectual and political debates. It was there that Popper's idea of an "open society" as distinct from closed totalitarian societies must have begun to take shape.

Since following the Nazi occupation of Austria in March

1938, the cultural life of the country entered an era of obscurantism and decline from which it never fully recovered—its best talents emigrated, were killed, or were silenced by censorship and terror—it is difficult to imagine that the Vienna where Popper began his studies, discovered his vocation for research, science, and dissidence, and became an apprentice cabinetmaker, a schoolteacher, and a socialist activist was perhaps the most cultured city in Europe, a world where Catholics, Protestants, integrated or Zionist Jews, freethinkers, Masons, and atheists coexisted, debated, and helped to revolutionize artistic forms, music primarily, but also painting and literature, social sciences, exact sciences, and philosophy. William Johnston's book *The Austrian Mind: An Intellectual and Social History 1848–1938* (1972) offers a rigorous reconstruction of this Tower of Babel where Popper at an early age learned to detest nationalism: he called it "a dreadful heresy" of Western civilization, one of his bêtes noires, which he always identified as the mortal enemy of the culture of freedom. By contrast he was always a firm defender of minorities, of the poor, and of the "culture clash" that, in his opinion, would be as enriching as the cultural collision between the Greek and Eastern cultures that produced the "Greek miracle" in the era of Pericles.

Popper's family, Jewish by origin, had converted to Protestantism two generations before he was born on July 28, 1902. His parental grandfather had an impressive library of some fifteen thousand books where, as a child, he developed his passion for reading and for books after he read—or had read to him—a book for children by Selma Lagerlöf. He never got over having had to sell that library when the family finances collapsed. During his childhood the family was still very prosperous. In his old age, when for the first time in his life he received some money from royalties, he tried, naively, to

reconstruct that library, but never managed to do so. His education was Protestant and stoic, puritan, and, although he
married a Catholic, a fellow student from the university named
Hennie, that strict, Calvinist morality with its renunciation of
sensuality, self-discipline, and extreme austerity stayed with
him all his life. According to the accounts compiled by Malachi
Hacohen, he criticized Marx and Kennedy more for having
lovers than for their political errors.

In the Vienna of his youth—red Vienna—liberal and democratic socialism prevailed, which favored multiculturalism,
and many assimilated Jewish families, like his, held important
positions in economic, university, and even political life. His
early rejection of all forms of nationalism—the return to the
tribe—led him to oppose Zionism and he always thought that
the creation of Israel was "a tragic error." In the draft of his
Autobiography he wrote this very strong comment, quoted by
Haim Hacohen: "I opposed Zionism initially because I was
against any form of nationalism, but I never expected the Zionists to become racists. It makes me feel ashamed in my origin: I feel responsible for the deeds of Israeli nationalists."*

He thought at the time that Jews should assimilate into the
societies in which they lived because "the idea of the chosen
people" seemed dangerous; it seemed to him to foreshadow the
modern visions of the Marxist "chosen class" and the Nazi
"chosen race." It must have been terrible for someone with his
views to see how in Austria, a society that he thought to be
open, anti-Semitism began to spread so quickly through the
ideological influence of Germany and to feel suddenly threatened, suffocated, and forced to go into exile. Soon after, in exile

* Malachi Haim Hacohen, *Karl Popper: The Formative Years, 1902–1945:
Politics and Philosophy in Interwar Vienna*, Cambridge University Press,
Cambridge, UK, 2000, p. 305.

in faraway New Zealand where, thanks to his friends Friedrich von Hayek and Ernst Gombrich, he had obtained a modest job as a lecturer at Canterbury College in Christchurch, he would hear the news that sixteen close relatives—aunts, uncles, cousins—as well as innumerable Austrian colleagues and friends of Jewish origin who, like him, thought that they were completely integrated, had been killed or had died in concentration camps, victims of demented Nazi racism.

In a private letter that he would make public in 1984, fourteen years after writing it, titled "Against Big Words," Popper summed up his early beliefs that would lead him from socialism to liberalism: "I started out as a socialist at secondary school but I did not find school very stimulating. I left school at sixteen and only returned to take the university entrance examination. At seventeen (1919) I was still a socialist but I had become an opponent of Marx (as a result of some encounters with Communists). Further experiences (of bureaucrats), led me to the insight, even prior to fascism, that the increasing power of the machine of the state constitutes the utmost danger for personal freedom, and that we must therefore keep on fighting the machine. My socialism was not just a theoretical stance; I learnt cabinetmaking (by contrast with my intellectual socialist friends) and took the journeyman's examination; I worked in children's homes; I became a primary school teacher; prior to the completion of my first book (. . .) I had no intention of becoming a Professor of Philosophy. *The Logic of Scientific Discovery* was published in 1934; I accepted an appointment in New Zealand at Christmas-time, 1936. (. . .) I am an anti-Marxist and a liberal."*

---

* "Against Big Words," in Karl Popper, *In Search of a Better World: Lectures and Essays from Thirty Years*, Routledge, New York and London, 1992, pp. 82–83.

Nazism, exile and the war were the context that led Popper to put aside his scientific research for some years and offer what he called his "intellectual contribution" to resistance against Hitler and the threat of totalitarianism. Before leaving Austria he had published *Logik der Forschung* (*The Logic of Scientific Discovery*, 1934), which would only be reprinted, in a much expanded edition, a quarter of a century later, in 1959. In this work he repudiated induction—that a scientific hypothesis can be validated through an accumulation of evidence that corroborates it—and he argued that scientific truths—which are always contestable—can only be considered truths if they pass the test of "falsifiability," that is, that they cannot be objectively refuted, a theory that he would develop and refine throughout his life.

THE OPEN SOCIETY AND ITS ENEMIES

It was in exile that he first wrote *The Poverty of Historicism* (1944–1945) and then his magnum opus, *The Open Society and Its Enemies* (1945). Malachi Haim Hacohen gives a detailed and absorbing account of the almost heroic conditions—he had to learn classical Greek to read Plato and Aristotle in their original language—in which Popper worked on these two books of political philosophy, finding time away from his classes and administrative obligations at the university, asking for bibliographical help from his European friends, and living in a poverty that at times bordered on destitution. His great help was the loyalty and commitment of Hennie, who deciphered the manuscript, typed it up, and also offered her own strong criticism.

The book traces the origins and development throughout history of the ideas that both drive and support the theories and doctrines that are opposed to human freedom. After five years of excessively hard work, the book that would make Popper the most daring liberal thinker of his age was published in 1945. It offers a hugely detailed description and a strong denunciation of the tradition that he called "historicist," which begins with Plato, is revitalized in the nineteenth century, enriched by the work of Hegel, and reaches its apogee with Marx. Popper sees at the heart of this current of thought the source of all authoritarian structures, an unconscious panic toward the responsibility that freedom imposes on the individual who tends to sacrifice this freedom to escape responsibilities. Hence the nostalgic desire to return to the collective, tribal world, to societies that are immobile and unchanging, to the irrationalism of magical-religious thought before the birth of individuals who freed themselves from the placenta of the tribe and broke with its resistance to change through trade, the development of reason, and the practice of freedom. The systematic questioning of all of Marx's predictions is devastating, but Marx is treated in the book with respect and, at times, admiration by his most implacable intellectual adversary. Popper recognizes his good intentions to eliminate exploitation and social injustices as well as his seriousness as a scholar and his intellectual honesty. He argues that one of Marx's greatest merits is to have freed sociology from "psychologism" and he goes so far as to state that, without knowing it, the author of *Capital* was a secret defender of open society. His great error was to succumb to *historicism*, to believe that history obeyed inflexible laws and could be predicted by a social scientist. He also questions Marx's theory that the "material conditions of production" (the social structure) explains and always precedes ideas (the cultural superstructure). And he shows how, at times, ideas anticipate social changes and the material conditions of production. He takes as an example the Russian Revolution itself, which probably would not have happened or taken the course that it did without the Marxist ideas that guided Lenin, its initial architect. Although by then these ideas had already deviated from the direction that Marx had conceived. He was convinced that communism would first take hold in more developed capitalist countries like Britain and Germany and not in a backward, semifeudal society like Russia.

The great villain of *The Open Society and Its Enemies* is Hegel, who Popper analyzes and discredits with a ferocity that is unusual for him (he calls him a "charlatan," "accommodating," "verbose," and "obscurantist," just as Schopenhauer had done before). Because this kindhearted, straightforward, and sensitive man was always intransigent in matters of freedom.

It is not just Plato who is criticized head-on in the book. Aristotle receives the same treatment and Popper sees his "essentialism" as being the most direct link between Ancient Greece and the philosophy of Hegel. Aristotle, the founder of "verbalism," pompous language that says nothing, bequeathed, according to *The Open Society and Its Enemies*, this tradition to Hegel, who developed it to terrifying lengths. Within the web of words with which Hegel constructed his system one can find all the foundations of the totalitarian state—collectivist, irrational, autocratic, racist, antidemocratic—originally conceived by Plato. And, in addition, perfected and perverted. For Hegel, the Spirit, the source of life, always in motion, over time becomes embodied in the state, the supreme form of modernity. This state, the manifestation of the *essence* of all that exists, is superior to the body of human beings that make up society; the pinnacle of the state is the monarch, an absolute sovereign who demands total obedience and submission. The state is strengthened through action, as was the case of the Prussian state. And the superior form of action is confrontation, war with other states that it must conquer to justify itself. Military victory will establish it as superior to others. Human progress is punctuated by heroes, men who carry out glorious deeds through which the state achieves fulfillment and grows in stature. The monarch—a leader or caudillo—is a superior being. He can deceive, lie, and manipulate the masses, as Plato authorized the guardians of *The Republic* to behave, to keep them submissive, and be implacable against those who might dare rebel, because the greatest crime that a citizen can commit is to rise up against the *spirit* that the state embodies, which, in turn, has the sovereign or supreme dictator as its quintessential manifestation. Is this not the best description of those supermen Hitler, Stalin, Mussolini, Mao, Fidel Castro?

The great novelty of this absolute masterpiece was that Popper found the origins and roots of all hierarchical and anti-democratic ideologies in Greece and in Plato. That is, in the very culture that laid the foundations for democracy and open society. The fear of freedom stems from this very culture and it was none other than Plato, the most brilliant intellectual of his time, who was the first to place reason at the service of irrationalism (the return to the closed culture of the tribe, to collectivist irresponsibility and to the political, slave-based, and racist despotism of the supreme leader). Popper mounts a fierce defense of rationalism and argues that irrationalism leads, sooner or later, to crime and that, although it begins with Plato, it is "the most poisonous intellectual disease of our own time"

Is it correct to identify irrationalism with collectivism and a nostalgia for the lost unity of the tribe? Is irrationalism not also integral to what it means to be human, the domain of the unconscious, of dreams, intuitions, instincts, and passions? It is true, as Popper argues, that it can take on destructive forms, like fanaticism and political and religious dogmatism, which cause oppression and terror. But irrationality also produced, in sublimated form, extraordinary artistic creations like the mystic poetry of Saint John of the Cross and the modernist poetry of Rimbaud and Lautréamont, and much of modern art is nurtured, at least partially, by this nonrational wellspring of humanity.

Did Popper offer an accurate interpretation of Platonic thought? Many Hellenists, philosophers, and political essayists question whether he did so. But even if Popper has gone too far in his criticism of Plato and Aristotle, his book will always remain an accurate analysis of the psychological and social mechanisms that induce sovereign individuals not to take up the risks that freedom demands but to prefer instead dictatorial regimes.

Malachi Haim Hacohen must have worked as hard researching the young Popper as Popper himself worked on his study of the origins of totalitarianism in classical Greece. For at times he gives the impression that over the course of these years of intense dedication, his devout and almost religious admiration for Popper was turning into disillusionment as he discovered in his private life his inevitable defects and obsessions, his intolerance, his lack of reciprocity with people who had helped him, his depressions, his relative inflexibility in accepting the arrival of new forms, ideas, and fashions of modernity. Some of these criticisms are unjust, but they have a place in a book dedicated to a man who always maintained that a critical spirit is the essential condition of true progress in science and in social life and that it is by submitting them to the test of trial and error—that is by trying to "falsify" them, to show that they are wrong—that one can learn the truth or lies of doctrines, theories, and interpretations that seek to explain the individual, either isolated or immersed in society.

Furthermore Malachi Haim Hacohen also firmly establishes, against what came to be believed during the years of the Cold War, that Popper was not in any way an innate conservative philosopher and that his theories about open and closed societies, historicism, "world 3," piecemeal social engineering, and the tribal spirit, and his arguments against nationalism, dogmatism, and political and religious orthodoxies, cover a broad liberal philosophical spectrum where all democratic political formations, from social democracy to conservatism, can be placed so long as they accept the separation of powers, elections, freedom of expression, and the free market. For example, the philosopher and former Labour MP Bryan Magee reclaimed Popper as a social democrat in his book *Popper*, an interpretation supported by Jeremy Shearmur, who was Popper's assistant at the London School of Economics, in his book *The Political Thought of Karl Popper*.* And Popper himself states in his brief and schematic autobiography, *Unended Quest*, that "if there could be such a thing as socialism combined with individual liberty, I would be a socialist still." But he adds, this is a "beautiful dream."†

Popper's liberalism is profoundly progressive because it is permeated with a desire for justice that, at times, is lacking in those who measure the scope of liberalism simply in terms of free markets forgetting that, in Isaiah Berlin's metaphor, freedom for the wolves can often mean death to the sheep. Eco-

---

* Bryan Magee, *Popper*, Fontana Modern Masters, Fontana Books, London, 1973, and Jeremy Shearmur, *The Political Thought of Karl Popper*, Routledge, London and New York, 1996.
† Quoted in Shearmur, p. 35.

nomic freedom, which Popper defended, must be enhanced by public education of the highest level and various initiatives in the social field, like the creation of institutions for the "protection of the economically weak from the economically strong"—retirement provision, insurance against unemployment and accidents at work, free education in state schools, a ban on child labor—and an intense cultural life accessible to the greatest number of people, in order to create an equality of opportunities that combats, in every generation, religious dogmas and the spirit of the tribe. In *The Open Society and Its Enemies* he is crystal clear: "Economic power may be nearly as dangerous as physical violence."*

Popper wrote his two great works of political philosophy in New Zealand and, in the years that followed, when he was back in Europe he would return to his scientific research and his philosophical interests without ever abandoning his social and political preoccupations. He saw the move to Britain in 1946 as decisive: "In 1944 I was travelling with my wife in a bitterly cold bus, returning from a skiing holiday on Mount Cook. The bus stopped in the middle of nowhere, at a snowed-in rural New Zealand post office. To my surprise, I heard my name called and someone handed me a telegram—the telegram that changed our lives. It was signed F. A. Hayek, and it offered me a Readership at the London School of Economics. The appointment followed in 1945 and in 1949 I was given the title of Professor of Logic and Scientific Method."†

Indeed it was his friend Hayek who had found him the job at the London School of Economics. In Britain he dedicated

* Karl Popper, *The Open Society and Its Enemies, Volume 2*, 5th edition, Routledge, London, 1990, pp. 124–126.
† Karl Popper, *All Life Is Problem Solving*, Routledge, Abingdon and New York, 1999, p. 57.

himself to research and teaching and to writing his books, articles, and lectures. Despite his inveterate discretion and modesty—when he opened the Mozart Festival in Salzburg in 1978, he stated that, since 1950, he and Hennie had lived a secluded life in the Chiltern Hills "without television or newspapers," but listening to good classical music—his genius was being recognized. In what would be his country of adoption he received multiple honors. He took British citizenship, was knighted by the queen, and was elected to membership in the British Academy and the Royal Society. His prestige in academic circles became so great as to rival that of his compatriot Ludwig Wittgenstein.

POPPER AND WITTGENSTEIN

These two eminent thinkers met just once face-to-face, on October 25, 1946, for scarcely ten minutes, and their verbal and almost physical skirmish was so intense that it has acquired mythic proportions. What really happened? What led to the meeting and what were its consequences, a meeting that, over the years, many see as a symbolic dividing line between the two central currents of modern philosophy?

Anyone wishing to know the circumstances leading to this clash of giants should read the book *Wittgenstein's Poker*, subtitled "The Story of a Ten-Minute Argument Between Two Great Philosophers," by David Edmonds and John Eidinow, two BBC journalists. Their book reads like detective fiction. Both men had been born in Austria to families of converted Jews (converted to Catholicism and Protestantism), and anti-Semitism and Nazism transplanted them—after the events that first took Wittgenstein to Norway and Popper to New Zealand—to Britain, which granted them both citizenship.

Wittgenstein belonged to a very rich family, but he had given away his entire fortune to his brothers and sisters and Popper came from a wealthy background, although both were compulsively drawn to a frugal and sheltered life, which Wittgenstein took to ascetic lengths. Despite their passion for ideas, they were both great proponents and practitioners of manual labor—Wittgenstein was a gardener, Popper a cabinetmaker—that they considered conducive to intellectual life. The puritanism of the society they were born into affected the sexual life of both men, which was characterized by sobriety and self-control, both in Wittgenstein's precarious homosexual relations and in the very austere marriage of Popper to Hennie, the only woman in his life. (The philosopher confessed to a friend in his old age that his mother had never kissed him and that he had never kissed his wife on the lips.) Both were indebted to Bertrand Russell—a witness and participant in the meeting of October 25, 1946—who had been instrumental in getting Wittgenstein's *Tractatus Logico-Philosophicus* published in Great Britain and his being offered a Chair at Cambridge, and who had also been an enthusiastic supporter of Popper's *The Open Society and Its Enemies*, published the previous year in Britain. And both were brilliant and incorruptible, satanically arrogant and full of resentments, although probably Wittgenstein's bouts of hysteria (as witnessed on that memorable occasion) dwarfed anything Popper might muster.

The differences were those of personality and, above all, philosophical. Wittgenstein's theory, according to which there were no philosophical problems properly speaking, just riddles and puzzles, and that the result of philosophy was not a number of "philosophical propositions" but rather "to make propositions clear," to purify language of all the psychological impurities, clichés, mythologies, and religious or ideological conventions that clouded thought, seemed to Popper intolerably frivolous, something that could cause philosophy to become a branch of linguistics or a formal exercise devoid of any meaning related to human problems. For him, human problems were the very stuff of philosophy and the mission of the philosopher was to search for answers and explanations to the most burning questions faced by humankind. This is what he had done, as a refugee in New Zealand, in *The Open Society and Its Enemies*, a work that contained many criticisms of Wittgenstein's philosophy—even accusing it of being contradictory and confused and his theory as being false—and in which there is a comment that must have outraged the author of *Tractatus*: "Clear speaking is speaking in such a way that words do not matter."*

These two contradictory versions of philosophy came up against each other that Friday, October 25, in the Cambridge Moral Science Club that Wittgenstein chaired, which had invited Popper—who had arrived in Britain a few months earlier—to give a presentation on the topic "Are there philosophical problems?"

The topic had been chosen to spark a debate between the two luminaries and, for that reason, on that evening, instead of the usual dozen or so lecturers and students that usually attended the Cambridge Moral Science Club, there were some thirty people, crammed together in the run-down set of rooms, H3, on the second floor of King's College. Popper arrived in Cambridge in the late afternoon and instead of going to the club he had tea with Bertrand Russell, which has led some mischievous people to allege—one of a thousand theories that do the rounds about this meeting—that Russell had

---

* Karl Popper, *The Open Society, Volume 2*, op. cit., p. 296.

encouraged Popper to attack head-on the puzzle theory of the author of *Tractatus*. But the truth is that he needed no such encouragement. Popper confesses in his 1974 autobiography, *Unended Quest*, that he had been for some time impatiently wanting to prove to Wittgenstein that philosophical problems did indeed exist and in what form. So he went that evening to the meeting at the Cambridge Moral Science Club with his sword unsheathed.

Popper began his presentation, speaking from notes, denying that the function of philosophy was to solve riddles and he had begun to list a series of issues that he thought were typical philosophical problems when an irritated Wittgenstein interrupted him, raising his voice (as was his wont). But Popper, in turn, also interrupted him and tried to continue with his talk. At this point Wittgenstein grabbed a poker from the fireplace and waved it in the air to demonstrate, in graphic fashion, his angry rejection of Popper's criticisms. An electric silence ran through the mild-mannered British philosophers present, unaccustomed to such demonstrations of Austrian colorful excess. Bertrand Russell intervened with a peremptory order, "Wittgenstein, put that poker down at once." According to one version of events, at this point, still with the poker in his hand, Wittgenstein screamed in Popper's direction: "Give me an example of a moral rule." To which Popper replied, "Not to threaten visiting lecturers with pokers." There was some laughter. Wittgenstein, flushed with anger, threw the poker onto the fire in the grate and left the room, slamming the door. According to another version, Popper made his joke once Wittgenstein had already left the room and both Russell and another philosopher present, Richard Braithwaite, were trying to calm the waters.

David Edmonds and John Eidinow have read all the

accounts written on this incident, compared the correspondence of the protagonists and witnesses, minutely analyzing, sometimes quite ruthlessly, the different versions, and their investigation—the most instructive part of the book—does not establish definitively the truth of what happened in those heated ten minutes but rather shows that we will never know with certainty what occurred. The ten or eleven living witnesses who attended the meeting have recollections that do not coincide and, which, at times, differ in radical ways. Some heard and others did not the remark of Bertrand Russell; some state that Popper's joke occurred before, and others after, Wittgenstein left the room like a furious gale. And nobody is very sure of the details of the comments and exclamations exchanged by the two protagonists. The student entrusted to transcribe the session, paralyzed by the unexpected turn in the debate, got into a complete muddle and came up with a general and insipid version that is open to the most wide-ranging interpretations.

Wittgenstein's Poker set out to write an account of an undoubtedly important cultural event and succeeded in doing so. But the two BBC journalists also unwittingly furnished an outstanding example of an old truth: that the fictitious component—be it imaginary or literary—in history is as inevitable as it is necessary. If an event that occurred so recently, with so many participants still among the living, can slip through the nets of scientific and objective research and become metamorphosed, through fantasy and subjectivity, into something very different—a most loyal disciple of Wittgenstein, present at the Moral Science Club that evening, has even categorically denied that anything occurred—think of what happens with historical accounts of past events, which over the centuries ideologies and religions, vested interests, passions, and human dreams have injected with more and more doses of imagination until they become closer to the realms of literature and even, at times, meld with literature. This does not deny the existence of history, of course; it just underlines that it is a discipline imbued with imagination.

SUSPECT TRUTH

For Karl Popper, truth is not discovered: it is in the process of discovery and this process is unending. It is therefore, always, a provisional truth, one that lasts only so long as it is not refuted. Truth can be discovered by an inquiring mind, it is hidden like a treasure in the depths of matter or in the abyss of space, waiting for a perceptive explorer to detect it and reveal it to the world like the statue of an immortal goddess. Popper's truth is fragile, continually under the barrage of tests and experiments that weigh it up and seek to undermine it—"falsify" in his term—and substitute it for another truth, a process that has occurred and will inevitably continue to occur in the course of that vast pilgrimage through time that we call progress, civilization.

The way in which this truth is established is very well described in an allegory that Popper deploys in *The Logic of Scientific Discovery*, his first book, to describe what science is: "Science does not rest upon solid bedrock. The bold structure of its theories arises, as it were, above a swamp. It is like a building erected on piles. The piles are driven down from above into the swamp, but not down to any natural or 'given' base; and if we stop driving the piles deeper, it is not because we have reached firm ground. We simply stop when we are satisfied that the piles are firm enough to carry the structure, at least for the time being."*

Truth is, in the first instance, a hypothesis or theory that attempts to solve a problem. Whether the result of laboratory experiments, the meditations of social reformers, or complicated mathematical calculations, it is presented to the world as objective knowledge of a specific province or function of reality. The hypothesis or the theory is—ought to be—subject to the test of trial and error, where it must be verified or refuted by those who are not persuaded by it. This is either an immediate or a very lengthy process, in the course of which the theory lives—always under the sentence of death like primitive little rulers who took the throne by killing and will be removed from the throne by being killed—and generates consequences, influences life, and causes changes, be it in medical treatment, the armaments industry, social organization, sexual behavior, or fashion. Until, suddenly, another theory emerges, "falsifying" it, and collapses what had seemed firm, like a castle of cards in a gust of wind. The new truth then takes to the field, to fight against whatever tests and challenges the mind and science might set; that is, to live the hectic, dangerous existence that truth and knowledge must endure in Popper's world.

He began to sketch out this theory in the 1930s, in his first book, *The Logic of Scientific Discovery*, and would continue to refine it for the rest of his life. The book set out to demarcate what is genuine scientific research and what is not. When he reflected on the border that separated the one from the other, he discovered an idea that he would develop until it became

---

* Karl Popper, *The Logic of Scientific Discovery*, Routledge, London and New York, 2002, p. 94.

the backbone of his philosophy: a scientific theory (which in essence is different from a metaphysical theory) can only be called such if it can be "falsified" or refuted; it must be subjected to criticism, forensically examined, its most intimate aspects assessed, its motivations and assumptions laid bare. If it stands up to this critical assault, then it will further our knowledge of nature and society. At least until another theory or hypothesis discredits it, pushing knowledge in a direction that the initial theory had excluded or had not caught sight of. In *The Logic of Scientific Investigation* there is already a description of the "trial and error" method that Popper from then on would continue to develop, extending it beyond science to social and political questions.

Of course, nobody has as yet successfully refuted that the world is round. But Popper advises us, against all evidence, to get used to thinking that the earth, in truth only, *is* round because in some way, at some time, the advance of knowledge could also unseat this truth, as it has done with so many truths that appeared unshakable.

However, Popper's thinking is not relativistic or skeptically subjective. Truth has one foot placed in objective reality, which he recognizes as existing independent of the human mind and this foot is—according to the definition of the Polish physician Alfred Tarski, which he adopts—the coincidence of the theory with the facts.

That truth has, or may have, a relative existence does not mean that truth *is* relative. While it lasts, until another "falsifies it," it reigns all powerful. Truth is precarious because science is fallible, since we humans are fallible. The possibility of error is always there, behind the knowledge that seems to us completely solid. But this awareness of fallibility does not mean that truth is unattainable. It means that in order to reach the truth we must be tireless in verifying and criticizing it, in the experiments that test it; and prudent when we have arrived at certainties, willing to revise and correct, and flexible toward those who challenge established truths.

· Popper always declared himself an optimist, convinced that the world today, with all its limitations, was the best that humanity had ever had: "From a historical point of view, we live, in my opinion, in the best world that has ever existed. Of course it is a bad world, because there is another that is better and because life urges us to search for better worlds. And we must continue this search for a better world. But that does not mean that our world is bad. In fact, the world is not only beautiful, but young people today have the opportunity to observe it in a way that they could never have done before."* And in his speech opening the Salzburg Mozart Festival he declared, "I am an optimist. I am an optimist in a world where among the intelligentsia it has become a strict rule that one must be a pessimist if one wants to be 'in.'"†

That truth exists is demonstrated by the progress that humanity has made in so many fields: scientific and technical but also social and political. By making mistakes and learning from those mistakes, men and women have come increasingly to understand nature and to know themselves better. This is an endless process in which we can move backward or sideways as well as forward. But even false hypotheses and theories may contain some information that brings us closer to knowing the truth. Is this not how progress has been made in medicine, in

---

* Karl Popper and Konrad Lorenz, *El porvenir está abierto*, Tusquets Editores, Barcelona, 1995, pp. 58–59. This is a translation of *Die Zukunft ist offen*, Vienna, Series papers, 1985.

† Karl Popper, *In Search of a Better World: Lectures and Essays from Thirty Years*, op. cit., p. 223.

astronomy, in physics? Something similar can be said about social organization. Through mistakes that it knew how to correct, democratic culture has managed to guarantee people in open societies better material and cultural conditions and greater opportunities to determine their own destinies. This is the "piecemeal approach" that Popper advocates, a gradual or reformist approach, at odds with a revolutionary outlook that would make a tabula rasa of everything in existence.

Although for Popper truth is always suspect—as in the wonderful title of the play by Juan Ruiz de Alarcón, *La verdad sospechosa*—while a truth holds sway, life is meekly organized around it and undergoes either minute or transcendent changes because of it. What is important, for progress to be possible, for knowledge of the world and of life to be enriched and not impoverished, is that the reigning truths must always be subject to criticism, exposed to tests, verifications, and challenges that confirm or replace them with others that are closer to that definitive and total truth (unattainable and perhaps nonexistent) whose lure has piqued our curiosity and appetite for learning ever since reason displaced superstition as a source of knowledge.

Popper makes criticism—the exercise of freedom—the foundation of progress. Without criticism, without the possibility of "falsifying" all the certainties, there can be no advances in scientific understanding or improvements in social life. If *truth*, if all truths are not subject to the test of trial and error, if there is no freedom for people to question the validity of all the theories that claim to give answers to the problems they face, the workings of knowledge become impaired and knowledge itself can be perverted. Then, instead of rational truths, myths, acts of faith, magic, and metaphysics hold sway. The kingdom of the irrational—of dogma and taboo—recovers its domain as before, when people were not yet rational and free individuals but rather an enslaved mass, scarcely even *a part* of the tribe. This process can take a religious form, as in Christian or Islamic fundamentalism—the Catholic nations of the Middle Ages, for example, or Iran and Saudi Arabia today—where no one can impugn the "sacred truths," or it can take a secular form, as in totalitarian societies where the official truth is protected from open examination in the name of the "scientific doctrine" of Marxist-Leninism. In both cases, however, as also in the cases of Nazism and fascism, a voluntary or forced abdication of the right to criticize—the exercise of freedom—causes rationality to deteriorate, culture to become impoverished, and science to turn into mysticism and enchantment. Beneath the jacket and tie of civilized men are the loincloths and magical markings of the barbarian.

The only way to progress is by stumbling, falling, and getting up, time and again. Error will always be there because the best decisions are always, to some extent, bound up in error. In the great challenge of separating truth from lies—a goal, perhaps the most human of all goals, that is perfectly possible to achieve—it is essential to bear in mind that in this task there can never be definitive achievements that cannot be challenged later, and no knowledge that cannot be revised. In the great forest of misperceptions and deceptions, mistakes and mirages, through which we roam, the only way that truth can clear a path is by rational and systematic criticism of what is—or passes for—knowledge. Without this privileged expression of freedom, the right to criticize, we are condemned to oppression, brutality, and also obscurantism.

Probably no other thinker has made freedom so essential a condition for humanity than Popper. For him freedom does more than guarantee civilized forms of existence and stimulate cultural creativity; it is the basic requirement for knowledge, which allows us to learn from our mistakes and overcome them, the mechanism without which we would still be living in the ignorance and confusion of our ancestors, eating human flesh and worshipping totems. "As against this, I think that the advance of science depends on the free competition of thought and thus upon freedom . . ."* For that reason, Popper was always opposed to exclusively state education, as Plato had argued in *The Republic*, and defended private education as a form of competition with the state system.

The theory of knowledge that Popper began to outline in *The Logic of Scientific Investigation* is the best philosophical justification for the ethical value that most characterizes democratic culture: tolerance that is, for example, the defining feature of all Isaiah Berlin's work. If there are no absolute and eternal truths, if the only way for knowledge to progress is by making and correcting mistakes, we must all recognize that our own truths might not be correct and what we think of as the errors of our adversaries might in fact be truths. To recognize that we might be wrong and others might be right is to believe that through discussion and dialogue—coexisting—it is much easier to identify truth and error than through the imposition of an official single truth to which we all must subscribe for fear of being punished or disgraced.

It remains a paradox that someone like Popper, who would later so passionately defend simplicity and clarity in expression and would criticize so severely intellectuals who used obscure, convoluted, and abstruse language, should have written a book so difficult to read as *The Logic of Scientific Investigation* and its

* Karl Popper, *The Logic of Scientific Investigation*, op. cit., p. 279.

numerous additions and postscripts. I am not referring exclusively to the difficulty for someone not familiar with the sciences—physics, mathematics, probability theory, the theory of relativity, theorems, or quantum theory—to read a book with so many references to these specialized subjects. Because even a top-level scientist at home with this material would have to make a great effort not to get lost in a work that branches off so often from its central arguments into footnotes—some written when Popper was correcting the proofs of the Austrian edition in 1935—that complicate, nuance, or refute these arguments, or else amplify them with notes, appendixes, and postscripts, often added many years later, creating veritable labyrinths. One becomes inevitably lost in many of its pages because there is no coherent line of argument. The explanation for at least part of this verbal tangle is that the first edition of *The Logic of Scientific Investigation* was written in German; the second, in English, was published a quarter of a century later, during which time Popper had continued researching—strengthening or correcting the ideas in his work—and he added very extensive footnotes and appendixes. The ideas on simplicity and clarity that he would defend with so much conviction are more successfully implemented (though not always) in his later work.

THE CLOSED SOCIETY AND WORLD 3

At the dawn of human history there were no individuals, only the tribe, the closed society. The sovereign individual freed from this collective body that jealously closed in on itself in order to defend itself from wild animals, lightning bolts, evil spirits, and innumerable other fears of the primitive world, is a late creation of humanity. It takes shape with the appearance of the critical spirit—with the discovery that the world and life are problems that can and must be solved—that is, with the development of rationalism and the right to exercise this rationalism independent of religious and political authorities.

According to Karl Popper's theory, outlined in *The Open Society and Its Enemies* (1945), this frontier moment in civilization—the passage from a closed to an open society— begins in Greece with the pre-Socratics—Thales, Anaximander, Anaximenes—and achieved decisive momentum with Pericles and Socrates. The theory has also sparked much controversy, but, names and dates aside, the substantive part of his argument remains persuasive: that at some point, by accident or as a result of a complex process, for certain people knowledge stopped being magical and superstitious, a body of sacred beliefs protected by taboo, and a critical spirit emerged that subjected religious truths—the only ones acceptable until then—to rational analysis and to comparison with practical experience. This transition, which occurred at the same time as trade broke up the isolation of the tribe, would lead to a prodigious flowering of science, arts, and technology, of human creativity in general, and also the birth of the singular, decollectivized individual and the foundations of a culture of freedom. For better or worse, since there is no way to prove that this move has brought us happiness, the detribalization of intellectual life would from then on gain pace and propel certain societies toward systematic development in every sphere. The beginning of an era of rationality and of critical thinking—of scientific truths—meant that, at that moment in history, it would be "world 3," in Popper's terms, that would have a decisive influence on social development.

Within the almost infinite series of nomenclatures and classifications that the wise and the fools have proposed to describe reality, Sir Karl Popper's is the most transparent: "world 1" is the world of natural and material objects; "world 2" is the world of private mental or psychological states; and "world 3" contains the products of the human mind. The difference between "world 2" and "world 3" is that the former encompasses the private subjectivity of every individual, their nontransferable ideas, images, sensations, and feelings, while the products of "world 3," although they stem from individual subjective experiences, have become public: scientific theories, legal institutions, ethical principles, characters in novels, philosophy, art, poetry, in short, our entire cultural heritage.

It is not fanciful to suppose that the most primitive state of civilization that regulates existence is "world 1." This world was organized on the basis of brute force and the rigors of nature—a lightning bolt, a drought, a lion's claws—which people were powerless to influence. In a tribal society, of animism and magic, the boundaries between "worlds 2" and "3" must have been very faint and continually erased as the chief or religious authority (almost always the same person) imposed their own subjective desires on their followers and denied them any individuality. Furthermore "world 3" remains almost static; the life of the tribe goes on within a strict routine of rules and beliefs that ensure the permanence and repetition of what already exists. Its main feature is, as in Plato's *Republic*, terror of change. Any innovation was seen as a threat, presaging the invasion of outside forces that could only bring the destruction, the dissolution into chaos, of the social organism that individuals cling to, out of fear and desolation, in their search for security. In this beehive, individuals had no responsibility and were slaves, they were parts irreparably linked to other parts in a social mechanism that preserved their existence and defended them against the enemies and dangers that lay in wait outside that fortress—the life of the tribe—that regulated all their actions and their dreams.

The birth of a critical spirit broke down the walls of closed society and exposed humanity to an unknown experience: individual responsibility. No longer a submissive subject, adhering without question to the complex system of prohibitions and rules that governed social life, the individual was now a citizen who could judge and analyze for him- or herself and eventually rebel against what seemed absurd, false, or abusive. Freedom, the mother and daughter of rationality and the critical sprit, places a heavy load on human beings: to have to decide for themselves what is beneficial and harmful to them, how to face up to the innumerable challenges of society, whether society is functioning as it should or whether it should be transformed. This burden is too heavy for many. And for that reason, argues Popper, at the very moment when open society emerged—when reason replaced irrationality, individuals became protagonists of history and freedom began to replace former slavery—a contrary impulse was born, articulated by such important thinkers as Plato and Aristotle, to impede and negate open society and to revive or preserve the old tribal society where human beings were bees within a hive, relieved of any responsibility to take individual decisions, to confront the unknown, to resolve at their own risk the infinite problems of a universe that was free of the gods and demons of idolatry and magic. This contrary impulse remained a permanent challenge to the reason exercised by sovereign individuals.

From that mysterious moment, humanity changed course. "World 3" began to prosper and proliferate with the products of a creative energy unencumbered by restrictions and censorship and to exert ever more control over "worlds 1" and "2," that is, over nature, social life, and the minds of particular individuals. Ideas, scientific truths, rationality, and trade were pushing back—albeit not without reversals, standstills, and detours that took people back to their starting point—brute force, religious dogma, superstition, and irrationality as the guiding principles of society and laying the bases of a democratic culture—of sovereign individuals equal before the law—and of open society. The long and difficult march of freedom through history would lead to the unstoppable development of the West on two fronts: with ships that traveled to the stars and medicines that defeated disease, along with human rights and the rule of law, but also chemical, atomic, and biological weapons—and suicide terrorists—capable of reducing the planet to ashes and a dehumanization of social and individual life as material prosperity and standards of living improve.

The fear of change, of the unknown, of the limitless responsibilities that are a consequence of the emergence of a critical spirit—of rationality and freedom—has enabled closed societies, adopting many different guises—the guise of "the future" or of a world without classes, or of "the city of God incarnate"—to survive until now and, at many moments in history, to hold sway over open societies, in forms equivalent to the obscurantism and gregariousness of primitive society.

The battle is not won, nor, probably, will it ever be won. The call of the tribe, the attraction to that form of existence in which individuals enslave themselves to a religion or to a doctrine or to a leader who assumes responsibility for solving all problems for them, and shy away from the arduous commitment to freedom and their sovereignty as rational beings, clearly touches chords deep within the human heart. For this call is heard time and again by nations and peoples and, within open societies, by individuals and collectivities that struggle ceaselessly to close these societies and negate the culture of freedom.

Contrary to what one might imagine, the most implacable intellectual opponents of the development of open societies are among the most direct beneficiaries of the critical sprit and freedom of thought and creation that open societies offer. These people have argued in different ways and under different guises for a return to the magic and primitive world of collective entities, of those "happy and irresponsible" individuals who are not sovereign beings, masters of their own destiny, but rather instruments of blind and impersonal forces that direct the march of history. The most serpentine and effective enemy of the culture of freedom, for Popper, is *historicism*.

HISTORICISM AND FICTION

In the first English edition of *The Poverty of Historicism* (1957), Popper explains that the central premise of his book, that one cannot predict the course of human history through any scientific or rational means, began to take shape in his head in the winter of 1919–1920; he completed the main outline in 1935; he presented his work as a paper in January or February 1936 in a private meeting at the house of his friend Alfred Braunthal in Brussels and later to the seminar run by F. A. von Hayek at the London School of Economics. Publication was delayed for some years because the manuscript was rejected by the philosophical journal to which it was submitted. It was finally published in three parts in *Economica*—numbers 42, 43, and 46 (1944–1945)—and only appeared in book form in Britain in 1957, with revisions, additions, a new prologue, and a dedication that reads, "In memory of the countless men and women of all creeds or nations or races who fell victims to the fascist and communist belief in Inexorable Laws of Historical Destiny."*

If you think that history is written before it happens, that it is the performance of a preexisting libretto, fashioned by God, by nature, by the development of reason or by class struggle and the relations of production (as Marxists argue); if you believe that life is a force or a social and economic mechanism that individuals have little or no power to alter; if you think that the movement of humanity through time is rational, coherent, and thus predictable; if in short, you consider that history has a secret meaning, that, despite its infinite episodic diversity, gives to everything a coordinated logic and arranges it like a jigsaw puzzle, where all the pieces fit together in their place, you are, according to Popper, a "historicist."

If you are a Platonist, Hegelian, Comtean, Marxist, or a follower of Machiavelli, Vico, Spengler, or Toynbee, you idolize history and, consciously or unconsciously, you fear freedom, and are afraid to assume the responsibility that comes with conceiving of life as a permanent creation, as malleable clay that each society, culture, and generation can shape in whatever way they want, thus taking responsibility and total credit for what might be achieved or lost in each instance.

History has no order, logic, sense, and much less a rational direction that sociologists, economists, or ideologues can detect in advance, scientifically. History is organized by historians; they make it coherent and intelligible through the use of points of view and interpretations that are, always, partial, provisional, and, in the final analysis, as subjective as artistic constructs. Those who think that one of the functions of social

---

* Karl Popper, *The Poverty of Historicism*, Routledge Classics, Abingdon and New York, 2002, p. xx.

sciences is to "forecast" the future, to "predict" history are victims of an illusion, for that is an unattainable goal.

What, then, is history? A constant multiple improvisation, an animated chaos to which historians give a semblance of order, an almost infinite contradictory multiplication of events that—so as to understand them—social sciences reduce to arbitrary schema, to syntheses and mappings that are always a very poor version and even a caricature of real history, that dizzying totality of human activity that always overspills rational and intellectual attempts at comprehension. Popper does not reject history books, nor does he deny that knowledge about what happened in the past can enrich us and help us to understand the future. He asks us to take into account that all written history is partial and arbitrary—a mere selection—because it reflects barely an atom of the unfinished social universe we inhabit, this "whole" that is always making and remaking itself, that cannot be restricted to politics, economics, culture, institutions, religion, and the like because it is the sum of all these aspects of human reality, without exception. This history, the only real history, cannot be countenanced or described by human knowledge. That is why Popper states that "history has no meaning."*

These ideas, which Popper outlined in *The Poverty of Historicism* (1944–1945) and extended in *The Open Society and Its Enemies*, and which he alludes to in many essays, are lucidly summarized in a text from 1961, "Emancipation Through Knowledge," where he argues that while history does not have a secret meaning, we ourselves can give it the meaning it lacks.†

* Karl Popper, *The Open Society and Its Enemies, Volume 2*, op. cit., p. 269.
† Karl Popper, *In Search of a Better World*, op. cit., pp. 137–150.

What we understand by history—but this, says Popper in *The Open Society and Its Enemies* is "an offence against every decent conception of mankind"—is usually "the history of international crime and mass murder (including, it is true, some of the attempts to suppress them)."* The history of the conquests, crimes, and other acts of violence perpetrated by caudillos and despots, whom books have turned into heroes, can only be a very pale reflection of the integral experience of all those who suffered or benefited at their hands. And it reveals very little of the effects and reverberations that the actions of every culture, society, and civilization have had on others, both their contemporaries and those that followed them. If the history of humanity is a vast current of development and progress with many meanderings, regressions, and obstructions (which Popper does not deny), it cannot, in any event, ever be encompassed in all its infinite diversity and complexity.

Those who have tried to isolate, within all this endless disorder, certain laws to which this human development is tied, have perpetrated what for Popper is the most serious crime that a politician or an intellectual can commit (but not an artist, for whom this is a legitimate right): fashioning an "unreal structure," an artificial entelechy that purports to present itself as scientific truth when it is nothing more than an act of faith, a metaphysical or magical proposal. Naturally not all historicist theories are equivalent: some, like Marx's, have a greater subtlety and weight than those, for example, of Arnold Toynbee, who reduced the history of humanity to twenty one civilizations, no more, no less.

The future cannot be predicted. The evolution of human-

* Karl Popper, *The Open Society and Its Enemies, Volume 2*, op. cit., pp. 270, 278.

kind in the past does not allow us to deduce any direction in human events. Not just in historical terms, but also from a logical point of view, this would be an absurd pretension. So Popper tells us, although there is no doubt that history influences the development of knowledge, there is no way of predicting, through rational means, the evolution of scientific knowledge. Therefore it is not possible to anticipate the future course of a history that will, to a great extent, be determined by technological and scientific inventions that we cannot know in advance.

International events in our day and age offer a good argument in favor of the unpredictability of history. Who could have foreseen, some years ago, the irresistible decline of communism in the world, the disappearance of the U.S.S.R., and the conversion of China into a capitalist society? And who would have predicted the mortal blow that the development of the new media would inflict on political censorship and thought control, for it is ever more difficult to tamper with or control these media?

But the fact that there are no *laws* of history does not mean that there are not certain *tendencies* in human evolution. And the fact that one cannot predict the future does not mean that *all* social predictions are impossible. In specific fields, social sciences can establish that, under certain conditions, certain events will inevitably occur. Inorganic increases in the money supply will always lead to inflation, for example. And there is also no doubt that in certain areas, like science, international law, and freedom, one can trace a more or less clear line of progress to the present day. But it would be imprudent to suppose that even in these concrete fields, there will be an irreversible progression into the future. Humanity can regress and fall, negating these advances. There were never in the past mass killings on the scale of the two World Wars and it is unlikely that terrorism has caused in the past worse human tragedies than those we witness today. And the Jewish Holocaust perpetrated by the Nazis and the extermination of millions of dissidents by Soviet and Chinese communism offer unequivocal proof that barbarism can grow again with unusual vigor in societies that appear to have reached high levels of civilization. The growth of Islamic fundamentalism and cases like Iran are proof, perhaps, of the ease with which history can transgress any sense of precision, follow uncontrollable paths, and regress rather than advance.

But even if the function of historians is to relate singular or specific events and not to unearth laws or generalizations covering human events, one cannot write or understand history without a point of view, a perspective, and an interpretation. The historicist error, says Popper, is to confuse a "historical interpretation" with a theory or a law. "Interpretation" is relative and, if it owns up to this fact, it is useful for ordering—partially—what otherwise would be a chaotic accumulation of stories. To interpret history as the result of class or race struggle, or of religious ideas, or as a conflict between an open and closed society, can be illustrative so long as none of these interpretations are assigned universal and exclusive validity. Because history admits many coincidental, complementary, or contradictory interpretations, but no "law" in the sense of a unique and inevitable course of events. What invalidates the interpretations of the "historicists" is that they give these interpretations the status of laws with which human events must meekly comply, just as objects submit to the law of gravity and the tides to the movement of the moon.

In this sense, there are no "laws" in history. History is, for better or worse—Popper and we liberals believe the former—"free," the child of the freedom of humankind and therefore uncontrollable, capable of the most extraordinary occurrences. Of course, a perceptive observer will note certain tendencies in history. But these presuppose a multitude of specific and variable conditions along with certain general (and regular) principles. When "historicists" highlight "tendencies," they usually omit specific and variable conditions and thus turn tendencies into laws. By proceeding in this way, they denaturalize reality and present an abstract all-encompassing model of history that is not a reflection of collective life as it develops over time but rather of their own inventiveness—their genius in some cases—and of their secret fear of what is unforeseeable. "It really looks," I quote from the final paragraph of *The Poverty of Historicism*, "as if the historicists were trying to compensate themselves for the loss of an unchanging world by clinging to the belief that change can be foreseen because it is ruled by an unchanging law."*

Popper's conception of written history seems exactly what I have always believed a novel to be: an arbitrary organization of human reality that protects men and women against the anguish produced by our intuition that the world, life itself, is a vast disorder.

To be persuasive, every novel must impose itself on the reader's consciousness as a convincing order, an organized and intelligible world whose parts mesh within a harmonious system, a "whole" that connects and refines them. What we call the genius of Cervantes, Tolstoy, Conrad, Proust, and Faulkner has to do not just with the energy of their characters, their slowly developing psychology, their subtle or labyrinthine

---

* Popper, *The Poverty of Historicism*, op cit., p. 161.

prose, their powerful imagination, but also, most significantly, with the architectural coherence of their fictitious worlds, their solidity, their intricate weave. This rigorous and intelligent order, where nothing is gratuitous or incomprehensible, where life flows in a logical and inevitable course, where all human activities are attainable, seduces us because it calms us. We unconsciously superimpose this order onto the real world and the real world then, fleetingly, ceases to be vertigo, confusion, immeasurable absurdity, bottomless chaos, multiple disorder, and becomes cohesive, rationalizing and ordering our surroundings, restoring the confidence that we are loath to give up, of knowing who we are, where we are, and, above all, where we are going.

It is no coincidence that the times when novels achieved their greatest heights preceded the great convulsive moments of history, and that the most fertile moments for fiction are those when collective certainties—faith in religion or politics, social and ideological consensus—break down or collapse, for it is then that ordinary people feel lost, with no solid ground beneath their feet, and look to fiction—the order and coherence of the world of fiction—to shelter them from drift and confusion, the great insecurities and unknowns that life now offers. It is also no coincidence that societies that have lived periods of the most acute social, institutional, and moral disintegration are those that have normally produced the most strict and rigorous, the best organized and logical narrative "orders": those of Sade, Proust, Joyce, Mann, Dostoyevsky, and Tolstoy. These fictional constructs that radically deploy free will are imaginary acts of disobedience against the limits imposed by the human condition. Similar symbolic deicides, like Herodotus's *The Nine Books of History*, Michelet's *History of the French Revolution*, or Gibbon's *The Decline and Fall of the*

Roman Empire—these wonders of erudition, ambition, elegant writing, and fantasy—are secret testimonies to the panicked fear that we feel when we suspect that our fate is to exercise freedom, as Benedetto Croce puts it. But these works are also formidable intellectual creations that seek to deny this fear. Fortunately this deep-seated fear of freedom has not only engendered tyrants, totalitarian philosophies, dogmatic religions, and "historicism," but also great novels.

REFORMISM, OR PIECEMEAL ENGINEERING

The Poverty of Historicism and *The Open Society and Its Enemies* are important not only because they refute the theories that history is written and follows a script conceived by God or is determined by social and economic forces against which individual actions cannot prevail, but also because in these works Popper lucidly defends the reformist method—both democratic and liberal—of a gradual and consensual transformation of society against the revolutionary desire to change society in an immediate, total, and definitive way. He calls the reformist way "piecemeal engineering" and the revolutionary way "utopic engineering."

His argument is clear and convincing. Piecemeal engineering, made by "small adjustments and readjustments that can continually be improved upon,"* is peaceful, seeks wide consensus, and is always exposed to criticism that oversees its actions and can accelerate them or delay them within the realms of possibility. Utopic or holistic engineering, which does away with such consensus, tends to steamroll its critics as unacceptable obstacles to its messianic goals, explaining that

---

* Ibid., p. 66.

in this way it will speed up the process; in truth, either imperceptibly or abruptly, it begins to replace the means by the ends, liquidating criticism (and sometimes critics) and imposing a dictatorship in which the utopian end, always postponed, merely serves to justify certain means, which, as they increasingly identify society with the state, curtail our freedoms and eventually do away with them.

"However, once we realise that we cannot make heaven on earth but can only improve matters a *little*, we also realise that we can only improve them *little by little*," he affirms in *The Poverty of Historicism*.* Little by little: through continually readjusting the parts instead of proposing a total reconstruction of society. Proceeding in this way has the advantage that at each stage we can evaluate the result achieved and correct any errors in time, and learn from them. The revolutionary method—historicist and holistic—shuts down this possibility because, by showing contempt for the particular and becoming excessively fixated on the whole, it very soon moves away from concrete experience. It becomes detached from reality, following an abstract model, divorced from experience. In its desire to match up to social reality, it ends up sacrificing everything else, rationalism, freedom, and, sometimes, even simple common sense.

The notion of *planning*, so detested by Hayek, is also one of Popper's bêtes noires. It is historicist through and through because it supposes that history cannot just be predicted but also directed and planned like a work of engineering. This is a dangerous utopia because therein lurks totalitarianism. There is no way to centralize all the knowledge scattered across the multitude of individual minds that make up society or of ascertaining the desires, ambitions, needs, and interests that together

* Ibid., p. 69.

will determine the historical evolution of a society. Planning, taken to its logical conclusion, leads to the centralization of power. It progressively dominates the development of all the disparate forces and aspects of social life and imposes an authoritarian control over the behavior of institutions and individuals. *Planning*, the controlled and scientific ordering of social evolution, is a pipe dream. Whenever it is imposed it always leads to the destruction of freedom and to totalitarian regimes in which those with central power, under the pretext of "rationalizing" resources in an efficient manner, take upon themselves the right to deprive citizens of any initiative or diversity and force them to behave in certain ways.

Popper shows that "historicism" and "social utopianism" always go hand in hand. Fascism and communism sought to interpret the laws of history with their policies toward achieving perfect societies, and both regimes practiced "utopian engineering" that was more an act of faith, a religion, than a rational philosophy, something essentially anti-scientific.

The Poverty of Historicism employs the method of "trial and error" in a periphrastic way first by presenting historicism in the most coherent way possible and then refuting it point by point. Popper shows how a certain historicist current attempts to differentiate its method from scientific methods, arguing that social actions do not always obey identical causes, and are not subject to the constant adjustments and readjustments of scientific inquiry; but that nonetheless these social actions also obey laws that, once discovered, can predict future historical events. This, for Popper, is the original sin of "historicism": to believe that there are laws that regulate social life equivalent to those discovered in nature and in science. There are no such things; all that can be identified in the fields of history and society are tendencies or developments that lack the constant, exact nature of the movements of the stars in space, that is, the rigorous proof of the laws of gravity discovered by Newton.

The "bad people" in Popper's book—the historicists he criticizes the most—are not Marx or Engels, who only get a passing mention, but rather Karl Mannheim, whose book *Man and Society in an Age of Reconstruction* is used as a model to illustrate the worst errors of historicism, and John Stuart Mill and Auguste Comte, historicists whom Popper accuses of having continued the ideological anti-democratic tendencies that had their origins in Plato, who, by establishing that historical evolution was predetermined and prophetic, laid the foundations for all totalitarian ideologies.

Popper often quotes Hayek to express how deeply their work chimes with each other's and *The Poverty of Historicism* can accurately be seen as a complementary work to *The Road to Serfdom*, which had been published a short time before it.

Popper would develop the central ideas of this book more robustly and with greater clarity in *The Open Society and Its Enemies*. The "free competition of thought," along with piecemeal or gradual engineering, offers the most solid basis for sustaining the democratic order, against the tyranny of messianic and utopian ideologies that identify the state with society and seek to detect a "common purpose" in history, something that leads inevitably to the abandonment of rational thought and to political tyranny.

Of course, in many free societies there are planning departments and these have not curtailed public freedoms. But this is because these departments only "plan" in very relative and symbolic ways; they usually just give advice and information about economic activity without compulsively imposing policies or goals. This is not, in a strict sense, planning but rather researching, advising, assessing: activities that are perfectly compatible with the functioning of the market and of democratic society.

Unlike the "utopian or holistic engineer"—the revolutionary—the "piecemeal engineer"—the reformist—admits that one cannot know "everything" and that there is no way to predict or control the movements of society without imposing a dictatorial regime in which, by censorship and force, everything is made to fit into a mold established beforehand by the powers that be. The "piecemeal engineer" puts the part before the whole, the present before the future, the problems and needs of men and women in the here and now before the uncertain mirage of humanity in the future.

Reformists do not claim to change everything or to act according to some remote global design. They look to improve institutions and to change concrete conditions in the present in such a way that partial but effective and constant progress can be made. They know that it is only by continually improving the parts that society as a whole can be improved. They look to reduce or abolish poverty, unemployment, and discrimination and to develop new ways of improving living conditions and security, and they are always sensitive to the complex diversity of conflicting interests and aspirations, seeking that necessary balance that will avoid injustice and create new opportunities. Reformists do not aspire to bring *happiness* to men and women because they know that this is a matter for individuals, not for the state, and that there is no way of encompassing within a norm all the heterogeneous multiplicity—in everything, including personal desires and aspirations—that we find in human society. Their aims are less grandiose and more realistic: to reduce injustice and the social and economic causes of individual suffering.

Why do reformists prefer to modify or reform existing institutions instead of replacing them as revolutionaries try to do? Because, as Popper says in one of his essays in his book *Conjectures and Refutations: The Growth of Scientific Knowledge*,* the way that institutions function never depends just on how they are composed—their structure, rules, the tasks or responsibilities assigned to them or the people in their charge—but also, as well, on the traditions and customs of the wider society. The most important of these traditions is the "moral framework," the profound sense of justice and social sensibility that a society has developed throughout its history. One cannot erase this. The delicate, deeply rooted psychology and mood of a society cannot be abolished or abruptly replaced as revolutionaries might wish. For in the final instance, it is the way in which institutions resonate with these traditions that determines whether they succeed or fail. However well thought out these institutions might be, they will achieve their goals only if they are closely attuned to that ineffable, unwritten "moral framework" that is so decisive in the life of a nation. The constant adjustment of institutions to this traditional and ethical base—which has evolved and changed much more slowly than the institutions themselves—is only possible through "piecemeal engineering" which, through its gradual approach to reforming society, allows it to make readjustments and corrections to prevent errors being perpetuated (something that "holistic," utopian methodologies cannot do).

Reformism is compatible with freedom. Further still, it depends on freedom because constant critical analysis is its main weapon. With its critical approach, reformism can al-

---

* Karl Popper, *Conjectures and Refutations: The Growth of Scientific Knowledge*, Routledge Classics, Abingdon and New York, 2002. The book was first published in 1963.

ways maintain a balance between the individual and power and prevent any increase in power that might crush the individual. By contrast, "utopian or holistic engineering" will lead, sooner or later, to the accumulation of power and the suppression of criticism. And the route to this eventual outcome—we might often be oblivious to it—is through *controls* that are, of necessity, an inevitable part of any policy that really seeks to "plan" the development of society. Economic, social, and cultural *controls* stifle initiative and freedom and do away with individual sovereignty, turning citizens into puppets. There are, of course, intermediate stages between a democracy regulated by a policy of partial or light controls and a totalitarian or police society, where the state controls practically 100 percent of all social activities. But it is important to bear in mind that, while it is evident that even in the freest of societies some form of power must place certain limits and conditions on individual behavior—for without them society would slide into anarchy or the law of the jungle—it is also true that any system of controls must be constantly monitored and balanced because they always contain the seeds of authoritarianism, the beginnings of a threat against individual freedom.

The state, Popper says, is a "necessary evil." Necessary, because without it there would be no coexistence or any redistribution of wealth that guarantees fairness—because freedom, in and of itself, is a source of enormous imbalances and inequalities—and corrects abuses. But "evil" because its existence imposes, in all cases, even in the freest democracies, significant limitations on individual sovereignty. And there is a constant risk that the state will grow and undermine the foundations—which are fragile, when all is said and done—on which, through history—and it is difficult to know whether men and women have become happier or more unhappy over this time—that most beautiful and mysterious of human creations has been built: the culture of freedom.

THE TYRANNY OF LANGUAGE

From a very young age, Popper was opposed to a fashion that, at the time, did not yet exist: the fashion for linguistic distraction. Much of contemporary Western thought, especially after the Second World War, would become obsessively preoccupied with the limitations and power of language, to such an extent that at a certain moment—in the 1960s—one had the impression that all the human sciences, from philosophy to history, including anthropology and politics, were becoming branches of linguistics (shades of Heidegger). And this formal perspective—words organized among themselves, disassociated from their referent, the objective world, life not spoken or written but lived—which was being recurrently used in every discipline, would end up turning Western culture into a kind of protoplasmic philological, semiological, or grammatical speculation. It became a great rhetorical fireworks display in which ideas and concerns about "the big issues" more or less disappeared, swept away by the exclusive preoccupation with expression itself, with the verbal structures of every science and form of knowledge.

Popper never shared this position and this doubtless explains in part why, throughout his long intellectual career, he was never a fashionable philosopher and why his ideas would be confined for a long time to academic circles. In *The Open Society and Its Enemies*, he had greatly criticized Aristotle for his "verbiage," the tendency to divert the discussion of important topics into sheer wordiness, something that, according to Popper, Hegel inherited and intensified, infecting philosophy with rhetorical obscurantism. For him language "communicates" things outside itself and one must try to use it functionally, without dwelling too much on whether words express exactly what the user intends them to mean. To become distracted by exploring language for its own sake, as something dissociated from the content that words have a duty to express, is not just a waste of time. It is also frivolous, a distraction from what is essential, which is the search for truth that, for Popper, is always *outside* words, something that words can communicate but never produce by themselves. "In my view, aiming at simplicity and lucidity is a moral duty of all intellectuals: lack of clarity is a sin, and pretentiousness is a crime," he wrote in his essay "Two Faces of Common Sense."* Simplicity, for Popper, means using language in such a way that words are not important, rather they are transparent and convey ideas without embellishment. Our "operational definitions" have the advantage of helping us shift the problem into a field where nothing, or little, depends on words. "Clear speaking is speaking in such a way that words do not matter,"† a sentence that brings to mind the famous expression of Ortega y Gasset, "Clarity is the courtesy of the philosopher." It is difficult to imagine a conviction more opposed to the decree issued by modern Western culture that we should mistrust words since they are capable of playing the most cruel tricks on us if we do not use them wisely and do not pay them sufficient attention.

Like Hayek, Popper had a very low opinion of intellectuals. But unlike Hayek, he did not reproach them so much for

* Essay in Karl Popper's *Objective Knowledge: An Evolutionary Approach*, Clarendon Press, Oxford, 1972. This sentence repeats, literally, something that Popper wrote in *The Open Society and Its Enemies, Volume 2*, op. cit., p. 296.

† Karl Popper, *Open Society, Volume 2*, p. 296.

being innate "constructivists" but rather for their tendency to write in a confused manner, in the belief that linguistic opacity was synonymous with depth, something that had turned contemporary philosophy into little more than an indecipherable logomachy. And he also condemned them for being pessimistic about, and unjustly criticizing, contemporary Western society, which he considered "the best of all existing worlds," causing young people today to feel downhearted and contemptuous toward "open society," which is the most free, prosperous, and just society that humanity has ever known.

On another occasion, Popper recalled that the idea had haunted him from an early age: "It must have been about 1930 when I made this light hearted comment. 'Many students come to university not with the idea that they are entering a great kingdom of knowledge where they might manage to carve out their own small piece of land but rather they come to learn *to speak in an incomprehensible way, to make an impression. This is the tradition of intellectualism.*' At that moment I was making a joke. Later, however, when I became a university professor, I was shocked to realize that this was indeed the reality. Unfortunately this really is what happens."*

It is not strange, therefore, that Popper should strongly criticize some of his contemporaries, like Adorno and Horkheimer, well-known members of the Frankfurt School. He thought that Adorno was a bad imitator of Karl Kraus, someone who "has nothing whatever to say" and says it very badly, imitating "Hegelian obscurantism." He considers Horkheimer more serious, but negative, since he was opposed to reforming "our so-called 'social system.'" He adds that the

---

* Karl Popper and Konrad Lorenz, *El porvenir está abierto*, op. cit., p. 58.

writings of the Frankfurt School are, in Raymond Aron's term, "the opium of the intellectuals."*

Despite all this, he believes that intellectuals could lend a service to humanity if they could radically change their ways: "Why do I think that we, the intellectuals, are able to help? Simply because we, the intellectuals, have done the most terrible harm for thousands of years. Mass murder in the name of an idea, a doctrine, a theory, a religion—that is all our doing, our invention: the invention of intellectuals. If only we could stop setting man against man—often with the best intentions— much would be gained. Nobody can say that it is impossible for us to stop doing this."†

Popper was a victim of a grave error: of undervaluing expressive form. It is certainly true that his belief that language should not be an end in itself, or even a dominant preoccupation, for it might profoundly distort the content of knowledge, which cannot not be completely identified with the language used to express it, could not be more pertinent. There is no identity between form and content, even where it might seem inevitable, in literature, because, as the Catalan poet Gabriel Ferrater wrote, one cannot confuse Dante's terza rima with the torments of hell. And it is also true that this belief guarded Popper against the temptation to which many famous intellectuals of his day succumbed, of giving less credence to big issues in favor of exploring marginal topics—and, at the end of the day, discussions about the formal expression of science or

---

* Karl Popper, *The Myth of the Framework: In Defence of Science and Rationality*, ed. M. A. Notturno, Routledge, Abingdon and New York, 1994, pp. 78–81.
† "Toleration and Intellectual Responsibility," essay in Karl Popper, *In Search of a Better World*, op. cit., p. 189.

philosophy are indeed marginal. Popper's thought has always dealt with fundamental issues, the big questions, truth and lies, objective and magical or religious knowledge, freedom and tyranny, the individual and the state, metaphysics and science, as do the great classics. But there is no doubt that this thought has been affected by this underestimation of the nature of words, by the rash assumption that they can be used as if they were not important.

Words are always important. If one undervalues them, they can take their revenge, introducing ambiguity, amphibology, double or treble meanings into a text that seeks to be aseptic and unequivocal. Popper's reluctance to consider language as an autonomous reality, with its own impulses and tendencies, has had a negative effect on his work, which, at times, despite its conceptual importance, can be imprecise and confusing. His use of terms and classifications is not always successful because they can be misunderstood. To use the term "historicism" for a totalitarian view of history or mere ideology is debatable since it suggests a challenge to history itself, or something close to this, which is far from Popper's philosophy. More questionable still is his use of the terms "piecemeal engineering" and "utopian or holistic engineering" for something that could more simply be called "reformism" and "radicalism" (or a "liberal approach" and a "totalitarian approach"). Hayek, for example, criticized Popper's use of the word *engineer* for a social reformer because of the unconscious association with communist vocabulary since Stalin had defined writers as "engineers of the soul." And there is an evident contradiction in his calling social reformers "engineers" since he had argued so persuasively against the idea of "planning," the illusion that one can organize society from a position of centralized power, something that, in the long or short term, leads to the curtailment and abolition of freedoms. And no less confusing is the defense of "protectionism" that Popper makes in *The Open Society and Its Enemies* (vol. 1, chapter 6) because he seems to be arguing for state intervention in the economy. This is clearly not the case, because he explains that he is talking about a "defence of freedom," but the danger of confusion would not have been there if he had used a more appropriate word than *protectionism*.

It is good that philosophers or scientists are not restricted just to analyzing the languages that they use, because this is usually a sterile and byzantine approach. But it is essential for thinkers to pay due attention to the way in which they express themselves so that, in every one of their texts, they are in control of words, in charge of their arguments and not passive servants of language. Popper's work, which ranks among the most suggestive and innovative of our time, has this blemish: his words, scorned by him, sometimes tangle and distort the ideas that the author did not always express with the rigor and nuance that their depth and originality required.

Someone at the opposite extreme to Popper with regard to his conception of language, Roland Barthes, wrote: "In the order of knowledge, for things to become what they are, what they have been, one needs the following ingredient, the salt of words. It is the flavour of words that makes knowledge profound and rich."* In Popper's functional language, there is no salt in the words, that perfect balance between content and expression that, paradoxically, was what he sought in his ideal of a "simple and lucid" language where words do not matter. In his books, even in those where the depth of his wisdom and analysis is most evident, the richness of a thought never comes

---

* Roland Barthes, *Leçon*, Éditions du Seuil, Paris, 1978, p. 21.

through to us in all its splendor, but is instead checked, watered down, and even confused as a result of the relative poverty and complexity of his writing. Unlike Ortega y Gasset, whose language fitted his ideas so well that it improved them, Popper's opaque and meandering prose sometimes does not do his ideas justice.

Putting Popper next to Roland Barthes is not completely arbitrary. On the question of language, they represent two blameworthy extremes, two costly points of excess. Unlike Popper, who thought that language did not matter, Barthes considered that, in the final analysis, language was all that counted, since it is the *center of power*, of *all power*. An essayist of immense talent but also frivolous and self-regarding, who showed off and vanished behind all those words—*discourse*, *text*, *langue*, *parole*, and so on—that he described with such brilliance and sophistry. Barthes ended up affirming— "demonstrating"—that it was not men and women who spoke, but rather language that spoke through them, molding them and subjecting them to a sinuous and invisible dictatorship: "Language . . . is not reactionary or progressive; it is, very simply, fascist, because fascism does not prevent speech, it compels speech."* Only literary works that break with the dominant language can escape this dictatorship, but only temporarily because they in turn will become the dominant language. Freedom, for Barthes, can only exist *hors du langage*. (Does this mean that the freest people are autistic or deaf and mute?) When one distills Barthes's thought, extracting it from the elegant texts that he wrote, one can see how superficial, light, provocative, playful, humorous, and often vacuous it is. But when one deals with these thoughts in their original

---

* Ibid., p. 14.

texts, embellished by the elegance of the prose, the control of nuance, the enchanting subtlety of the sentence, it seems deep, it seems to express some transcendent truth: a beautiful rhetorical mirage.

Because it is not true that language is the seat of all power. What nonsense! Real power kills and words, at best, merely bore, hypnotize, or scandalize us. His elegant prose and iridescent style gave Barthes's ephemeral thought the appearance of depth and permanence, while Karl Popper's ambitious and profound system of thought has been to some degree constrained and diluted by a style that was never at the level of what he expressed. Because although ideas are not made up just of words, as Barthes believed, without the appropriate words to embody and communicate them, ideas will never be all that they might be.

THE VOICE OF GOD

If someone were to put together a book of current idiocies for the use of politically correct intellectuals, similar to the *sottissier* that Flaubert wrote in the nineteenth century, two instructions should take pride of place: (a) attack consumer society and, (b) see television as a source of a widespread lack of culture, violence, and stupidity.

Of course it is everyone's inalienable right to condemn consumerism, but, to be consistent, those who do the condemning must accept that the austere society that they are proposing, where people would only buy what is indispensable for survival, without any superfluous products—that is, a society almost without industries—would be a primitive world made up of unemployed and hungry crowds, at the mercy of disease and the law of the strongest, in which the precariousness of existence would not leave much time for the vast majority of people to have a spiritual and intellectual life. The return to the tribe would have been accomplished. Because the truth is that the more citizens consume industrial products—and, in open societies, whether these products are superfluous or indispensable is up to the consumer to decide—the more work there will be, education will be better and more widespread, and there will be more leisure time, for without these things, there can be no meaningful spiritual or intellectual life.

The question of television is infinitely more thorny than that of consumerism. There is no doubt that television has colossal power in today's society and it has contributed decisively to creating the "society of the spectacle" that I myself have criticized.* Popper thought that, in our day and age, television was "the most important power of all," to such a degree that it appeared to "have replaced the voice of God." These remarks appear in one of the last texts that he wrote, commenting on the study by the psychologist John Condry on the effects of television on children in the United States. Both these texts were brought together in a book published by Anatolia in France with the belligerent title *La Télévision: un danger pour la démocratie.†*

I will say briefly now what I hope I have made clear in the preceding pages, that I consider Karl Popper to be the most important thinker of our time, that I have spent much of the past thirty years reading and studying him, and if I were asked to name the most stimulating and enriching work of political

---

* Mario Vargas Llosa, *Notes on the Death of Culture: Essays on Spectacle and Society*, Faber & Faber, London, 2015.

† Karl Popper and John Condy, *La Télévision: un danger pour la démocratie*, Editions 10/18 Anatolia, Paris, 1994. All subsequent quotations are from this edition.

philosophy of the twentieth century, I would not hesitate one second in saying *The Open Society and Its Enemies*. I will also say that my admiration for this extraordinary intellect had me trembling at the knees the day when Pedro Schwartz, his former student, took me to meet him in his orderly small house in Kenley, on the outskirts of London, where I was moved to hear him talking enthusiastically about Kant and about the twenty-first century. Though I must confess that my emotion turned to surprise when we moved from philosophy and history to literature and I heard Sir Karl rail against Kafka and his compatriots Musil and Roth, and explain to us that he preferred the healthy and agreeable novels of Trollope to that boring and sickly literature. One of my best intellectual experiences was when I participated in a "Meeting with Karl Popper" in Santander, in August 1991, when the philosopher celebrated his eighty-ninth birthday and I had the opportunity to debate some ideas with him during a roundtable discussion.

A great philosopher has all the right in the world to his literary tastes, but is it conceivable that the most intransigent defender of individual freedom against the abuses and interference of the state could propose, as a solution to the problems that television brings to open society, a corporate system of licenses and controls to prevent the producers of programs and films from continuing to fill the small screen with the three poisons of "violence, sex and sensationalism"?

Popper argues that democracy will not survive if it does not place effective controls on television to reduce the unlimited power that it exerts today in shaping our cultural and moral environment. His analysis is based on the research of Professor Condry which, of course, makes one's hair stand on end: U.S. children watch an average of forty hours of television a week—four to five hours a day from Monday to Friday and seven to eight a day on Saturdays and Sundays—and this dependency causes many physical, moral, and intellectual disorders: a decrease in metabolism, obesity, passivity, lack of ethical standards, a stereotyped view of values, an inability to differentiate between fantasy and reality, a solipsistic outlook on life. Among all these effects, Popper highlights what he considers the most pernicious: the incitement to violence. And arguing that civilization is based fundamentally on being able to reduce violence, he proposes that the evil should be attacked at its source.

His solution goes against all liberal anti-state, anti-control assumptions and chimes completely with the constructivist and interventionist theories of social democrats, socialists, and communists (which he demolished in *The Open Society and Its Enemies*). It proposes giving compulsory professional training to all potential producers of TV programs, which would allow the state to enlighten them "on the fundamental role of education" and the "way in which children receive these images, how they absorb what television presents to them and how they try to adapt to an environment shaped by television." After this instruction, they will receive "a patent or a licence" without which they would not be able to work in television and which would be suspended or taken away if their work violated this "ethical oath," something like the Hippocratic oath for doctors, which they would take at the beginning of their career. An "order" or a council similar to that used by lawyers or doctors would be set up to oversee the correct use of this consultation code.

One shivers at the thought of what would happen if Popper's proposal had been successful and had been adopted by open societies. From that moment they would be significantly less open, that is for sure. Perhaps in their television schedules there would be less violence on the lines of Tarantino or James Bond films. But what of the *other* violence that would replace it? The violence of mediocrity and stifled talent that comes with the bureaucratization of a creative activity, the violence of the exclusion of any rebellious or disaffected sentiment, and censorship for all types of experimentation or search for new forms and content. The resulting television programs would be, perhaps, as healthy and anodyne as those broadcast in China, Cuba, or North Korea, or those that entertained TV viewers in Franco's Spain or Pinochet's Chile, where only professionals duly credited by the state—always through some sort of a corporative "decree"—could produce films or programs that met a strict code designed to defend society against its enemies. Would this solve the problem or would the cure be worse than the illness?

The problem exists, of course, and there is no doubt that it has become more acute with the massive development of new communication technologies, because it is true that television, and now the internet and the so-called social networks, exert an unprecedented influence over modern life. And it is essential to take certain precautions, for example regarding children, so that this influence does not become harmful. It is quite legitimate to establish watershed times for the broadcast of certain films or programs whose content could be harmful for younger viewers and that these programs should be classified so that parents can decide whether they are appropriate for their children, although, of course, with today's audiovisual revolution, these precautions might be useless. In any event, if these limitations went to the extreme of providing the state with a means of controlling the audiovisual media, the result would be, inevitably, the exploitation of the media by those in power, that is, a violence as destructive for the mind and for morality as the violence it seeks to eradicate.

Whether we like it or not, television, the internet, and social networks are here and will be here for some time yet. It is senseless to ask whether it would have been better had they not been invented. Whatever the statistics say, I suspect that, as happens with books, the much talked-of violence on our screens is more an effect of than a cause of the violence in society and that, therefore, it is not by banning access to screens but rather by stifling the roots of violence in real life, through education, that it will be combated effectively. This is a complex topic, of course, and perhaps it has much more to do with the murky and violent depths that—despite what this good and wise man Sir Karl Popper believed—also reside in the human soul, as with the bad examples offered by the fictions of literature, film, television, and the internet.

In any event it is not too much competition but rather the lack of competition that prevents television from producing more original and creative programs and that produces so much stupidity and low intellectual content. If television were to display the same diversity and nuance that exists in books, magazines, newspapers, and (in some countries) on radio stations, then refined, exquisite, demanding, and extravagant viewers would find on the small screen what is now so notably lacking. The disappearance of media borders and the dominance of information superhighways (that include entertainment and fiction) will perhaps bring us closer to this ideal.

RAYMOND ARON (1905–1983)

H e was a small man with big ears, blue eyes, and a melancholic gaze, always extremely courteous. He had been born into a secular, assimilated, and quite well-off Jewish family. He spent his childhood in Versailles, in a house with a tennis court, and in his early years he was quite a successful tennis player until his intellectual calling took him away from sporting activities. But he remained a rugby enthusiast, though he only followed games on television. In the École Normale, where he studied in the 1920s, he obtained the best marks in his year but he was so discreet and cautious in class discussions that his friend and fellow student Jean-Paul Sartre said to him one day: *"Mon petit camarade, pourquoi as-tu peur de déconner?"* (My little friend, why are you so afraid of putting your foot in it?). Sartre never knew this fear and throughout his life, he often put his foot in it, with all the force of an intelligence that disguised the worst sophisms as truths. Raymond Aron, by contrast, maintained his decorum throughout his productive life, which ended in late September 1983 in the Paris Palais de la Justice, where he had gone to testify on behalf of his friend Bertrand de Jouvenel in a libel case. Then, as always, he gave his opinions with the same moderation and good manners he had shown from his early years. The only exception, perhaps, was his response to the student revolution of May 1968, which made him furious.

At a young age he became interested in German philosophy, learned German, and in 1930, on completing his studies at the École Normale, he set off for the land of Goethe. He taught in Cologne for a couple of years and then spent a further two years at the Französische Akademiker-Haus in Berlin. He was there in 1932, the year of Hitler's electoral triumph. Some time later he witnessed, along with his friend, the historian Golo Mann, the auto-da-fé in which the Nazis burned thousands of "degenerate" books at the gates of the University of Humboldt. These traumatic political events did not distract him from his intellectual work, which, on his return to Paris, led to the publication of two key books on philosophy and sociology that introduced to a French audience figures such as Dilthey, Simmel, Husserl, Heidegger, and Max Weber: *Essai sur une théorie de l'histoire dans l'Allemagne contemporaine* and, more significantly, his doctoral thesis, *Introduction a la philosophie de l'histoire* (both published in 1938).

He was a somewhat eccentric thinker within the French tradition that adores extremes: he was liberal and moderate, a champion of that Saxon political virtue common sense, an amiable skeptic who, without always much luck, but with great wisdom and lucidity, defended for more than half a century in books, articles, and lectures—in academia and in journalism—liberal democracy against dictatorships, tolerance against dogmas, capitalism against socialism, and pragmatism against utopias. In an era fascinated by excess, iconoclasm, and insolence, the good sense and urbanity of Raymond Aron were so unostentatious, so against the whirlwind of frenetic fashion, that even some of his admirers seemed in secret to concur with the malicious phrase coined by someone in the sixties that "it was better to be wrong with Sartre than right with Aron." During the fifties and sixties, in the midst of the intellectual tumults in France, when the left had the monopoly over cultural life, he was a sort of exile within his own country. Later, from the seventies, when his predictions about, and analysis of, the U.S.S.R. and its satellite countries were confirmed, he was increasingly recognized, and his 1983 *Mémories* met with almost universal acclaim. But it did not last long. Although this vindication must have pleased him, he did not show it: he was too focused on editing his final masterpiece, the two hefty volumes of *Penser la Guerre: Clausewitz* (1976).

He was a dispassionate intellectual, with a penetrating but unshowy intelligence and a cold and clear prose, who could reflect serenely on the most burning questions and comment on current affairs with the same lucidity and objectivity as when he was teaching in the Sorbonne about industrial society or about his masters Montesquieu and Tocqueville. But he could be at times a master of irony and sarcasm as in his lecture on the one hundred and fiftieth anniversary of Marx's birth, delivered at UNESCO in the midst of the May 1968 revolution, when he stated that Berlin students were preparing for the peaceful society of their Marxist future by "defenestrating their professors." The only thing that made him impatient, like Valéry's Monsieur Teste, was *bêtise*, or human stupidity. Once, commenting on the populist demagogy of the Poujade movement, he wrote: "Quand ça devient trop bête, je cesse de comprendre" ("When it becomes too stupid, I cease to understand").*

---

* Raymond Aron, *Histoire et politique: Textes et témoignage*, Julliard, Paris, 1985, p. 230.

With his passing, we have lost one of the last great European intellectuals, and one of the most accessible to nonspecialists, a moralist, philosopher, and sociologist of the highest order who, at the same time, worked in journalism and had the talent—which is today very rare among intellectuals—of being able to elevate commentary on current affairs to the category of a creative essay and to imbue his academic writing and his sociological or historical reflections with the clarity of a good newspaper column. A professor in the Collège de France, a columnist who for more than half a century commented weekly on political affairs first in *Combat*, then in *Le Figaro*, and finally in *L'Express*, he was living proof that specialists could also be good communicators. Intellectuals today are, and write for, specialists; there is a seemingly unbridgeable chasm between their knowledge, which is trapped behind often esoteric language, and the ever cheaper and more bankrupt intellectual offerings disseminated by the media. One of Raymond Aron's great achievements was that throughout his life he could be a bridge between the two sides of this precipice that is widening at an alarming rate.

A tireless worker, Aron's life forced him continually to test his ideas against the proof of reality. A Germanophile intellectual from his student days, he found himself living in Germany, learning about the sociology and philosophy of that country, when the development of Nazism and its seizure of power led him to discover his own situation as a Jew, something that he had been scarcely conscious of before. The Judaism of Raymond Aron requires a separate mention. Like Sir Isaiah Berlin, with whom he shares a similar outlook on so many issues, his ideas on this topic, which is so often distorted by passion and prejudice, are instructive. Born and raised in a family that had stopped practicing religion and was assimilated, and as an agnostic himself (his parents never took him to a synagogue), Aron often criticized the religious intolerance and the nationalist extremism of those he called, somewhat humorously, his Jewish "co-religionaries." He never had faith in the "chosen people" and the "sacred history" of the Old Testament. But when in a press conference in 1967, de Gaulle called Jews "an elite people, self-assured and domineering," Aron responded with a book that is one of the most intelligent descriptions of the Jewish condition and the problem of Israel: *De Gaulle, Israel et les Juifs* (1968).

Among the many homages written at his death, *Libération* stated that "Raymond Aron saved the right from drowning in stupidity," an example of the French obsession with classification and its often cheap leftism. Pigeonholing him in this way erases the nuances of Aron's thought. Quoting Ortega y Gasset, he once said that right and left were "two equivalent hemiplegias." Considered right wing, he was so in a very particular way, a very liberal way. After the defeat of France in 1939, he was one of the first intellectuals to leave for London to join the Free French forces, but de Gaulle did not allow him to become a combatant, as he had intended, and made him the editor in chief of the Resistance magazine, *La France Libre*. His support of de Gaulle was always independent, mistrustful, and critical: he was often a severe critic of the Fifth Republic and of the general himself, accusing both of being authoritarian. After the student revolution of 1968, which he opposed with a passion that was rare in him, he wrote in *La Révolution introuvable* (1968) that he was not a Gaullist and that General de Gaulle had a particular dislike for him.*

* Raymond Aron, *La Révolution introuvable: réflexions sur les événements de Mai*, Fayard, Paris, 1968. Text references are from the Spanish edition, *La revolución estudiantil*, Editorial Desclée de Brouwer, 1970.

Furthermore, he was the first intellectual who dared to argue that the independence of Algeria was inevitable, in *La Tragédie algérienne* (1957), a book written at a time in which almost the entire French left, including the Socialist Party, had a reactionary, nationalist position on the issue. Michel Winock has analyzed the scandal that erupted in the right-wing press at Raymond Aron's stance against the jingoistic nationalism—from the socialists to the extreme right in France—that demanded the preservation of Algeria under French sovereignty and the extermination of the insurrectionary FLN.* Aron's ideas were coherent and incontrovertible: one cannot defend liberalism and democracy and, at the same time, an imperialist and colonialist policy against a people claiming their right to be independent. It is true that when France invaded and occupied Algeria in the nineteenth century, the most progressive minds in France (in all of Europe) thought that "colonizing" was to guarantee progress in societies living in feudal obscurantism, was to fight against slavery and to bring literacy, modern science, and technology to these societies, in short all the myths deployed to give the colonial powers a clear conscience. But in the twentieth century, these fabrications had been exposed by a cruel and flagrant reality—the harsh exploitation of the colonized by the racist, discriminatory, and abusive policies of the colonizers—and Aron explained all this with his customary objectivity and intelligence: France, the champion of freedoms, could not deny Algerians their right to create their own state and elect their own governments.

Practically the entire right in France felt betrayed by the man they considered their most significant intellectual spokes-

---

* Michel Winock, *"La tragédie algérienne"* in Raymond Aron, *Histoire et politique: Textes et témoignage*, op. cit., pp. 269–273.

man. Insults were rained on Aron, with critics calling him "a cerebral intellectual lacking in humanity" (D. Arlon), condemning his "glacial stoicism" (Jules Monnerot), his "desiccated realism" (G. Le Brun Keris) and his "icy clarity" (François Mauriac). Others accused him of having become a "spokesman for US capital" and there were also anti-Semitic attacks, like an article in *Réveil de la France* that compared him with Mendès France and Servan-Schreiber (both of Jewish origin) and complained of "these Frenchmen who were still not used to France."

THE OPIUM OF THE INTELLECTUALS

But Raymond Aron was in the main opposed to the radical left thinkers of his generation. He was a tenacious, and for many years, almost solitary critic of the Marxist and existentialist theories of Sartre, Merleau-Ponty, and Louis Althusser, as can be seen in his polemics, essays, and articles collected in the volumes *Polémiques* (1955) and *D'une sainte famille a l'autre* (1969) and his splendid analysis of Marxism and culture, *L'Opium des intellectuels*, published in 1955, which François Furet described very well as "a combative and philosophical work."*

In it this "incorrigible liberal," as he called himself, surveys the attitudes of intellectuals toward power and the state since the Middle Ages, and he describes the similarities and differences between intellectuals in the Soviet Union, subject to the dogmas of the Communist Party, and the "skeptical" intellec-

---

* Raymond Aron, *Polémiques*, Gallimard, Paris, 1955. Raymond Aron, *D'une sainte famille a l'autre*, Gallimard, Paris, 1969. Raymond Aron, *L'Opium des intellectuels*, Calman-Levy, Editeurs, Liberté del'Esprit, Paris, 1955.

tual, which was his way of saying "free": "If they can abolish fanaticism, let us pray for the advent of the skeptics."*

For Aron, Marxism is, as was Nazism, a typical "secular religion" of our time, a definition that he first used in several articles published in *La France Libre* in 1944. Among the most interesting pages in this book is his close analysis of how dogmatic Marxism has become. It was Marx who called religion the "opium of the people." Aron argues that Marxism offers many great similarities with the Catholic Church, at least at first sight: both share a messianic optimism—a classless society will herald the end of history and will begin a heavenly era of peace and justice for all of humanity. In the ideological dogma of Marxism, history is the work of class struggle with the Communist Party at the vanguard, a war in which the proletariat represent the righteous men and women in society, the custodians of all that is good and the instrument through which the exploitative bourgeoisie will be defeated and the last shall become first. The book was written when the "worker priests," who had offered a bridge between Catholicism and communism, had been called to order by the Vatican, and Raymond Aron offers a subtle analysis of these believers, whose principal mouthpiece was the journal *Esprit*, who argued that Marxism and Christianity were compatible and who were among the most prominent "fellow travelers" of the Communists. Their alliance, for Aron, was an insoluble contradiction because the Church, whether it likes it or not, always "consolidates established injustice" and "the Christian opium makes the people passive" while the "communist opium incites them to revolt" (p. 300). But at least in some respects the two

---

* Aron, *L'Opium*, p. 334. All the quotations from this book have been translated from this French edition.

religions—the sacred and the secular—are alike because the "Stalinist religion," like the Christian religion, justifies all sacrifices, excesses, and abuses in the name of paradise, "a future which recedes as one approaches it, a moment in which the people will harvest the fruits of their long patience" (p. 301).

Taking all this into account, we should point out that *L'Opium des intellectuels* is directed not so much at communists, but at crypto-communists, fellow travelers, or useful idiots represented in postwar France by left-wing Christians and existentialists, above all Jean-Paul Sartre and Maurice Merleau-Ponty, who are subjected to incisive criticism.

Aron illustrates that both the right and the left are fraught with so many divisions that it is fanciful to talk of a united left, heirs to the great revolution of 1789, which is secular and in favor of an egalitarian, liberal society. And that, among the left, the arguments revolve around the issue of freedom. He notes that in Britain the Labour Party in government since 1945 had put through great social reforms, "ruining the rich," without doing away with public freedoms, while Stalinism did away with these freedoms when it extended the control of the state over economic life.

He describes the failure of the Fourth Republic, when Gaullism was defeated at the polls. The myth of revolution, embodied in the U.S.S.R., had seduced a great number of intellectuals as can be seen in the 1952 polemic between Sartre and Francis Jeanson on the one side and Albert Camus on the other, about the concentration camps in the Soviet Union. Aron's position, which is very close to Camus's, is extremely critical of Sartre, who did not deny the existence of the Gulag—this term was not yet in common currency, until Aleksandr Solzhenitsyn disseminated it some years later—but justified it because, in his opinion, the U.S.S.R., despite everything, represented the defense of the proletariat in its struggle to the death against the bourgeoisie. Aron underlines the paradox that violence was ever more seductive to the intellectual class at a time when, in terms of French politics, the revolution was becoming ever distant and fading. And he asks whether this passion for violence does not have a great deal in common with the attraction that it always held for the extremist European right, that is, fascism and Nazism.

The most persuasive and brilliant of the topics analyzed in *The Opium of the Intellectuals* is "the myth of the proletariat," this proletariat that, Marx argued, would have the function of saving humanity from injustice and exploitation and establishing a classless society, just and free of contradictions. Aron shows the messianic, Judeo-Christian origins of this conviction, an act of faith that lacks any scientific base. Why would the working class be the only class capable of saving humanity? For one thing, the conditions of the workers in 1955 are very dissimilar to those of workers in Marx's early years, in the middle of the nineteenth century, and, furthermore, the standard of living and rights for industrial workers in countries like the United States, Sweden, and Great Britain, although different, are also vastly superior if one compares them to those in the least developed and third world countries.

It is also not true that when the workers obtained power in the U.S.S.R., they became "liberated": they are still slaves, not now to capitalists, but to political leaders who proclaim themselves as representatives of history, who pay them miserable wages, do not allow them independent unions, and repress any working-class protest as a political crime. Aron comments ironically on existentialist and Christian intellectuals, many of whom had never seen a worker in their lives and lived in the free and affluent societies of the West, spreading the myth of the militant and revolutionary proletariat in countries where the majority of workers aspired to less transcendent and more practical things: to having their own home, a car, social security, and paid holidays, that is, to becoming bourgeois. The true victims of social injustice in present-day society, he argues, are the Jews and other minorities who are victims of racial prejudice, those who live in near slave conditions in African countries and the Middle East, and the peasants living in feudal conditions on large estates throughout the third world.

Another splendid chapter, titled "Churchmen and the Faithful," studies communism as a secular religion with its orthodoxies and heterodoxies, its sects, its deviations, and its inquisition. His interpretation of the "Stalinist show trials" in the 1930s is very relevant. In these trials Kamenev, Bukharin, Zinoviev, and other comrades of Lenin were forced to declare themselves "agents of Hitler and the Gestapo" before being executed. It is incredible that respectable philosophers like Merleau-Ponty in his book *Humanisme et terreur* would validate these legal monstrosities—in essence legally sanctioned murders—in the name of the "essential truth" of the class struggle and of the Communist Party as the representative and vanguard of the proletariat. We should point out that, unlike Sartre, Merleau-Ponty later changed his opinion and would break with Sartre precisely because of his persistent defense of Marxism as the "unsurpassable horizon of our time." His book *Les Aventures de la dialéctique* (1955) is a very severe critique of Sartre's essay "Les Communistes et la paix," to which Simone de Beauvoir responded with a no less virulent attack, "Merleau-Ponty et le pseudo-sartrisme" (1955). Aron offers an implacable denunciation of the fallacy of considering the Communist Party—he calls this fallacy "sacred history"— with all its comings and goings, its contradictions and changes of political behavior, its recantations and repressions, as the eternal representative of historical truth and social justice.

In his chapter "The Meaning of History," he refutes the idea of the "churchmen" and the "faithful" that history has a single meaning and it will disappear with the class struggle when the exploitation of man by man no longer exists. The "end of history," he argues, is a religious idea and, furthermore, it is simplistic to believe that the motor of history is just the struggle between the bourgeoisie and the proletariat, ignoring the multiplicity of social, cultural, traditional, religious, psychological, family, and personal factors that exist alongside economic factors, without which it would be impossible to understand historical events like the Battle of Austerlitz or Hitler's attack on the U.S.S.R. in 1941. Only an "act of faith" could lead a philosopher—he is still referring to Merleau-Ponty—once the Communist Party takes power, to accept what he had previously condemned: the lack of electoral and press freedom, the trampling of human rights, including torture: "the sublime end excuses the revolting means."

Aron criticizes the "Idolatry of History," denying that this offers the absolute explanation for humanity. One of the most successful aspects of this book is its fusion of philosophical and political wisdom, where serene and thoughtful reason is combined with a polemical and even sometimes propagandist tone with respect to both the past and the present. His pages continue to be a warning against ideological dogmatism that seeks to legitimate the Marxist myths of the proletariat, of revolution, and of the Communist Party and the so-called omniscience and omnipotence of the Central Committee and the Secretary General, introduced by Lenin and used, above all, by Stalin.

This book and others by him, like *Marxismes imaginaires*

(1969), sought to offer a brave and reasoned counterweight to the ideologized fervor of the time, showing the relativism and the myths underlying theories that purport to offer definite and absolute answers about society and humankind. They did not, unfortunately, have the impact they deserved, especially among young people. This was because these books, like others he wrote that were dictated by current concerns—for example, *République impériale* (*The Imperial Republic*) and his critique of the disturbances of the so-called student revolution of May 1968 in France, *La Révolution introuvable* (*The Elusive Revolution*)—were written simply to dismantle the ideologies in vogue rather than to offer in their place an all-embracing theory, which he did not believe in. In that, as well, he was a genuine liberal. In our day and age, when we find healthy critical reappraisal replacing the utopian illusions of the fifties and sixties, the pragmatic realism and the reformist and liberal ideas of Raymond Aron should receive a more sympathetic hearing.

THE ELUSIVE REVOLUTION

In May 1968 in France there was student unrest at the University of Nanterre, which then spread to the Sorbonne, to the remaining universities in the country, and to colleges and schools. This is how the "student revolution" began, and it sparked similar movements in different parts, which is why it became so important the world over. Nearly sixty years on, such a reaction seems excessive when one considers its real significance: it led to a certain freedom in behavior, especially sexual freedom, the disappearance of standards of polite behavior, the multiplication of swear words in communications, and not much more. Not only did French society continue as before but in the university sector things became more rigid and not more democratic, former academic standards plummeted, and all the problems have still not been resolved.

In its early days the events of May 1968 had the look of a libertarian—in any event, anti-Stalinist—revolution in French society, led by students. Lecturers and professors as well as other university employees joined the rebellion, local universities were occupied, communes were established and barricades erected, there were almost daily noisy assemblies, which voted for likable but crazy proposals (the most popular slogans were "power to the imagination" and "it is forbidden to forbid"), and theaters and cultural centers were taken over. Echoes of the mobilization even reached the Cannes Film Festival, provoking an incident in which the filmmaker Jean-Luc Godard, flattened by a punch to the chin, was one of the few victims of the revolt. The efforts of the students to connect with the workers and involve them, despite the resistance of the communist trade unions, was partially successful because a wave of strikes paralyzed many factories in different parts of France, forcing the Communist Party, which was very reticent at the beginning, to declare a general strike. In this curious revolution there were no deaths but there were, instead, intense debates in which Trotskyists, Marxist-Leninists, Maoists, Castroists, Guevarists, anarchists, progressive Christians, and all sorts of groups and groupuscules of the extreme left (with the exception of what Cohn-Bendit, one of the leaders of May 1968, would call, "la crapule staliniénne") exchanged ideas, plans, and incendiary proclamations without coming to blows. But all this, however, was eclipsed in an unexpected way when, in the elections called in the midst of this revolutionary effervescence, the Gaullists swept the polls and gained their highest ever victory, greatly increasing the absolute majority that they already held in parliament. The famous revolution deflated as if by magic, confirming once again Raymond Aron's theory that, both in the nineteenth and the twentieth centuries, all French revolutionary crises "are followed, after the phase of the barricades or of lyrical illusions, by an overwhelming return of the party of order."*

And it goes without saying that the "May revolution," which was interpreted as the materialization of the sociological theories of Herbert Marcuse, had the support of almost the entire intellectual class, led by Sartre, Simone de Beauvoir, Althusser, Foucault, and Lacan, with manifestos, speeches, visits to the barricades, and even a symbolic attack by a group of writers on a hotel. The exception was Raymond Aron who, from the first moment, declared himself categorically—and, for the first time in his life, furiously—against what he saw not as a revolution but as a caricature, a comic opera that would not lead to any change in French society but rather to the destruction of the university system and of the economic progress that France was making. He received such strong criticism for this view from Sartre that a group of intellectuals, headed by Kostas Papaioannou, circulated a manifesto defending him.

The book that he subsequently published, *La Révolution introuvable: Réflexions sur les événements de mai* (1969), contains a long interview with Alain Duhamel, a framing essay, and a compilation of all the articles that he wrote in *Le Figaro* in May and June 1968. Aron declares his hostility from the outset toward what he saw as a chaotic movement that would lead to the "Latin-Americanization" of French universities. He sees the event as being charged with "passion and delir-

---

* Raymond Aron, *La revolución estudiantil*, op. cit., p. 87.

ium," on the verge of being controlled by extremist groups and groupuscules, who looked to use it to revolutionize society according to models inspired by different forms of Marxism—Trotskyism, Castroism, Guevarism—something that, in the short or long term, would serve only to "increase the prevailing confusion" and, in the worst case, plunge France into a dictatorship. He thought this final outcome improbable and in his analysis, punctuated by quotations illustrating the skepticism and frustration that his inspiration Alexis de Tocqueville had felt about the 1848 revolution, he pointed out the paradox that in their desire to create "direct democracy," the revolutionary students, despite declaring themselves Marxists, were more anti-Soviet than anti-capitalist.

In this book he defends himself against the charge that he had moved to a "reactionary position" and frequently points out that he had proposed an integral reform of the French university system, looking to modernize it, not hold it back, unblocking it, freeing it from asphyxiating state control, establishing a greater control over student admissions, because the current greatly increased student numbers worked against young people achieving academic success and receiving the training that universities can give them to allow them to successfully enter the job market. The declaration of the rebels against consumer society reveals, he argues, their blindness and dogmatism because "the consumer society is the only thing that allows tens of thousands of students to be enrolled in universities" (p. 207). He also rejects the idea that the revolution is democratic: "Who is going to believe that votes by a show of hands in plenary or general assemblies are the free will of professors and students?" (p. 210). He states that the majority of the young people in the movement are peace-loving and reformist, but that they are neutralized by the revolutionary groups and groupuscules seduced by the example of Mao's China and Castro's Cuba, and these latter groups, he argues, must be resolutely opposed without worrying about becoming unpopular as a result. It is true that his standpoint led Raymond Aron to be roundly criticized in those days and months, but time would also prove him to be right in this instance: the May revolution did not improve one iota the situation of the French university system, which continues to this day in a chaotic and insoluble crisis.

Although he was skeptical of great political passions, Aron, who described himself as a committed observer, did, however, believe in progress. For him, although without holding out too many hopes in this regard, progress was represented by modern industrial society, which had completely changed the economic and social structure that Marx had studied, and which had led him to develop theories about the working class, for example, that modernity had made obsolete. Raymond Aron analyzed and defended this new society in a volume that brought together his lectures at the Sorbonne in 1956 and 1957, and which became one of his most widely read books: *Dix-huit leçons sur la société industrielle* (*Eighteen Lectures on Industrial Society*, 1963). In this text and in the lectures that he published with the title *Essai sur les libertés* (*An Essay on Freedom*, 1965), we find much of Raymond Aron's political thinking.

Can we sum up this thinking in a few sentences? If all ideas about building paradise on earth are senseless, it is perfectly legitimate, by contrast, from what the development of humanity through history has taught us, to conclude that men and women have progressed to the extent that they are less prone to religious servitude, despotism has been weakened, and the gregarious mass has become transformed into a community of individuals who have been given certain rights and allowed to take initiatives. The technological and scientific development of the West has been the motor force of this process of individual emancipation, and industrial, modern democratic nations have developed as a result. The great technological revolution has served, on the one hand, to accelerate development and, on the other hand, to ameliorate the excesses and abuses of the old capitalist system. With all the defects that can be laid at the door of modern industrial societies, they have managed to achieve unprecedented levels of prosperity, justice, and freedom that cannot be matched by other contemporary regimes, in particular communist regimes. These industrial societies have shown that "there is no incompatibility between political freedoms and wealth, between the mechanisms of the market and the rise in living standards: quite the reverse, the highest living standards have been achieved in countries that have political democracy and a relatively free economy."* But this panorama does not justify optimism, because developed, democratic society is under threat today. Its main enemy is the state, an entity that is essentially voracious, oppressive, and bureaucratic, always on the lookout, at the slightest opportunity, to grow and destroy everything that puts the brakes on and limits its power. Its second enemy is totalitarian states—the U.S.S.R. and China—for which the mere existence of a democratic society poses a grave risk. The ability of modern men and women to resist the growth of the state and totalitarian threats will determine whether history in the future will either continue its gradual evolution toward better living standards or else take crab-like steps

---

* Raymond Aron, "De quoi disputant les nations," in *Polémiques*, op. cit., p. 245.

toward the obscurantism, intolerance, and poverty that most of the planet still experiences.

Let us not forget that Raymond Aron lived and wrote during the Cold War, which witnessed, in France above all, a considerable group of intellectuals and important democratic sectors joining the neutrality and peace campaigns promoted by the Soviet Union and the communist parties. His position on this was blunt and unequivocal: *"Dans la guerre politique, il n'y a pas et il ne peut pas y avoir de neutres"* ("In the war of politics, there is no, and can be no, neutrality"). In his opinion Stalin and the U.S.S.R. would have taken over Western Europe some time ago were it not for the fear that this occupation would unleash a nuclear war with the United States. But we should not deceive ourselves: the imperialist tendencies of the U.S.S.R. were very apparent, as could be seen in all the satellite countries in Central and Eastern Europe, and the West could not lower its guard. This is why Aron defended the Atlantic Alliance and he argued that European union, which he always supported, must never lead to any break with, or distancing from, the United States. North American society might be far from being perfect, as could be seen, for example, in its discrimination against Blacks, but weighing everything up, at least in the United States there was respect for the right to criticize and the openness of the system allowed for reforms, while the totalitarianism of Stalin would have forced free and democratic Europe into total submission.

Is there anything that we can reproach the admirable Raymond Aron for? Perhaps there is. That all his thought focused on Europe and the United States and that, like Albert Camus, he showed an almost complete lack of interest in the third world, that is, in Africa, Latin America, and Asia. Had he arrived, deep down, at the conviction that for our countries, so bound up in conflicts and tremendous problems, there was now no hope? For a thinker who was in so many respects universal, his lack of curiosity about what was happening to the other two-thirds of humanity is surprising.

RAYMOND ARON AND JEAN-PAUL SARTRE

They were contemporaries, fellow students, and friends in their early days, and later bitter rivals. And for anyone not blinded by ideological myopia it is interesting to compare the cases of Raymond Aron and Jean-Paul Sartre as the two most important intellectual figures of modern France.

I was in Paris in 2005, when the centenary of their birth was celebrated. France celebrated in style the one-hundred-year anniversary of the birth of the author of *Being and Nothingness*. There were documentaries, programs, and debates on Sartre's intellectual and political legacy on the radio and television, special supplements in newspapers and magazines, a profusion of new books on his life and work, and, the jewel in the crown, an exhibition, *Sartre and His Century*, in the Bibliothèque Nationale, a model of its kind. I spent three hours there and there still was a lot left to see.

In the exhibition one could follow step by step, quite objectively, all the aspects of a life that encompassed the twentieth century, which Bernard-Henri Lévy has called, in exaggerated fashion, *le siècle de Sartre*, and whose books, ideas, and positions on important issues had an influence in France and most of the world that is now difficult to imagine. (In Peru in the 1950s, I spent half of my salary on a subscription to Sartre's journal *Les Temps Modernes* and I studied it every month from beginning to end.) One of the lessons the spectator could draw from the exhibition was to realize how precarious this intellectual dominance of Sartre proved to be, seemingly so extensive fifty years ago, but now almost nonexistent. It was all there in the glass exhibition cases: from when, as a boy, at ten years old, he discovered his ugliness through the eyes of his mother, who was widowed and had remarried, to his decision, when he was (after Aron) the star student at the École Normale, not to give up either of his two vocations, literature and philosophy, and to become "at the same time, Stendhal and Spinoza." Before he was forty, he had achieved this and, furthermore, something he had not foreseen, he had become a media figure, who appeared in gossip magazines and was the object of tourist attention in Saint-Germain-des-Prés, along with Simone de Beauvoir, Juliette Gréco, and Edith Piaf, as one of the icons of postwar France.

Posters and photographs documented the premieres of his plays, the publication of his books, the criticism of these works, the interviews he gave, the publication of *Les Temps Modernes*, and there were the manuscripts of his philosophical essays and of his short stories and novels that he wrote in school exercise books or on loose pages in cafés, on a table apart from but alongside the one where his "morganatic" partner, Simone de Beauvoir, worked. His most famous polemic, with Albert Camus, on the Soviet concentration camps, was very well laid out, as were the repercussions of this debate in intellectual and political circles, inside and outside France. Also his journeys across half the world, his fractured love affair with the Communists, his anti-colonialist struggle, his insistence on joining the May 1968 movement, and the extreme and rather embarrassing radicalization of his final years when he went to visit the German terrorists of the Baader-Meinhof group in prison, when he sold the Maoist newspaper

La Cause du Peuple in the streets, or when, by now blind, he stood on a barrel and perorated the workers at the gates of the Renault factory at Billancourt.

The exhibition was splendid and, for someone like me, who was very personally involved for a number of those years, and participated in the debates and dedicated many hours to reading Sartre's books and articles, and devoured all the issues of *Les Temps Modernes* and tried to follow the chiaroscuro ideological twists and turns of the author of *The Roads of Freedom*, it was also rather sad. But I don't think that it will spark much interest among young people in rediscovering Sartre nor will it bring him any greater respect or admiration. Because, except on the issue of anti-colonialism, where he always had a crystal-clear and lucid viewpoint, the exhibition, despite its obvious hagiographic intent, revealed how clumsy and wrong he was in almost all the political positions that he defended or attacked.

What is the use of such a dazzling intelligence if, after his return from his tour across the U.S.S.R. in the 1950s, in the worst period of the Gulag, he could state, "I have ascertained that there is a complete freedom of criticism in the Soviet Union." In his polemic with Camus, he did something worse than deny the existence of Stalinist concentration camps for real or imagined dissidents: he justified them in the name of the classless society that was being built. His diatribes against his old friends like Albert Camus, Raymond Aron, or Maurice Merleau-Ponty, because they refused to become, like him, a "fellow traveller" of the communists at different times, prove that his booming declaration that "every anti-Communist is a dog" was not a one-off remark but a profound conviction.

It seems unbelievable that someone who, scarcely fifty years ago, justified, in his essay on Frantz Fanon, terror as therapeutic, through which the colonized would regain their sovereignty and dignity, and who, proclaiming himself a Maoist, bestowed his respectability and prestige onto the genocide that the People's Republic of China committed during the Cultural Revolution, could have been considered by so many (and I declare myself guilty, I was one of them) the moral conscience of his time.

The celebration of the hundred years of Raymond Aron, who practically never left the catacombs of academia and the former journal *Commentaire* that he founded and edited, was much more discreet, not to say clandestine. Aron and Sartre were friends and classmates and there are photos that show the two "petits copains" arm in arm, playing around. Until the outbreak of the Second World War they had a similar trajectory. Then, with the Nazi invasion, Aron was one of the first Frenchmen and -women to travel to London and join the Resistance. He was always a dedicated supporter of reconciliation between France and Germany and of the construction of Europe but—and in this he differed from much of the French right—he never believed that European unity should weaken Atlanticism, the close collaboration between Europe and the United States that he always promoted.

Unlike Sartre's work, which has aged on par with his political opinions—his novels owe their technical originality to John Dos Passos, and, with the exception of *Huis Clos*, his plays would not today pass muster on the stage—Aron's writings remain fresh and topical. His essays on philosophy, history, and sociology and his tenacious defense of liberal doctrine, of Western culture, of democracy, and of the market at a time when most European intellectuals had succumbed to the siren song of Marxism, were fully borne out by what happened in the world following the fall of the Berlin Wall, which was the symbol of the disappearance of the U.S.S.R., and the conversion of China into an authoritarian capitalist society.

Why then, if his ideas have not survived, does the media glamour surrounding the unreadable Sartre remain alive, while almost no one is attracted to the figure of the sensible and convincing Raymond Aron? The explanation has to do with one of the features that culture has acquired in our day and age: it has become theatrical, it has become banal and frivolous by being drawn into the world of publicity and the gossip columns of the celebrity and gossip magazines. We live in the civilization of the spectacle and the intellectuals and writers who are the most popular are almost never popular because of the originality of their ideas or the beauty of their creations, or, in any event, not just for intellectual, artistic, or literary reasons. They are popular above all else for their histrionic ability, the way in which they project their public image, their exhibitionism, their rudeness, their insolence, all that farcical and noisy dimension of public life that passes itself off as rebellion (but which, in fact, masks a complete conformism), which the media can exploit, converting authors, like artists and singers, into spectacles for the masses.

In the Bibliothèque Nationale exhibition, there is an aspect of Sartre's biography that has never been completely clarified. Was he really a member of the Resistance against Nazi occupation? Yes, he belonged to one of the many organizations of intellectuals that supported the Resistance, but it is obvious that his membership was more theoretical than practical because during the occupation he was very busy: he was a teacher, even replacing a teacher who had been expelled from a school for being Jewish—this episode has been the subject of virulent discussions—and he wrote and published his books and premiered his plays with the approval of the German censors, as André Malraux would later point out. Unlike Resistance members like Camus or Malraux who risked their lives during the war, Sartre does not appear to have risked very much. Perhaps unconsciously he wanted to blot out this uncomfortable past with the ever more extreme positions that he adopted after the liberation. One of the most recurring themes of his philosophy was bad faith which, for him, conditions bourgeois life, inducing men and women from that social class to cheat and hide their true personality behind lying masks. In his best book, *Saint Genet, comédien et martyr*, he analyzed with great acuity the psychological-moral system through which, according to him, the bourgeois hide from themselves, constantly retreat into vigorous denial, fleeing from this murky conscience that always accuses them. Perhaps this was true in his case. Perhaps this fearsome enemy of democrats, this incorrigible anarcho-communist, this incandescent "Mao" was just a desperate bourgeois ever increasing his poses so that nobody would remember his apathy and prudence in the face of the Nazis when things were hotting up and commitment was not just a rhetorical conjuring trick but a life-and-death decision.

Many things have happened in France and the world since the death of Raymond Aron. Have these events proved his ideas to be right or wrong? The Communist Party, which in his day was the most important party in the country, has shrunk in size and has become marginal, which must count as one of his posthumous victories. Another victory is that the current French intellectual class is as distant from Marxism as he always was. What is surprising is that the former communist voters, like the workers of the "red belt" around Paris, now vote for the Front National, which has moved from being the ultra-right fringe party of some years back to being a strong force within the political mainstream. This is something that Aron and nobody else could have imagined, although perhaps Hayek might have done so, for he always argued that, despite their mutual hatred, communists and fascists shared a common denominator: statism and collectivism. In the most recent French elections a young man who was fighting his first campaign in the political arena, Emmanuel Macron, generated a great deal of enthusiasm, especially among the younger generation, with center-right ideas that, at first glance, seem quite close to those that Raymond Aron espoused all his life. Will France today rediscover in this solitary democratic and liberal twentieth-century intellectual a precursor and an intellectual guide to what seems a new and interesting stage of its political evolution?

The powerful Soviet Union, which Aron fought against all his life, has died out, a victim of its own incapacity to satisfy the ambitions of its millions of citizens, and has been replaced by an authoritarian and imperial regime, of gangster and mercantilist capitalism, which seems a continuation of the old authoritarian and overbearing czarist system. China stopped being communist and became a model of authoritarian capitalism. However, to say that history has proved Raymond Aron right would be somewhat premature. Because although the threat of communism, which he relentlessly opposed, has ceased to be a threat for democracies around the world—only a lunatic would take as models for their country, the regimes of North Korea, Cuba, or Venezuela—democracy has not won the contest and will probably never completely do so. It is true that, in the Western world, the European Union, despite Brexit, has remained solid, and much of Latin America has been won over to democracy. But it faces new threats like the fanatical and extremist Islamism of al-Qaeda or ISIS, whose large-scale terrorism sows insecurity, and with this comes the risk that, in the name of security, public freedoms will be eroded in those countries most threatened by terrorism, the advanced democracies. Furthermore, within the heart of these open societies, poisons like corruption and populism are growing to such an extent that, if they are not contained in time, they can distort and destroy from within everything that is most positive and liberating in these societies.

On all these problems, including the mass migration from Africa into Western Europe, which is giving rise to chauvinist and racist movements that we had thought had died out, we miss the opinions and analysis of Raymond Aron: his intelligence, his culture, the depth of his thought, the breadth of his vision would doubtless help us understand these challenges more clearly and discern the best way to face up to them. That there is no one today capable of replacing him is the greatest proof of his extraordinary intellectual and political capabilities and of how lucky we were to have benefited from all that he managed to achieve in recent times.

SIR ISAIAH BERLIN (1909–1997)

THE DISCREET PHILOSOPHER

I discovered Isaiah Berlin many years ago when I read his book on Marx, which was so clear, suggestive, and unprejudiced that I spent a long time looking for other books by him. I discovered that his work was difficult to find because it was scattered, if not buried, in academic publications. With the exception of his books *Vico and Herder* (1976) and *Four Essays on Liberty* (1969), which were available in the English-language world, most of his work had led the quiet life of the library and the specialist journal. Some time later, thanks to a former student of his, Henry Hardy, who began to collect his essays, these were made available to the wider public in a number of volumes: *Concepts and Categories* (1978), *Russian Thinkers* (1979), *Against the Current* (1979), *Personal Impressions* (1980), *The Crooked Timber of Humanity: Chapters in the History of Ideas* (1990), *The Magus of the North: J. G. Hamann and the Origins of Modern Irrationalism* (1993), *The Sense of Reality: Studies in Ideas and Their History* (1996), *The Roots of Romanticism* (1999), *The Power of Ideas* (2000), *Freedom and Its*

Betrayal: Six Enemies of Human Liberty (2002). And finally, his correspondence.

This was an important event because Isaiah Berlin, a Latvian educated in Britain, where he would become professor of social and political theory at Oxford and president of the Royal Academy, was one of the most exceptional minds of our time. He was an extraordinarily erudite political thinker and social philosopher, whose work provides a rare pleasure in its skill and brilliance as well as offering an invaluable guide for understanding in all their complexity the moral and historical problems faced by contemporary reality.

Berlin believed passionately in ideas and in the influence that ideas have on the behavior of individuals and societies. Yet at the same time, as a good pragmatist, he was aware of the space that usually opens up between ideas and the words that seek to express them, and between the words and the deeds that put them into practice. Despite their intellectual density, his books never seem abstract to us—unlike the later works of Michel Foucault and Roland Barthes—or the result of a speculative and rhetorical virtuosity that has, at some moment, cut its moorings with reality. Instead Berlin's essays are deeply rooted in common experience. The collection of essays titled *Russian Thinkers* is an epic fresco of intellectual and political thought in nineteenth-century Russia; yet the most outstanding characters are not people but ideas. These shine, move around, challenge one another, and change with the vivacity of the heroes of a good adventure novel. In another book on a similar theme, *To the Finland Station* by Edmund Wilson, the thoughts of the protagonists seem to transpire from the persuasive and multicolored portraits that the author draws of his characters. Here, by contrast, it is the concepts that they formulated, the ideals and arguments with which they confronted one another, their intuitions and knowledge that define the figures of Tolstoy, Herzen, Belinsky, Bakunin, and Turgenev and make them plausible or reprehensible.

But even more than *Russian Thinkers*, the collection *Against the Current* will doubtless remain as one of Isaiah Berlin's greatest contributions to the culture of our time. Furthermore, each essay in this magisterial work reads like a chapter of a novel whose action takes place in the world of thought and in which the heroes and the villains are ideas. Thanks to this scholar, who never loses a sense of balance and who can see clearly the forest for the trees, Machiavelli, Vico, Montesquieu, Hume, Sorel, Marx, Disraeli, and Verdi are seen to have a great contemporary significance, and the things that they believed, advocated, or criticized illuminate in a powerful way the political and social conflicts that we considered to be specific to our age.

The most surprising thing about this thinker is that he appears, at first sight, not to offer ideas of his own. It might seem nonsense to say this, but it is not nonsense because when one reads him, one has the impression that in these essays Berlin achieves what, after Flaubert, and thanks to him, most modern novelists have tried to achieve in their works: to erase themselves, make themselves invisible, to offer the illusion that their stories are self-generated. There are many techniques for making the narrator "disappear" in a novel. The technique that Berlin uses to make us feel that he is not behind his texts is "fair play." That is, the scrupulous attention with which he analyzes, puts forward, summarizes, and quotes the thoughts of other people, considering all their arguments, weighing the attenuating circumstances they faced, the constraints of the age, never pushing their words or ideas in one direction or another to make them appear similar to his own. This objectivity in transmitting the inventions and discoveries of other people leaves us with the fantastic impression that, in these books that say so many things, Isaiah Berlin himself has nothing of his own to say.

This is, of course, a rigorously false impression. "Fair play" is only a technique that, like all narrative techniques, has just one function: to make the content more persuasive. A story that seems not to be told by anyone in particular, that purports to be creating itself, by itself, at the moment of reading, can often be more plausible and engrossing for the reader. A thought that seems not to exist by itself, that reaches us indirectly, through what certain eminent men from different epochs and cultures thought at specific moments in their lives, or one that professes to be born not out of the creative effort of an individual mind but rather out of the contrasts between the philosophical and political conceptions of others and the gaps and errors in these conceptions, can be more convincing than a thought that is presented, simply and arrogantly, as a single theory. The discretion and modesty of Isaiah Berlin are, in fact, a wily strategy.

Many years ago I lost my taste for political utopias, those apocalypses—like Sendero Luminoso in Peru in the 1980s—that promise to bring heaven down to earth and which, instead, cause worse injustices than those they seek to remedy. From that time on I have thought that common sense is the most valuable of political virtues. Reading Isaiah Berlin I saw clearly something that I had only intuited in a rather confused way. True progress, which has forced back or overthrown barbarous practices and institutions that were the source of infinite suffering for men and women, and has established more civilized relations and styles of life, has always been achieved through a partial, heterodox, distorted application of social theories. Social theories, *in the plural*, which means that different and even irreconcilable ideological systems have brought about identical or similar forms of progress. The prerequisite was always that these systems should be flexible and could be amended or reformed when they moved from the abstract to the concrete and came up against the daily experience of human beings. The filter at work that separates what is desirable from what is not desirable in these systems is the criterion of practical reason. It is a paradox that someone like Isaiah Berlin, who loved ideas so much and moved among them with such ease, was always convinced that it is ideas that must give way if they come into contradiction with human reality, since if the reverse occurs, the streets are filled with guillotines and firing-squad walls and the reign of the censors and the police begins.

THE MAN WHO KNEW TOO MUCH

If, in addition to his brilliance, Isaiah Berlin had not been so well-liked or held in such high regard, then it is quite possible that he would never have been the universally recognized intellectual figure that he had become at the time of his death, and that most of his work would remain unknown to the vast majority of his readers outside a handful of academic colleagues and students at Oxford and at American universities where he taught. His was a unique case in terms of his Olympian lack of interest in whether or not his essays were read or published—he sincerely believed that they were not important enough to merit that honor—and also in terms of his decision not to write his autobiography or write a diary, as if he were not remotely concerned about the image that he might leave for posterity (*Après moi, le déluge*, he liked to say).

Those of us who did not attend his classes and yet feel ourselves to be his students will never be able to thank enough Henry Hardy, the philosophy postgraduate at Wolfson College, Oxford (where Isaiah Berlin was the founding president and ran the college from 1966 to 1975), who, in 1974, proposed to his supervisor that he should collect, edit, or re-edit his writings. However incredible it might seem, up until that date he had published only three books. The rest of his vast written work was unpublished, packed in dusty boxes in his office, or buried in scholarly journals, *Festschriften*, in folders containing testimonials, lectures, reports, reviews, obituaries, or in archives of official institutions, feeding the worms. Thanks to Hardy, who managed to overcome Isaiah Berlin's tenacious reticence to excavate his own bibliography, and to Hardy's titanic research and rigorous editing, those ten books that have cemented Isaiah Berlin's prestige inside and outside innumerable universities have been published and volumes of correspondence have also begun to appear. And without Michael Ignatieff, another friend and persistent follower of the professor from Latvia, he would still be a mere ghost, without flesh or blood, shielded behind a scattered bibliography.

Just as the volumes compiled by Hardy proved to the world that the insinuations of his rivals were absolutely false when they implied that Isaiah Berlin was merely a brilliant conversationalist, a salon philosopher, without the patience or energy to undertake work of great intellectual scope, so, thanks to Ignatieff—a journalist and historian born in Canada, a graduate of the University of Toronto and Harvard, resident in Britain and in Boston, a leader for a time of the Canadian Liberal Party, a professor at Harvard and now rector of the

Central European University in Budapest—we know* that the author of *The Hedgehog and the Fox* had an interesting and at times dramatic and adventurous life. His life was not just spent, as might first appear, submerged in the peaceful cloisters of the elegant unreality of Oxford, for he was involved, sometimes directly and sometimes indirectly, in the great events of the century, like the Russian Revolution, the persecution and extermination of Jews in Europe, the creation of Israel, the Cold War, and the great ideological conflicts between communism and democracy in the post–Second World War period. The character that emerges from Ignatieff's book—an affectionate and loyal book but also an independent work because, true to Berlin's ethical principle par excellence, that of fair play, he does not hesitate in pointing out his errors and defects along with his virtues and excellent qualities—is no less attractive and warm. Here is a modest, cordial, amenable, and sociable man, around which the legend that followed him throughout his life was built. But the picture is also more complex and contradictory, more human and more profound, of an intellectual who, despite having received the highest honors in Great Britain—president of the Royal Academy, rector of an Oxford college, recipient of the Order of Merit, the highest decoration in the UK honors system, and of a knighthood from the queen—always felt deep within himself that he was an expatriate and a Jew, supporting a tradition and a community that had been, from time immemorial, subjected to discrimination, danger, and prejudice. This outlook contributed decisively to the insecurity that shadowed him throughout his life. And it also doubtless shaped his prudent stance, his desire

---

* Michael Ignatieff, *A Life: Isaiah Berlin*, Chatto & Windus, London, 1998.

to integrate into society and to go unnoticed, away from the glare of power and success, and also shaped his systematic defense of tolerance, pluralism, and political diversity and his hatred of fanatics of whatever stripe. Behind the conversationalist who enchanted guests at dinners and parties with the richness of his stories, his fluency, and extraordinary memory, there hid a man torn by the moral conflicts that he described before, and better than, anyone else: freedom and equality, justice and order, the atheist Jew and the practicing Jew, and a liberal fearful that unrestricted freedom might lead to "the wolf eating the lambs." The clear, serene, and luminous thinker suggested in his writings comes out in the portrait painted by Michael Ignatieff. But beneath the shining clarity of his ideas and his style there appears a man often overwhelmed by doubt, who made mistakes and was tortured by these mistakes, who lived in a state of discreet but constant tension that prevented him from feeling totally integrated into any society, despite all appearances to the contrary.

Although he never even considered writing his autobiography, Isaiah Berlin agreed to talk to his friend Michael Ignatieff in front of a tape recorder about all the events in his life, on condition that Ignatieff would only publish his research after Berlin's death. The conversation lasted ten years, Berlin's final decade, and ended in the last week of October 1997, a few days before his death, when Sir Isaiah, very fragile and racked by illness, invited his biographer to Headington House, his country house in Oxford, to correct some facts that his memory had clarified, and to remind Ignatieff, insistently, that his wife, Aline, had been the center of his life and that he was forever in her debt. Ignatieff has rounded out these personal memories with very detailed research in Russia, the United

States, Israel, and Britain, interviewing dozens, perhaps hundreds of people associated with Berlin and combing newspapers, books, and archives, so his biography, without being definitive, is a very complete account of the life of the great thinker, linking it to the development of his interests, convictions, ideas, and intellectual work. It is a literary biography in which the life and the work are melded.

Although Isaiah Berlin spent only his first twelve years in Russia (he was born into a well-off Jewish family in 1909 in Riga, at a time when Latvia belonged to the Russian Empire), the experiences of those early years of his childhood, affected by tremendous social convulsions and family upheavals, left an indelible impression and shaped two aspects of his personality: his horror of totalitarianism and dictatorships, and his Judaism. The main event of this childhood was, without doubt, the Bolshevik revolution, which he saw close-up in Saint Petersburg, where his family had taken up residence after fleeing from the insecurity and threats that the Jewish community was subject to in Riga. In Saint Petersburg he witnessed, at age seven and a half, scenes of street violence that made him immune forever to revolutionary enthusiasm and "political experiments." In this period his hostile attitude toward communism was born, and he remained faithful to it throughout his life, even at the time of the Cold War, when the great majority of the intellectual community of which he was part was Marxist or close to Marxism. He never yielded to this temptation and his anti-communism led him to extreme positions that were rare in him, like defending the United States during the unpopular Vietnam War and refusing to sign a protest against Washington in response to the Bay of Pigs invasion of Cuba in May 1961. (Castro "may not be a Communist," he wrote to

Kenneth Tynan, "but I think he cares as little for civil liberties as Lenin or Trotsky."*) This attitude led him to commit an act that was not very consistent with his pluralist ethic: he used his academic influence to block the appointment to a Chair in politics at the University of Sussex of Isaac Deutscher, an exiled Jew like himself, but an anti-Zionist and a left-wing intellectual, the author of the most famous biography of Trotsky. His somewhat questionable response to those who accused him of behaving in this affair like "the anti-communist witch hunters" was that he could not recommend for a Chair anyone who subordinated scholarship to ideology.

Fleeing once more, this time not only from fear but also from hunger, the Berlin family returned to Riga for a short time in 1920 and on the train there they were subjected to insults and attacks from anti-Semitic passengers and officials which, according to Berlin, made him realize for the first time—and forever—that he was not Russian or Latvian, but Jewish, and would always be so. Although he was an atheist and was educated in England in a secular environment, he was always committed to the community and the culture of his ancestors, even to the extreme of strictly observing Jewish religious rituals at home. He was a curious practicing nonbeliever. And, as a Zionist, he collaborated closely with one of the founders of the State of Israel, Chaim Weizmann, although, unlike a number of his relatives, he never thought of becoming an Israeli citizen. A lot of this work was done during the Second World War, when Isaiah Berlin was serving as an analyst and political adviser to the British government, in New York and in Washington, which must have caused him much anguish and many dilemmas given the tense relationship that existed be-

* Ignatieff, p. 234.

tween the Foreign Office, which was pro-Arab, and the Zionist leaders. In the collection *The Power of Ideas* (2000) there are two long essays in which Berlin defends Zionism and the creation of Israel with solid arguments; but in both he fails even to mention the fundamental issue of the Arab presence in Palestine over many centuries, when the first waves of European Zionists arrived, and how, in his opinion, one should deal with the problem of the future coexistence of both communities.

Knowing in detail the contradictions in Isaiah Berlin's personal life helps us to understand the secret origins of one of his most famous theories: that of "contradictory truths."

CONTRADICTORY TRUTHS

A constant in Western thought is the belief that one true answer exists for every human problem and that once we find this answer, then all others must be rejected as mistaken. A complementary belief, as old as this one, is that the most noble and inspiring ideas—justice, freedom, peace, pleasure—are compatible with one another. For Isaiah Berlin, these beliefs are false, and many of the tragedies that have befallen humanity can be laid at their doorstep. From this skeptical base, Professor Berlin produced a number of powerful and original arguments in favor of freedom of choice and ideological pluralism.

Faithful to his indirect method, Isaiah Berlin sets out his theory of contradictory truths, or of irreconcilable ends, by analyzing other thinkers who have touched on this question. Thus, for example, in his essay on Machiavelli, he tells us that Machiavelli detected in an involuntary, casual way this "uncomfortable truth" that not all values are necessarily compatible, that the idea of a single, definitive philosophy underpinning a perfect society is materially and conceptually impossible. Machiavelli reached this conclusion by studying the mechanisms of power and discovering that they were at variance with the values of Christianity that, nominally, regulated life in society. To lead a "Christian life" and to apply rigorously the ethical norms laid down by that belief system meant condemning oneself to political impotence, at the mercy of unscrupulous and calculating people. If one wanted to be politically adept and construct a "glorious" community like Athens or Rome, then one had to replace Christian education with something more appropriate to this desired end. For Berlin what was important was not so much that Machiavelli had pointed out this dilemma but rather his intuition that both aspects of the dilemma were equally persuasive from a moral and social point of view. That is, the author of *The Prince* saw that men and women could be torn between aspirations that were equally appealing and yet incompatible.

Every social utopia—from Plato to Marx—is founded on an act of faith: the belief that human ideals, the great aspirations of individuals and societies, can be harmonized, that achieving one or several of these goals does not preclude achieving others. Perhaps nothing expresses this optimism better than the rhythmic motto of the French Revolution: "Liberty, Equality, Fraternity." That well-intentioned movement, which sought to establish a government of reason on earth and put into practice these simple and unquestionable ideals, demonstrated to the world, through repeated slaughter and frustrations, that social reality was more tumultuous and unpredictable than French philosophers had proposed when they prescribed abstract solutions for human happiness. The most unexpected outcome—that still today many refuse to accept—was that these ideals sabotaged one another from the very moment they moved from theory into practice; instead of being mutually supportive, they were mutually exclusive. French revolutionaries discovered, to their surprise, that liberty was a source of inequality, that a country whose citizens had complete or extensive freedom of initiative and control over their own actions and possessions would, sooner or later, be a country torn by many material and spiritual differences. In order to establish equality, there was no option but to sacrifice liberty and impose the coercion, the surveillance and the all-powerful bulldozer actions of the state. That social injustice was the price of liberty, that dictatorship was the price of equality, and that fraternity could be achieved only in a relative and transitory fashion, for more negative than positive reasons—as when a war or some other catastrophe brought people together—is painful and difficult to accept.

However, for Isaiah Berlin, what is worse than accepting this terrible dilemma of human destiny is refusing to accept it (burying one's head in the sand). For however tragic it might be, this reality allows us in practical terms to learn worthwhile lessons. The philosophers, historians, and political thinkers who have intuited this concept—the concept of contradictory truths—have been better able to understand the process of civilization. For example Montesquieu, through a different route from that of Machiavelli, saw that a central feature of the development of humanity was that men and women had many different goals, which were often incompatible, and that these incompatibilities were at the root of conflicts between civilizations and disputes between different nations. They also led to rivalries between classes and groups within a single society and even to crises and anguish within individuals themselves.

Like Montesquieu in the eighteenth century, the great

Russian writer and nonconformist Alexander Herzen understood this dilemma in the nineteenth century and this allowed him to analyze with greater lucidity than his contemporaries the failure of the European revolutions of 1848 and 1849. Herzen is one of Berlin's favored spokesmen, the affinities between the two are great, and Berlin has written one of his most brilliant essays on this philosopher. The skepticism they both share has a curiously positive and stimulating effect: it is a call to arms because it is both pragmatic and, at times, optimistic. Herzen was one of the first to reject—since it would lead to criminal behavior—the notion that humanity had a splendid future ahead and that current generations should be sacrificed to achieve this end. Like Herzen, Berlin often reminds us, with examples taken from history, that no justice has ever stemmed from political injustice and that liberty has never been born out of oppression. For that reason both men believe that, on social issues, small but effective achievements are always preferable to great, all-encompassing solutions, which they condemn as illusory.

The fact that there are contradictory truths, that human ideals can be in conflict, does not mean, according to Berlin, that we must despair and feel powerless. It means that we must be aware of the importance of freedom of choice. If there is not one but several answers to our problems, we must be ever alert, testing the ideas, laws, and values that govern our world, comparing them and weighing the impact that they have on our lives, choosing some and rejecting others or, after difficult compromises, modifying the rest. And while this is an argument in favor of responsibility and freedom of choice, Isaiah Berlin also sees it as an irrefutable reason for tolerance and pluralism, not just as moral imperatives but as practical requirements for the survival of the human race. If there are truths that are rejected and ends that must be denied, we must admit to the possibility of error in our lives and be tolerant to the errors of others. We must also admit that diversity—of ideas, actions, customs, morals, and cultures—is the only guarantee we have that, if error becomes enshrined, the havoc it causes will be contained because we have not *one* but many solutions to our problems, all of them precarious.

The Latvian Jewish community, into which Isaiah was born, spoke Russian, Latvian, and German and although the child learned these three languages, he identified most with Russian, a language and a literature that he used and studied all his life. In England, while he was educated at a distinguished Christian independent school, St. Paul's in London, and then, thanks to his outstanding grades, at Oxford, he continued studying the Russian language alongside philosophy so that although the umbilical cord that bound him to his native land was cut when he was twelve years old, when he began to be a British citizen and to assimilate into the culture of his second country, his intellectual sympathy and love for Russian language and literature remained. We can see this in the remarkable assurance and knowledge that he brought to his many essays on Russian writers and thinkers, among them those dedicated to Tolstoy, Turgenev, or his admired model, the liberal Alexander Herzen. On his return to Russia for a few months, in 1945, as a British diplomat—a journey that would have an incalculable effect on his emotional and political life—two great writers he met, Boris Pasternak and Anna Akhmatova, were literally astonished at the fluent elegance with which this professor from another world spoke the cultured Russian of former times, and also that he was so well acquainted with a literature and with authors who were beginning to become ever more invisible or remote in this society that was subject to the iron censorship of Stalin.

IN WASHINGTON

The Second World War radically changed the private world of Isaiah Berlin. Without it, it is very likely that his life would have been spent, like those of other dons at Oxford, among the halls where he first gave classes on philosophy and later on political and social theory, in libraries, and in his rooms in the most prestigious and traditional of all the colleges in the university, All Souls, where he had been elected Fellow at the incredible age of twenty-three (the first Jew to be given an appointment at that college). But when the war broke out this "asexual and erudite" life underwent an abrupt transformation: the young don, whose fame as a polyglot and specialist in European cultures—Russian and German in particular—was already widespread in academic circles, was sent to the United States by the British government, to New York and Washington, to act as an adviser to the Foreign Office and the embassy in its dealings with the White House. Between 1941 and 1945, Sir Isaiah did extraordinary work for his country of adoption through his analyses of the international situation and the delicate diplomatic relations between the Allies, which are perhaps the most read among all the Foreign Office briefing papers. (In 1944, Churchill himself was so impressed by them that he wanted to know who had written them. Anthony Eden replied to him: "Mr Berlin, of Baltic Jewish extraction, a philosopher." And he added, in his own hand, that while the summaries are well written they had "perhaps a too generous oriental flavour.")* He also established a network of contacts in the highest social, academic, and political circles in the United States, thanks to his personal charm and ease in society: a pyrotechnic conversationalist, he was the toast of diplomatic dinners and meetings and, apart from hypnotizing and amusing people with his good humor, his stories, and his knowledge, he left his interlocutors with the gratifying feeling that, by spending time with him, they were immersing themselves in high culture. This snobbish aspect of his life—which was always full of social engagements, dinners, galas, and receptions in the highest echelons of society—curiously did not affect in any way his intellectual work, in which he never made concessions or lapsed into banality. It is not out of the question to see this somewhat frivolous aspect of his personality as a compensation, a substitute for sex, of which it appears that he had little or no experience until his later years. All his friends at Oxford were sure that he was a confirmed bachelor.

THE NIGHT WITH AKHMATOVA

Perhaps this is the reason why he was so affected by an entire night that he spent in November 1945, in a soulless flat in Leningrad, with the greatest living Russian poet, the unfortunate Anna Akhmatova. Isaiah Berlin had been sent for a few months to the British Embassy in Moscow and he took a nostalgic trip to Leningrad in search of books and memories of his childhood. In a bookshop, someone overheard him asking

* Ignatieff, p. 125. A section of these important briefings, many of them substantial political essays, were published in 1981: *Washington Despatches, 1941–1945: Weekly Political Reports from the British Embassy.* Ed. H. G. Nicholas, with an introduction by Isaiah Berlin, London 1981.

after the poet and offered to take him to her apartment, which was close by. Anna Akhmatova was fifty-six years old, twenty years older than Berlin. She had been a great beauty and a very famous poet from before the revolution. Now she was in disgrace and since 1925 Stalin had not allowed her to publish a single line or give any recitals. Her tragic life was one of the saddest stories of those terrible years: the Soviet regime shot her first husband and imprisoned her third husband in a Siberian labor camp. Her son, Lev, a talented young man with whom Isaiah Berlin spoke briefly on that night, would be sent to the Gulag for thirteen years, and the Soviet commissars blackmailed Akhmatova, offering to keep him alive if she wrote abject odes in adulation of the dictator who was tormenting her. Because the suffering of the great poet greatly increased after that night, Isaiah Berlin would always feel remorse that he had been involuntarily responsible for this. (In the archives of the KGB, there is a memorandum on the conversation, in which Stalin remarks to the cultural commissar Zhadanov, "So now our nun is consorting with British spies, is she?"*)

He always emphatically claimed that the eleven or twelve hours that he spent with Akhmatova were chaste, full of intense and sparkling conversation, and that in the course of the night she recited to him a number of the celebrated poems from the book *Requiem* that—in defiance of persecution—she was writing from memory, a book that would come to represent one of the greatest testimonies of spiritual and poetic resistance against the Stalinist tyranny. The talk was of literature, an evocation of the great pre-revolution authors, many of them dead or in exile, about whom Berlin could give her information, and, discreetly, they touched on Anna's very difficult situation, her

* Ignatieff, p. 167.

life always in the balance, seeing repression all around her and waiting for it to fall on her at any moment. But it is a fact that, even though there was not the slightest physical contact between them, at noon the following day the austere Isaiah Berlin returned to the Hotel Astoria jumping with joy and proclaiming, "I am in love, I am in love." From that moment right up to his death, he would always say that this had been the most important event in his life. And Akhmatova's reflections on that visit can be found in the beautiful love poems in *Cinque*. A story of impossible love, of course, because, from then on, the regime cut all communication and contact between the poet and the outside world, and in the following six years Berlin could not find out where she was living. (When he asked the British Embassy in Moscow to make inquiries for him, he was told that it would be better for Akhmatova if he did not even try to contact her.) Many years later, in 1965, at the beginning of the thaw in the Soviet Union, Isaiah Berlin and other dons proposed the great Russian poet for an honorary doctorate in Oxford and the Soviet authorities allowed her to travel to England to be awarded the doctorate. She was by now an old woman, but her prolonged persecution had not managed to break her. Their meeting was cold and when she looked around the sumptuous residence, Headington House, where he lived with his wife, Aline, she could not contain a pained caustic remark: "So the bird is now in its golden cage."*

THE TWO LIBERTIES

The word *freedom* must have been used two hundred different ways. Isaiah Berlin has contributed two definitions of his own

---

* Ignatieff, p. 233.

to help clarify what he has rightly called a protean word: negative freedom and positive freedom. Although the distinction is subtle and somewhat elusive when approached theoretically, the distinction between these two forms of freedom becomes very clear when we assess concrete options, historical situations, and specific policies. And the difference also throws into relief problems that are often hidden by artificial distinctions such as "formal" and "real" freedom—a distinction people usually make when they are looking to repress formal freedoms.

Freedom is closely linked to constraint, to what denies or limits liberty. We are freer to the extent that we find less obstacles in the way of organizing our lives according to our own criteria. The less authority imposed on my actions, the more I can choose from among my own motivations—my needs, ambitions, and personal fantasies—without the interference of outside forces, the freer I am. This is the "negative" concept of freedom.

This concept is more individual than social and is absolutely modern. It develops in societies that have achieved a high level of civilization and a certain degree of affluence. It is based on the supposition that the sovereignty of the individual must be respected because personal freedom is, in the final instance, the source of human creativity, intellectual and artistic development, and scientific progress. If the individual is suffocated, constrained, and mechanized, then that source of creativity is cut off and the result is a gray and mediocre world, peopled by ants or robots. Those who embrace this notion of liberty believe that power and authority pose the greatest danger to society but since authority and power are inevitable, they argue, their sphere of influence should be kept to a minimum, just what is necessary to avoid the breakup of society, and that they should be scrupulously regulated and controlled.

Certain philosophers like John Stuart Mill and Benjamin Constant defended this concept of liberty most passionately, and nineteenth-century liberalism was its most evident political expression. But it would be wrong to think that "negative" freedom ends there. In fact it covers something much greater, more diverse, and more permanent; it is the underlying assumption of countless political programs, intellectual formulations, and ways of behaving. This "negative" concept of liberty informs all democratic theories, in which the coexistence of different points of view or creeds is essential, along with respect for minority opinions. It also encourages the conviction that freedom of the press, of religion, of movement, freedom to work—and today freedom of sexual behavior—must be safeguarded for without them life becomes impoverished and degraded.

Ideas as disparate as literary romanticism, monasticism, mysticism, some anarchist tendencies, social democracy, the market economy, and liberal philosophy are connected, despite their obvious discrepancies, since they share this concept of liberty. But in the political arena it is not just democratic systems that bring about such freedom. Isaiah Berlin shows that, however paradoxical it might seem, certain dictatorships that we find repugnant can accommodate negative freedom and even, in part, put it into practice. We have witnessed this in Latin America just as Spaniards witnessed it in Franco's final years. Certain right-wing dictatorships that emphasize economic freedoms, despite the abuses and crimes they commit, like the Pinochet dictatorship in Chile, generally offer a wider margin of "negative" freedom to their citizens than do socialist or socialist-leaning democracies, like Cuba and Venezuela in our day and age.

While "negative" freedom wants to limit authority, "positive" freedom looks to take control of, and exert, authority.

The focus here is on society rather than the individual, based on the (very fair) idea that each individual's possibility for realizing his or her own potential is largely determined by social causes beyond any one person's control. How can an illiterate person benefit from freedom of the press? What use is freedom of movement to someone living in dire poverty? Does freedom to work mean the same to the owner of a company as to someone who is unemployed? While "negative" freedom mainly concentrates on the fact that individuals are different, positive freedom emphasizes above all their similarities. The one argues that liberty is preserved by respecting variants and particular cases, the other that liberty is increased in social terms when there are fewer differences in society, when a community is more homogeneous.

Ideologies and beliefs that are all-embracing and are convinced that there is one ultimate, unique goal for a given community—a nation, a race, a class, or the whole of humanity—share this "positive" notion of freedom. It has brought mankind a great number of benefits and thanks to it we have a social consciousness: an awareness that drastic economic, social, and cultural inequalities are an evil that can and must be corrected. Notions of human solidarity, social responsibility, and justice have been enriched and expanded thanks to the "positive" concept of freedom, which has also served to curb or abolish abuses ranging from slavery to racism and discrimination.

But this concept of freedom has also generated its corresponding abuses. Just as General Pinochet and General Franco (in the years of Spain's economic growth) could speak, with some justification, about "negative" liberty, so Hitler and Stalin could state, without too much exaggeration, that their respective regimes were establishing true ("positive") freedom in their nations. All social utopias, left or right wing, religious or secular, are based on a "positive" concept of liberty. They are convinced that in every person there is, alongside a specific, distinct individual, something more important: an identical social "I" who aspires to a collective ideal, which will become a reality in a given future, to which everything that impedes it or obstructs it must be sacrificed. For example, particular cases that are deemed a threat against social harmony and homogeneity. For that reason, in the name of this "positive" liberty— this future utopia, or the triumph of the human race, or a society without classes and states, or the city of the blessed— the most cruel wars have been waged, concentration camps have been set up, exterminating millions of human beings, asphyxiating regimes have come to power, and all forms of dissidence and criticism have been eliminated.

These two notions of freedom are at odds with each other, they mutually reject each other, but there is no sense in trying to demonstrate that one is true and the other false because although the word that they both use is the same, it refers to different things. This is one of those cases of "contradictory truths" or "incompatible goals" that, according to Berlin, underlie our human condition. In theory one can stack up an infinite number of arguments in favor of one or the other concept of liberty, all equally valid or questionable. But in practice—in social life, in history—the ideal is to try to achieve some kind of transaction between the two. The societies that have managed to find a compromise between these two forms of freedom have achieved a more decent and just (or less indecent and less unjust) standard of living. But this is a very difficult transaction and it will always be precarious because, as Berlin points out, "negative" and "positive" freedom are not two interpretations of a concept, but something more:

two profoundly divergent and irreconcilable attitudes toward human development.

IN A GOLDEN CAGE

The fact that the seemingly confirmed bachelor Sir Isaiah would, in 1956, come to marry Aline Halban, who belonged to an aristocratic and very wealthy Jewish family, was not just a surprise to his innumerable friends; it was the culmination of a bizarre sentimental adventure that could provide rich material for a delightful comedy of manners.

When his diplomatic mission ended in 1945, Isaiah Berlin returned to Oxford, to his classes, his lectures, his intellectual work. He was already beginning to be known on both sides of the Atlantic and from that time on began to spend semesters at North American universities, above all Harvard, as well as making periodic trips to Jerusalem. He was showered with distinctions and the British establishment opened their doors to him. And then, well into his forties, sex seems to have made an appearance in his life, in a manner that could only be described as tortuous and academic: through adulterous liaisons with wives of his university colleagues. An irresistible humor fills the pages in which Ignatieff—with great affection and indulgence—describes a first affair, lasting several years, with meetings in churchyards, libraries, corridors, parks, and even in his parents' bedroom. Overcome with remorse, Berlin went to the husband and told him the truth: "I'm in love with your wife." The aggrieved husband dismissed the matter with an emphatic "That's not possible," and changed the subject.*

The second adventure was more serious. Aline was married

---

* Ignatieff, p. 211.

to an eminent physicist, Hans Halban, an Austrian by birth, who had worked on French nuclear programs before teaching at Oxford. She was attractive, cultured, rich, and passionate about classical music and social life, like Isaiah himself. The close friendship forged as a result of these shared interests began to evolve in a "guilty" way. The physicist found out what was happening and tried to put an end to Aline's outings. Isaiah Berlin paid him a visit. While (I am sure) they had tea, they discussed the problem that had arisen. Meanwhile Aline waited in the garden to hear the outcome of the conversation. The philosopher's logic was persuasive and the physicist recognized this. They both went out to the garden to walk among the rosebushes and hydrangeas and inform Aline of their agreement: she could see her lover once a week with the approval of her husband. And so it seems that friendly triangular harmony persisted until Hans Halban had to return to Paris. Then the couple decided to divorce and Isaiah and Aline were free to marry. The marriage was a very happy one. In Aline, Berlin had found more than a wife: she was his accomplice, who shared his tastes and interests and helped him in his work, a woman capable of organizing life with the confidence that comes with wealth and experience, and creating an agreeable, well-ordered existence in which social life—summers spent in Paraggi in Italy, the music festivals at Salzburg, Pesaro, and Glyndebourne, the dinners and outings with distinguished people—coexisted with the mornings and afternoons spent reading and editing his essays.

THE HEDGEHOG AND THE FOX

Among the preserved fragments from the Greek poet Archilochus, there is a line that says: "The fox knows many things, but the hedgehog knows one big thing." This formula, according to Isaiah Berlin, can serve to isolate two kinds of people, artists and human beings in general. There are those who possess a central, systematized vision of life, an organizing principle that makes sense of, and assembles into a structure, historical events and everyday actions, the individual and society. There are others who have a scattered and multiple view of reality and of men and women, which they do not form into a coherent explanation or order because they see the world as complex and diverse, where specific acts or events might have their own logic and coherence, but where the whole is tumultuous, contradictory, and ungraspable. The first of these is a "centripetal" view, the latter a "centrifugal" view. Dante, Plato, Hegel, Dostoyevsky, Nietzsche, and Proust are, according to Berlin, hedgehogs. And the foxes are Shakespeare, Aristotle, Montaigne, Molière, Goethe, Balzac, and Joyce.

Isaiah Berlin himself is, without doubt, one of the foxes. Not just for his open, pluralist, vision of humanity but also because of the cunning with which he presents his formidable intuitions and intellectual discoveries indirectly, as simple rhetorical figures slipped into lectures, or as mere working hypotheses. The metaphor of the hedgehog and the fox appears at the beginning of his magisterial essay on Tolstoy's theory of history and its similarities with the conservative thinker Joseph de Maistre. As soon as Berlin formulates the metaphor, he is quick to warn us of the dangers of any classification of this sort. For these can be artificial and even absurd.

But not in his case. Quite the reverse. Here the metaphor is absolutely appropriate and is as illuminating a way of understanding two attitudes toward life that are present in all fields of culture—philosophy, literature, politics, and science—as his distinction between "negative" and "positive" was for understanding the problem of freedom. It is true that there is a centripetal view, the hedgehog's, that explicitly or implicitly reduces everything that happens and everything that is to a well-wrought nucleus of ideas, through which the chaos of life becomes order and the opacity of things becomes transparent. This outlook has been based at times on faith, as in the case of Saint Augustine or Saint Thomas, and in other instances on reason, as in the work of the Marquis de Sade, Marx, or Freud. And despite the very great differences in form, content, and intention (and, of course, in talent) among these writers, there is a kinship among them. This is, above all else, their all-encompassing viewpoint, a universal organizing principle that allows them to identify and structure all experiences. This principle, this key—grace, the unconscious, sin, the social relations of production, desire—offers the general structure that underpins life and also the framework within which men and women develop, suffer, or find pleasure, as well as offering an explanation of why and how they act in this way. In the outlook of the hedgehog, chance, accident, and arbitrary events disappear from the world or are given such marginal status as to become insignificant.

Unlike this world in which generalities are the norm, the fox is confined to the particular. For the fox, the "general" does not exist: there are only particular cases, so many and so diverse that bringing them together does not lead to any significant unity but rather to dizzying confusion, a magma of contradictions. The literary examples that Berlin provides, Shakespeare and Balzac, are typical. The work of both these writers offers an extraordinary throng of individuals who bear no resemblance to one another in terms of their private intentions or their public actions, a vast panoply of different behaviors and moral outlook, of human possibilities. Critics who try to identify "constants" in these worlds and offer a unifying vision of their characters and their lives leave us with the distinct impression that they are impoverishing or betraying Shakespeare and Balzac. For these writers did not have *one* single viewpoint but several, contradictory viewpoints.

Whether it is disguised or explicit, in every hedgehog there is a fanatic, in every fox a skeptic and an agnostic. Those who believe that they have found an ultimate explanation for the world end up barricading themselves within this explanation and not wanting to countenance any others; while those who are incapable of conceiving an explanation of this sort, end up, sooner or later, questioning whether such an explanation can exist. Thanks to hedgehogs, extraordinary deeds have been undertaken—discoveries, conquests, revolutions—because for this type of enterprise one needs, almost visibly, the zeal and heroism that the centripetal, teleological viewpoint, like that of Christians, Jews, Muslims, or orthodox Marxists, often inspires in its followers. Thanks to the foxes, our "quality" of life has improved, because people who are unwilling to accept that there is a single, unique order, and tacitly admit that there are different, dissimilar outlooks on life, find it much easier to accept and, in some cases structure their lives around, ideas of tolerance, pluralism, mutual respect, permissiveness, and freedom.

There are certain arenas in which hedgehogs have naturally predominated. In politics, for example, where all-embracing, clear, and coherent explanations to problems are always more popular, and, apparently at least, more effective when it comes to governing. In the arts and literature, by contrast, foxes are more numerous, but not so much in sciences, where they remain a minority.

Berlin shows that in the case of Tolstoy, a hedgehog and a

fox can coexist in the same person. A novelist with a genius for describing specific details and events, this prodigious observer of human diversity who depicted all the different individual cases that comprise society, this fierce challenger of the abstractions offered by historians and philosophers who endeavored to explain human development in terms of a rational system—Tolstoy the fox—was hypnotically tempted by the ambition of arriving at a unified, central view of life, and achieved this, first with the historical determinism of *War and Peace*, and more notably in the prophetic religious phase of his final years.

I think that the case of Tolstoy is not unique, that all of us foxes always envy the hedgehogs. For them life is more livable. Although the vicissitudes of existence fall identically on both groups, for some mysterious reason suffering and dying are less difficult and intolerable—and sometimes easier—for those who feel that they possess a central universal truth, a gleaming part of the mechanism that we call life, a mechanism whose workings they think they understand. But the existence of foxes is also a constant challenge to hedgehogs, the siren song that confused Ulysses. Because although it is much easier to live in clarity and order, there is an irremediable human facet that looks to deny such simplicity and, quite often, seeks out the shadows and disorder.

HEROES OF OUR TIME

What influence does the individual have in history? Are the great collective events, the development of humanity, the result of impersonal forces, of social mechanisms over which isolated people have little or no influence? Or, by contrast, is everything that happens fundamentally the result of the vision, the genius, the fantasy, and the exploits of particular men and women, as Carlyle argued? These are the questions that Isaiah Berlin addresses in the essays collected in *Personal Impressions* (1980).

The book contains fourteen texts, written between 1948 and 1980, mainly in praise of politicians, academics, and writers, penned to be read at university events or published in journals. Despite their occasional nature and the fact that some were written to fulfill an obligation, they are all elegant and intelligent, displaying the vast erudition and the stimulating insights of his most wide-ranging essays. As a whole they comprise a gallery of representative figures whom Berlin considered to be the most admirable and worthy of respect of his contemporaries, his personal anthology of heroes of our time. The most immediate impression the reader takes from this curious and sometimes unexpected fellowship where celebrities like Churchill and Pasternak rub shoulders with unknown Oxford bibliophiles—is that one can say of Berlin what Einstein, one of his models, was reputed to have thought: that if we are going to pay homage to certain individuals, it should be to those who have achieved something important in the field of knowledge and culture rather than in the areas of conquest and power.

Between the individualist, romantic view of history and the collectivist, abstract view of positivism and socialism, Berlin prefers the former although, as always, his argument is nuanced because, for him, any rigidly unilateral position is unthinkable. He does not deny that there are "objective forces" in social processes. But there is no doubt, as his chapters on Churchill, Roosevelt, and Weizmann make explicit, that, in his opinion, the intervention of individuals—leaders, ideologues—in history is both fundamental and decisive. And that these individuals can push these "objective forces" into the background, often shaping the development of a people, modeling their behavior, their intentions, and instilling in them the energy, determination, and the spirit of sacrifice to defend certain causes and bring about specific policies. The formidable and, for a long time, the solitary resistance of the British against Nazism would not have been the same without Churchill. The New Deal in the United States, that great social experiment in interventionist politics, would not have been what it was without Roosevelt, and modern Zionism and the creation of the State of Israel would not have taken the form they did without Chaim Weizmann. We could also add the remarkable case of Nelson Mandela in bringing about peaceful change in South Africa.

Isaiah Berlin is only too aware how warped the concept of the hero in history has become, the demagogy that surrounds it, from Carlyle's study to the justification of absolute leaders who are seen to personify their people, like Hitler, Stalin, Franco, Mussolini, Mao, and so many other little demigods of our time. It is precisely his convinced anti-totalitarianism that leads him to emphasize that these three "heroes" are admirable for the most part because, although they were great men with an extraordinary ability to influence their fellow citizens and provoke changes in society, they always acted within a democratic framework and the constraints of law, tolerant of criticism and obedient to the ballot box. It is this shared quality of leaders who are respectful of law and liberty that, for Berlin, unites the conservative Churchill, the democrat Roosevelt, and the liberal Weizmann over and above their doctrinal differences.

But history is not just made up of politicians and does not draw merely on objective facts. In Berlin's civil pantheon, scholars, thinkers, teachers—that is, all those who produce, criticize, or disseminate ideas—are given a privileged position. As in his other books we see here clearly Berlin's conviction that these people are the driving force of life, the backdrop on which all social events are inscribed, and the key for understanding both outer reality and inner lives. That is why he expresses unreserved enthusiasm for those like Einstein, who radically transformed our understanding of the physical world, or like Aldous Huxley, Maurice Bowra, and the poets Anna Akhmatova and Boris Pasternak, who spiritually enriched the time they lived in, questioning established intellectual values and exploring new critical issues, or creating works whose beauty and depth give pleasure and understanding to us all.

Isaiah Berlin was a moralist as well as a convinced rationalist. Although he did not say this in so many words, it is clear from his glowing portraits that, for him, it is difficult, perhaps impossible, to disassociate the intellectual and artistic greatness of individuals from their ethical probity. All the people that populate these reverential pages are seen as positive both intellectually and morally to such an extent that at times we get the feeling that the two terms, for Berlin, seem to be synonymous. It is true that some of his exemplary figures, like the historian L. B. Namier, have difficult temperaments and appear, at times, insufferable, but all of them, deep down, display noble feelings and are generous, upright, and decent in their dealings. Isaiah Berlin is so persuasive that, when we read him, we are even inclined to believe that talent and virtue go together. Is this always the case?

THE MAGUS OF THE NORTH

Isaiah Berlin was a democrat and a liberal, one of those rare tolerant intellectuals capable of recognizing that his own convictions could be misguided while those of his ideological adversaries could be correct. And the best proof of his open and sensitive nature, which always contrasted his ideas with reality to see if reality supported or contradicted them, was the fact that he dedicated most of his effort to studying not so much the philosophers and thinkers close to the culture of liberty as to its most bitter enemies, for example Karl Max and communism, the subject of much of his book *The Sense of Reality*, or Joseph de Maistre, the ultra-reactionary precursor of fascism, to whom he dedicated one of his most luminous essays. He had a passion for knowledge and when it came to those who promoted things that he hated, like authoritarianism, racism, dogmatism, and violence, before refuting them he wanted to understand them, to find out how and why they had come to espouse causes and doctrines that increased injustice, barbarity, and human suffering.

A good example of this is the volume *The Magus of the North: J. G. Hamann and the Origins of Modern Irrationalism* (1993), a collection of notes and essays that Berlin had not written as an organic text and that had been selected and edited by Henry Hardy.

What is extraordinary about the notes, articles, and sketches that he dedicated to the German theologian and philosopher Johann Georg Hamann (1730–1788), a mortal enemy of the Enlightenment and a passionate spokesman for irrationalism, is that through the course of these pages this convinced and confessed reactionary appears a sympathetic and in many ways almost modern figure. His defense of unreason—the passions, instinct, the depths of personality—as an integral part of humanity and his idea that all philosophical systems that are exclusively rational and abstract are a bowdlerization of reality and life are completely valid. And his audacious theories, for example on sex and on linguistics, to some extent prefigure libertarian and radical anarchic viewpoints like those of Michel Foucault. He was also prophetic when he argued that if it continued along the path it had taken, the philosophy of the future would sink into an indecipherable obscurantism, a mask for vacuity and inanity that would place it beyond the reach of the common reader.

Where these coincidences end is at the crossroads where God appears. Hamann subordinates all of existence to God, who is, for the German mystic, the single and final justification and explanation for social history and individual lives. His rejection of generalizations and abstractions and his defense of what is specific and concrete made him an advocate of individualism and a mortal enemy of the collective as a social category and a marker of identity. In this sense he was, Berlin argues, on the one hand a precursor of romanticism and what would two centuries later be termed existentialism (especially in the Catholic version of Gabriel Marcel) but on the other hand one of the founders of nationalism and even, like Joseph de Maistre, of fascism.

Hamann was born in Königsberg, the son of a barber-surgeon, into a pietist Lutheran family and his childhood was spent among religious and stoic people whose forebears mistrusted books and intellectual life. He, by contrast, was a voracious reader and he managed to get into university, where he studied a broad, somewhat extravagant, range of topics—history, geography, mathematics, Hebrew, and theology—as well as learning French and writing poetry in his own time. He began to earn his living as a tutor of the sons of the prosperous local bourgeoisie and for a time seemed seduced by ideas that were coming out of France: Voltaire and Montesquieu. But not long after, during a stay in London where he was linked to a mysterious political conspiracy, and after several months of dissipation and excess that bankrupted him, he experienced the crisis that would change his life.

It happened in 1757. Living in poverty, isolated from the world, he buried himself in the study of the Bible, convinced, he wrote later, that the sacred book of Christianity was "an allegory of the inner history of the soul of each individual man." He came out of this experience transformed into the solitary and argumentative conservative and reactionary who, in a series of polemical pamphlets, like a combination of punches, fiercely criticized all manifestations of modernity wherever it might appear: in science, in customs, in political life, and, above all, in religion. He had returned, and with burning zeal, to the Lutheran Protestantism of his ancestors. He made enemies everywhere due to his intractable nature. He also picked quarrels with people who admired him and wanted to help him, like Kant, who read him and tried to get him a post at the university. Hamann called Kant "a nice little homunculus, agreeable to gossip with but clearly blind to the truth." He never had any intellectual regard for Herder, who was his confessed admirer and considered himself his disciple. It is not surprising, therefore, that he spent his life in almost complete anonymity, with few readers, and in great austerity, since he made only a humble living from minor bureaucratic posts.

After his death, the Magus of the North, as Hamann liked to call himself, was soon forgotten by the small group that knew his work. Isaiah Berlin asks himself, "What is there about him that is worth rescuing today?" He gives an answer in the best chapter of the book, "The Central Core." Hamann's true originality, he explains, is his conception of the nature of humanity, which was the polar opposite to the optimistic and rational vision being promoted by the French Enlightenment encyclopedists and philosophers. The human being is a divine creation, sovereign and unique, and cannot be subsumed into a collectivity as happens when people invent theories ("fiction," Hamann calls them) about the evolution of history toward a future of progress, in which science would displace ignorance and abolish injustice. Human beings are distinct as are their destinies; and their greatest source of wisdom is not reason or scientific knowledge but rather experiences, the sum of those lived experiences that they accumulate throughout life. In this sense, the thinkers and academics of the eighteenth century seemed to him to be authentic "pagans" farther from God than "thieves, beggars, criminals and vagabonds," beings leading "irregular" lives who through the very instability and upheavals of their hazardous lives could often reach divine transcendence in a deeper and more direct way.

He was a Puritan, yet in matters of sex, he promoted ideas that scandalized all his contemporaries. "Why are the glorious organs of generation objects of shame?" he asked. In his opinion any attempt to domesticate sexual passions weakened human spontaneity and spirit and, for that reason, anyone who wanted to know themselves fully should explore everything and even "descend to the depths of the orgies of Bacchus and Ceres." However, while he showed himself to be very open on this issue, in other areas he argued that the only way to guarantee order was through a vertical and absolute authority that would defend the individual, with the family and religion acting as tutelary and intangible institutions of society.

WISE, DISCREET, AND LIBERAL

Unlike France, which turns its great thinkers and writers into media figures and popular icons, Britain hides them away and keeps them in the shadows as if, were they to be exposed to the public glare and to the embrace of publicity, their intellectual and artistic achievements would become impoverished. From this diametrically opposed treatment of their famous personalities in the fields of knowledge and creativity, we can draw some conclusions about the elitist nature of British culture and the democratic nature of French culture or, more precisely, about cultural snobbery which, since at least the eighteenth century, has been a very distinctive marker of French life and, the complete opposite, the anti-cultural snobbery that is pronounced in British society.

In any event, there is no doubt that if, instead of taking up exile in Great Britain, the Berlin family had taken refuge in France, the death of Isaiah Berlin in 1997, at eighty-seven years of age, would have seen lavish funeral rites and a fanfare of obituaries like those that greeted Sartre and Foucault. In his country of adoption, by contrast, Isaiah Berlin was buried with the discretion with which he lived and wrote, in the cloistered solitude of Oxford, the university to which he dedicated his entire life.

He was an extraordinary essayist and thinker but his work—so rich and thought-provoking from a political and intellectual point of view—has been very little read outside the English-speaking world. But the reason for this lies both in Berlin's extreme modesty—he was the only very talented writer I have known to give the impression of lacking any of the vanities that afflicted his peers and of believing, very seriously, that his work in the fields of philosophy, history, and criticism were mere *pièces d'occasion*, of no great importance— which was as much to blame as the mania for secrecy and the catacomb nature of British academic life. And yet within this modest, kindhearted professor, with his shining bald head, there resided a very great wisdom. He moved with ease across a dozen languages, from Russian to Hebrew, from German to English and the main Romance languages, and across disciplines and sciences as disparate as philosophy, history, literature, the physical sciences, and music. He had original insights into all these areas and wrote about them with depth, elegance, and complete transparency.

As well as being wise and modest, he was a great liberal. This clearly is a matter of pride for those of us who think that liberal doctrine is the symbol of democratic culture—of tolerance, pluralism, human rights, individual sovereignty, and legality—the flagship of civilization. Having said this, we should add that among the different currents of thought within liberalism, Isaiah Berlin did not agree with those like Friedrich von Hayek or Ludwig von Mises who saw the free market as the guarantee of progress, not only economic but also political and cultural, the system that could best harmonize the almost infinite diversity of human expectations and ambitions within an order that safeguards freedom. Isaiah Berlin always harbored social democratic doubts about laissez-faire policies, which he reiterated a few weeks before his death in the splendid conversation—a kind of testimony—with Steven Lukes, repeating that he found it very difficult to defend unrestricted economic freedom that filled coal mines with children.

Berlin's liberalism consisted, above all, in the exercise of tolerance, in his constant endeavor to understand his ideological enemy, to explore and explain their ideas and arguments often in such an over scrupulous manner that he disconcerted his colleagues. How was it possible that such an incorruptible defender of the democratic system, so hostile to any form of collectivism, could write one of the most impartial studies of

Marx? It was possible and it was also the case that this great enemy of intolerance wrote the best modern essay on Joseph de Maistre and the origins of fascism. And that his aversion to nationalism did not prevent him but rather propelled him to study, with a zeal that one could call loving, the Reverend Herder, the cornerstone of the regionalist, anti-universalist vision of society.

The answer is very simple and describes Berlin to a T. As an intellectual discipline, he said, "I am bored by reading people who are allies, people of roughly the same views . . . What is interesting is to read the enemy, because the enemy penetrates the defences, the weak points, because what interests me is what is wrong with the ideas in which I believe—why it might be right to modify or even abandon them."* Those of us who have read Isaiah Berlin know that there is no affectation in these remarks, that his thought was always being sharpened and enriched through the study of his adversaries.

His intellectual work, which was rich and prolific, was concentrated in essays and articles, lectures and reviews, not in great syntheses, ambitious, organic works, or long-term projects. This was not, as Ignatieff convincingly argues, because he led a dispersed life full of many different obligations: like Borges, brevity and the small scale were his hallmark. In the 1980s, as if to prove those critics wrong who reproached him for not bringing out a major work on a wide-ranging theme, he decided to expand the 1965 lectures he had given on the origins of romanticism (published posthumously as *The Roots of Romanticism*) and worked for many months in the British Library, filling hundreds of index cards. In the end, he gave it

* Isaiah Berlin, "In Conversation with Steven Lukes," *Salmagundi* 120, Fall 1998, p. 90.

up: large-scale projects were not his style. He lacked the ambition, the enormous faith in himself, that touch of obsession and fanaticism that masterpieces require. The short essay was more conducive to his modesty, his skeptical view of himself, his complete disregard for appearing to be a genius or a sage, to his conviction that what he had done was very little in the dazzling firmament of universal thought.

That was not true, of course, because in those relatively short texts that interpreted and reread the great thinkers, historians, and writers of classical and modern Europe, this born essayist—he is similar, in this respect, to another great liberal, José Ortega y Gasset—has left a work that is seminal to the culture of our time and to liberal thought. And among liberals, along with Ortega y Gasset, he was the best writer. His style is as transparent and readable as that of Stendhal, another prolific writer, who dictated rather than wrote his texts, and, quite frequently, the richness and vividness of his ideas, his quotations, and his examples, the liveliness and elegance with which he organized his thought, give his essays a novelistic quality, full of infectious humanity.

Of the authors I have read in the past thirty years, Isaiah Berlin is one of those who has impressed me the most. His philosophical, historical, and political ideas have always seemed illuminating and instructive. However, I feel that while few people in our time have seen in such a penetrating way what life is—the life of the individual in society, the life of societies in their time, the impact of ideas on everyday experience—there is another dimension of men and women that does not come out in his worldview, or does so in a furtive way: the dimension that Georges Bataille described better than anyone else, that is, the world of unreason, which underlies and sometimes clouds and kills reason: the world of the unconscious, which, in ways that are always unverifiable and very difficult to detect, impregnates, directs, and sometimes enslaves consciousness; the world of those obscure instincts that, in unexpected ways, suddenly emerge to compete with ideas and often replace them as a form of action and can even destroy what these ideas have built up.

Nothing could be further from the serene, harmonious, lucid, and healthy view of man held by Isaiah Berlin than this somber, confused, sickly, and fiery conception of Bataille. And yet I suspect that life is probably something that embraces and mixes these two enemies into a single truth, in all their powerful incongruity.

I saw him twice in my life. I have already mentioned the first time, in the 1980s, at a dinner at the house of the historian Hugh Thomas, at which the star guest was the prime minister, Margaret Thatcher. The second time was in Seville, in 1992, at a congress devoted to the quincentenary of the discovery of America. People showered him with compliments, which he accepted with a blush. I had written a series of articles on him, which would later become the prologue to the Spanish edition of *The Hedgehog and the Fox*, in which I committed the major gaffe of stating that he had been born in Lithuania instead of Latvia. "Well, it's not serious," he said, offering me some good-natured support, "because, when I was born, all that was Russia." Thank you, maestro.

JEAN-FRANÇOIS REVEL (1924–2006)

I f we were to identify a notable contribution made by contemporary France in the field of ideas, we would not look to the structuralists or deconstructionists or the "new philosophers," who are more showy than consistent, but to the work of a journalist and political essayist: Jean-François Revel. His books and articles, which are both thoughtful and iconoclastic, original and incisive, were always a refreshing alternative to the stereotypes, prejudices, and conditioned responses that have asphyxiated political debate in our day and age. With his independence, his ability to see when theory stops expressing life and begins to betray it, his courage in standing up against intellectual fashion, and his systematic defense of freedom wherever it is threatened or diminished, Revel seems like an Albert Camus or a George Orwell for our times. Like theirs, his struggle was quite misunderstood and lonely.

As was the case of the author of *1984*, Revel's harshest criticisms were aimed at the left, despite his being, for most of his life, a socialist, and he received his most bitter attacks from that quarter. It is well known that the strongest hatreds in political life can be stirred by one's closest relative. Because if anyone could justifiably earn the title—much debased today—of a "progressive" in the intellectual field, it was him, for he always looked to strip away the clichés and the routine thinking that prevented contemporary political vanguards from understanding social problems, and to offer solutions to these problems that were both radical and achievable. In order to carry out this demolition work, Revel, like Orwell in the thirties, opted for a relatively simple approach, but one that few thinkers today have adopted: a return to the facts, prioritizing life over thought. Deciding the validity of political theories on the basis of concrete experience is revolutionary today, because what usually happens, and this has doubtless been the greatest stumbling block of the left, is the very opposite: determining the nature of events through theory, which usually means twisting the events to fit the theory. Nothing could be more absurd than to believe that truth spreads from ideas into human actions rather than that human actions imbue ideas with truth, for this ends up divorcing ideas from actions. This divorce could be seen most clearly in Revel's time (especially in the countries of the so-called third world) in the ideologies of the left, which stood out as being tremendously unrealistic.

Facts interested Revel more than theories and he never had the slightest hesitation in refuting theories if they were not confirmed by the facts. Our political alienation must be very deep indeed if someone who merely introduced common sense into thinking about life in society—for this is what insisting on subjecting ideas to the acid test of concrete experience really means—is viewed as an intellectual iconoclast.

WHY PHILOSOPHERS?

He was born in Marseilles in 1924 and had filled all the requirements for a high-level academic career in France: École

Normale, graduate in philosophy, active in the Resistance during the Nazi occupation. And he had taught in French institutes in Mexico and Florence, where he learned Spanish and Italian, two of the five languages that he spoke perfectly. His official biography says that his first book was *Pourquoi des philosophes?* ("Why Philosophers?," 1957), but in fact he had published a novel before then, *Histoire de Flore*, that he never republished because he was excessively self-critical. This study along with its sequel five years later, *La Cabale des dévots* ("The Cabal of the Believers"), revealed to the world a formidable pamphleteer in the style of Voltaire, cultured and pugnacious, ironic and lapidary, where the richness of his ideas and his questioning spirit were expressed in a terse and at times incandescent prose. More than half a century after its first publication, this book has retained all its ferocity, and perhaps seems even more ferocious since some of the figures that it attacked, like Heidegger, Jacques Lacan, and Claude Lévi-Strauss have since become untouchable intellectual reference points.

As he himself would later say, *Pourquoi des philosophes?* marked his stormy break with philosophy. And with the French university system and its humanities professors, another of his targets, whom he accused of being very far behind North American and German universities, made lethargic by their cronyism and their ever more incomprehensible and boring rhetoric. This book took Revel out of an academic world where he might have vegetated far from the concerns of the day, and turned him into the formidable journalist and political thinker that we know. His articles and essays, alongside those of Raymond Aron, were a model of lucidity in the second half of the twentieth century, which, in France, was almost completely dominated by Marxism and its variants, which both men opposed in the name of democratic culture. Nobody has replaced them and without them French newspapers and journals seem more timid and despondent.

The word *pamphlet* today has something of a shameful connotation, referring to a vulgar, clumsy, and insulting text, but in the eighteenth century it was a highly respected creative genre, which the most distinguished intellectuals employed to air their differences. Among the thousand and one activities undertaken by Jean-François Revel, he edited for the independent publishing house run by Jean-Jacques Pauvert an excellent collection of pamphlets called "Libertés," which featured Diderot, Voltaire, Hume, Rousseau, Zola, Marx, Breton, and many others. Many of his books can be placed in this tradition, like *Pourquoi des philosophes?*, a settling of scores with the thinkers of his time and with philosophy itself which, according to his analysis, had become less and less readable due on the one hand to discoveries in science and, on the other hand, to the lack of inspiration and originality and the obscurantism of modern philosophers. Revel knew what he was talking about; he had a profound knowledge of the Greek classics as can be seen in his splendid *Histoire de la philosophie occidentale* (1994). This entire book is full of comparisons between what it meant to "philosophize" in the Greece of Plato and Aristotle, or in the Europe of Leibniz, Descartes, Pascal, Kant, and Hegel, and the modest and specialized activity confined often to linguistics that has usurped the name of philosophy today.

The book does not just strongly criticize contemporary philosophers; it also praises some. Sartre, for example, whose *Being and Nothingness* is, for Revel, a profound work of great speculative daring, and Freud, whom he robustly defends against certain psychoanalysts like Jacques Lacan who, in his opinion, grotesquely complicates Freud's ideas and uses them to erect a vain monument to himself. However, his attacks on Claude

Lévi-Strauss are unjust. He questions his *Elementary Structures of Kinship*, accusing the author of being a good psychologist but of contributing nothing, from a sociological point of view, to our knowledge of primitive man. He extends this assertion to all of Lévi-Strauss's studies of marginal societies, arguing that by reducing his entire analysis to describing the primitive mentality, concentrating on its psychological traits, he did not investigate what is most important from a social point of view: why the institutions of traditional society had certain characteristics, how they differed from each other, what needs were satisfied by the rituals, beliefs, and institutions of each community. The work of Lévi-Strauss was still evolving when Revel wrote his essay and perhaps his assessment of the great anthropologist would have been different if he had had a broader perspective on his work.

In 1971, for a re-edition of *Pourquoi des philosophes?*, Revel wrote a lengthy prologue assessing what had happened in the intellectual field in France in the previous fourteen years. He did not correct anything that he had written in 1957; quite the reverse, he found in structuralism, which was in vogue at the time, the same shortcomings and deceptions that he had denounced in existentialism. He levels his most acerbic criticism at Althusser and at Foucault, especially Foucault, who was on everyone's lips following the publication of *The Order of Things* and who had declared that "Sartre was a man of the nineteenth century" and whose flamboyant declarations—"the humanities do not exist" and "man is an invention of recent date and one perhaps nearing its end"—became the toast of the bistros of Saint Germain. (He would soon start throwing stones at the police and denying the existence of AIDS.)

In this text, Revel warned that fashion was dragging philosophy into seemingly suicidal levels of artificiality and esotericism, beginning with the sustained attack of the new philosophers on humanism. But what piques his sarcastic humor the most is the strange alliance between political snobbery—let's say Marxism, or even more serious, Maoism— and the ever more complex speculations of the "theories" produced by the proponents of structuralism that encompassed so many disciplines and genres, which meant that nobody could understand what they were writing about. In this regard, the journal *Tel Quel* carried off all the prizes and its presiding genius, the subtle Roland Barthes, had just explained, in his lectures at the Collège de France, that "language is fascist." The analysis that Revel makes of an issue of *Tel Quel*, ridiculing the pretensions of the disciples of Barthes and Derrida, that their literary theories and linguistic experiments would help the proletariat to defeat the bourgeoisie in the battle that they were waging, is both hilarious and devastating.

In line with the criticism that he leveled against his philosopher colleagues, Revel always sought to combine intellectual rigor with a clarity of expression. In this he went even further than Raymond Aron, his friend and mentor, from whom he had inherited the responsibility of being the great champion of liberal ideas in a country at a point in time when the "opium of the intellectuals" (Aron's term for Marxism) had bewitched French thinkers. All of Revel's books, without exception, are within reach of moderately educated readers, despite the fact that some of them discuss matters of intricate complexity, such as theological doctrines, erudite polemics on philosophy or aesthetics, scientific discoveries, or theories of art. He never resorted to specialist jargon or confused obscurity with depth. He was always clear without ever being superficial. That he managed this in his books is commendable; even more so that this was the main feature of the hundreds of articles that he wrote on current affairs each week for over half a century in *France-Observateur*, *L'Express* (where he was the editor), and *Le Point*.

SOCIALIST AND LIBERAL

In an attempt to discredit him, his opponents often labeled him a conservative. He was never a conservative. In his youth he was a socialist and, for that reason, he offered an acerbic critique of the Fifth Republic of General de Gaulle (*Le Style du Géneral*, 1965) and in 1968 he stood up against reactionary forces in France in merciless fashion (*Lettre ouverte à la droite*). The previous year he had been a parliamentary candidate for François Mitterand's party. He was his entire life an atheist and an anticlerical republican, a most severe critic of the dogmatic nature of all churches, in particular the Catholic Church, and a defender of the secularism and rationalism inherited from the Enlightenment; he developed these ideas with great wisdom and humor in a book-length discussion with his son Matthieu, a Buddhist monk and a translator of the Dalai Lama: *Le Moine et le philosophe* (*The Monk and the Philosopher*, 1997). Among the variants of liberalism, Revel was always close to an anarchist position without ever completely espousing it, as the insolent declaration at the beginning of his memoirs suggests: "I abhor the family, both the one I was born into and the one I founded."

THE TOTALITARIAN TEMPTATION

He lived amid polemics. One of the great scandals was the publication of *La Tentation totalitaire* (*The Totalitarian Temptation*, 1976), a persuasive demonstration—with facts accessible to everyone, but which no one had taken the trouble to evaluate until then—of this unexpected conclusion: that the main obstacle against the triumph of socialism on the planet was not capitalism but communism. It was a stimulating book, because, despite being a merciless critique of communist countries and parties, it never felt like a reactionary essay, in favor of stasis, but rather the reverse. It was an attempt to put the struggle for justice and freedom in the world back on the right path, a struggle that had lost its bearings and had forgotten its goals more through the internal defects of the left than through the power and ability of its opponents.

Revel was at his most suggestive when his analysis focused on an area that was somewhat masochistic: a self-criticism of the defects and ailments that the left nurtured within itself that led to intellectual stagnation: its fascination with dictatorship, its blindness toward the roots of totalitarianism, its inferiority complex toward the Communist Party, its ineptitude in formulating socialist projects different from the Stalinist model.

Despite some pessimistic pages, Revel's book had a constructive message in his determination to present reformism as the shortest and most effective route to achieving revolutionary social goals and his defense of social democracy as the system that has proved itself in practice as capable of simultaneously developing social and economic justice and political democracy. It was a book that was good for us to read in the seventies in Peru because it appeared at a time when we were living firsthand through some of the evils that he denounced. The dictatorial regime of General Velasco Alvarado had, in 1974, assumed state control over the press, suppressing all critical outlets in the country. And yet the traditional left celebrated the move as progressive and just. This was the time when Peruvian political exiles—APRA party members and populists—

were not able to present their case to the Russell Tribunal on the violation of human rights in Latin America that was meeting in Rome because, as the organizers told them, their situation was not comparable to that of the victims of the Chilean and Argentine dictatorships: perhaps the Peruvian military dictatorship might be seen as "progressive"?

WITHOUT MARX OR JESUS

While he was a social democrat and a liberal, Revel also had a libertarian streak that nuanced these positions, as can be seen in *Ni Marx ni Jésus* (*Without Marx or Jesus,* 1970), a book that is both amusing and provocative. He argues, with telling examples, that the most important manifestations of social and intellectual rebelliousness in the contemporary world have developed outside the political parties of the left and not in socialist countries, but rather in the citadels of capitalism, like the United States and Great Britain. The revolution, which had become sclerotic in "revolutionary" nations and parties, was alive, Revel states, thanks to movements like those of young people in industrial societies who questioned the very bases of institutions that were thought untouchable—the family, money, power, morality—and thanks to the political awakening of women and of cultural and sexual minorities fighting for their rights, who attacked the bases on which social life had functioned for centuries.

When he discussed the control of information, his analyses were always apposite, as when he declared that "the great battle of the end of the twentieth century, the one on which all the others depend, is the battle against censorship." He maintained that when the freedom to express oneself freely within any society or institution is curtailed, then everything begins to fall apart. Not only does criticism disappear, without which any social system or organism becomes paralyzed and corrupted; this warped attitude is interiorized by individuals as a survival strategy and, as a result, all activities (except perhaps strictly technological activities) suffer the same damage. This, in the final analysis, Revel argued, is the explanation for the crisis of the left in the world: it has lost the custom of freedom, not only as a result of repression inflicted by outside enemies, but because it has adopted the suicidal conviction that being effective is incompatible with freedom. "All power is right wing or becomes right wing," he argued. "It will only become the domain of the left if it can be controlled. And without freedom, there can be no control."

HOW DEMOCRACIES PERISH

Revel's most successful book after *The Totalitarian Temptation* was *Comment les démocraties finissent* (*How Democracies Perish*, 1983). I read it during breaks at a congress of journalists in Cartagena, Colombia. To escape interruptions, I took refuge on the hotel beach, under some canopies that gave the place a Bedouin look. One evening, someone asked me, "Are you reading that modern Cassandra?" It was a professor from Stanford who had recently read *Comment les démocraties finissent*. "I was so depressed that I had nightmares for a week," he added. "But it's true that you can't put it down."

No, I could not put it down. Just as when I was in school and read Verne and Salgari in math classes, I spent most of the sessions of the congress immersed in Revel's arguments, hiding the book among copies of lectures. I continued reading it on the interminable flight that took me to London. I finished it when the plane landed. It was a sunny day and the English countryside between Heathrow and the city was greener and more civilized than ever. Arriving in Britain always produced in me (until Brexit) a feeling of peace and optimism, of well-being, of stepping into a world where, despite its problems and crises, a bedrock of harmony and social solidarity allowed institutions to function, and for words like *respect for the law*, *individual freedom*, and *human rights* to have substance and meaning. Was all this condemned to disappear in the near future? Would tomorrow's Britain become that kingdom of lies and horror that Orwell described in *1984*?

The reader of *How Democracies Perish* emerges from its pages with the impression that—save for a radical and improbable change in liberal societies—very soon this "brief parenthesis" and this "accident" of democracy in the evolution of humanity would come to an end, and that the handful of countries that enjoyed the fruits of democracy would become melded with those countries who never emerged from the ignominy of despotism that has accompanied humankind from the dawn of history.

A modern Cassandra? Revel, heir to that tradition of polemicists and iconoclasts personified by the encyclopedists, wrote with elegance, gave reasoned arguments, and maintained an attentive curiosity for what was happening in the rest of the world, something that was once a hallmark of intellectual life in France and which, unfortunately, many contemporary French intellectuals seem to have lost. His references to Latin America in this book are surprisingly exact; his examples from Venezuela, Peru, the Dominican Republic, Cuba, and El Salvador are very well documented. All of Revel's books have been heterodox, but *How Democracies Perish*, alongside his usual persuasiveness, irony, and acute analyses, has something that the other books do not contain: an overwhelming pessimism.

The argument of the book is that Soviet communism had practically won the war against the democratic West, destroying it psychologically and morally through the introduction of harmful bacteria that, after paralyzing it would hasten its fall, like an overripe fruit. The responsibility for this process, according to Revel, could be found in the democracies themselves, which, through apathy, unawareness, frivolity, cowardice, or blindness had collaborated irresponsibly with their adversary in forging their own ruin.

Revel mapped the extraordinary growth of Soviet influence in Europe, Asia, Africa, and Latin America and what he thought was the irreversible nature of this process. Once a country fell within its sphere of influence, the Western countries—he said—regarded this as definitive and sacrosanct, without taking any account of the views of the inhabitants of the country in question. Would anyone, in Washington or London, have dared, at the beginning of the 1980s, to have talked of "liberating" Poland, without being considered a pterodactyl looking to start a nuclear war by provoking the U.S.S.R.? Moscow, by contrast, was not bound by such scruples. Its policy of helping countries to "liberate themselves" from capitalism was coherent, permanent, not obstructed by any type of internal opposition, and it adopted many different tactics. The direct intervention of its troops, as in Afghanistan; indirect intervention, through Cuban or East German forces, in Angola and Ethiopia; military, economic, and promotional support, as in Vietnam and in countries where there were guerrilla or terrorist movements, regardless of their ideological stripe, all served the global strategy of the U.S.S.R.

At the end of the Second World War the military superiority of the Western countries over the U.S.S.R. was overwhelming. In the 1980s the reverse was true. Soviet supremacy was enormous in all areas, including the nuclear field. This formidable buildup of arms met with no internal obstacles; the citizens of the U.S.S.R. did not even have a clear idea of what was happening. In the West, by contrast, the peace movement, against nuclear arms and in favor of unilateral disarmament, had gained considerable momentum and influenced large democratic parties, like the British Labour Party and the German social democrats.

Revel's analysis covers the fields of diplomacy, politics, culture, and journalism. His most incisive pages described the effectiveness with which the U.S.S.R. carried out its campaign of disinformation in the West. The proof that it had won this battle, he stated, was the hundreds of thousands of democratic citizens who turned out in North American, British, French, and Scandinavian cities to protest against "Yankee intervention" in El Salvador—where there were fifty U.S. assessors—but who would not have even thought of protesting in the same fashion against the one hundred and thirty thousand Soviet troops in Afghanistan or the thirty thousand Cubans in Angola.

Does anybody in the West, he asked, still think that democracy has any purpose? To judge by the way in which its intellectuals and political leaders, its unions and the press criticize the system from within, subjecting it to continuous and merciless condemnation, it would seem that they had internalized the criticisms formulated against democracy by its enemies. How else to explain the misleading use of formulas like "the Cold War," which was always linked to the West— when it was in this period that the U.S.S.R. gained military supremacy—as well as "colonialism" and "neo-colonialism," only seemed to be applied to Western countries and never to the U.S.S.R. While in the subconscious of the West, notions of "liberation," "anti-colonialism," and "nationalism" always seemed inevitably linked to socialism and to what Moscow stood for.

The problem posed by Revel in his book seemed almost insoluble. The only way that democracy could avert the danger, he pointed out, would be by giving up what makes it preferable to a totalitarian system: the right to criticize, controls over power, pluralism, being an open society. It is because democracy allows freedom of the press, political struggle, elections, and protest that its enemies can easily "infiltrate" it, manipulate information, exploit its intellectuals and politicians. But if, in an attempt to avoid this risk, a democracy strengthens its grip on power and systems of control, then its enemies win again, by imposing their methods and practices.

Is there no hope, then? Would men and women of my generation have to witness the entire world sink into barbarism, full of missiles and computers? Luckily it has not turned out that way. For two reasons that, in my opinion, Revel did not sufficiently consider. The first: the economic, scientific, and technological superiority of the Western democracies. This advantage—despite the Soviet military might—was increasing while censorship continued to regulate academic life in the U.S.S.R. and bureaucratic planning continued to stifle its agriculture and industry. And second: the internal factors that led to the disintegration of the Soviet empire. When one read in those years the works of the dissidents or the manifestos of Polish workers, one discovered that, behind the iron curtain, despite the repression and all the risks, there was a heartening and ever growing love of freedom that citizens of free countries had allowed to stagnate.

USELESS KNOWLEDGE

After the death of Jean-Paul Sartre and Raymond Aron, Jean-François Revel became both the intellectual leader and the moral compass of France, that typically French phenomenon known as the "mandarin." Since I am well aware of his lack of appetite for publicity and his suspicion of fraud in any shape or form, I imagine how uncomfortable he must have felt to be placed in this predicament. But there was no way of avoiding it: his ideas and pronouncements, his stance on different issues, and his criticisms had made him a *maître à penser* who fixed the terms of the political and cultural debate around which his contemporaries defined themselves ideologically and ethically by either agreeing with or rejecting his point of view. Without its "mandarin," intellectual life in France would seem to us hollowed out and shapeless, a chaos awaiting form.

Every new book of Revel's caused polemics that went beyond the world of specialists because his essays went to the heart of contemporary issues and always challenged the totems erected by prevailing fashions and prejudices. The book he published in 1988, *La Connaissance inutile* (*The Flight from Truth: The Reign of Deceit in the Age of Information*), was the object of diatribes and controversy because of the mercilessness of his analyses and the way in which some untouchable figures of contemporary culture emerged from its pages battered and bruised. But beyond the gossip and the anecdotal, *La Connaissance inutile* was read by tens of thousands of people across the world because it is one of those books that offers a salutary lesson to our times through the depth of its analysis, its moral courage, and the ambition of its design.

The thesis of *La Connaissance inutile* is as follows: the driving force of society in our day and age is not truth but lies. Our society, more than any other on the long road of civilization, has access to very detailed information about all the knowledge acquired by science and technology. This should mean that rational and successful decisions are made in all areas of society. But, Revel argues, this is not the case. The prodigious development of knowledge and information, which is accessible to everyone who takes the trouble to make good use of it, has not prevented those who organize other people's lives and determine the direction society takes from committing the same errors and causing the same catastrophes, because their decisions are still being dictated by prejudice, passion, or instinct rather than by reason, as in the times that (with a large dose of cynicism) we still dare to call "barbarous."

Revel's accusation was directed, above all, at the intellectuals of the developed societies of the West. The worst and perhaps most noxious opponents of liberal society are not, for Revel, their outside opponents—the totalitarian regimes of the East and the *progressive* satraps of the third world—but the vast conglomeration of objectors from within, drawn from the intelligentsia of free societies, and who seem principally motivated by hatred of freedom as it is understood and practiced in democratic societies.

Gramsci's contribution to Marxism was, above all, to confer on the intelligentsia the historic and social function that, in the texts of Marx and Lenin, was the monopoly of the working class. This function was redundant in Marxist societies where the intellectual class—like the working class as well—was a mere instrument of the elite or *nomenklatura* that had expropriated power for their own benefit. Reading Revel's essay, we gain the impression that the Gramscian theory of the role of the "intellectual" as someone who shapes and influences culture was only applicable, in a sinister way, in societies that Karl Popper called "open." I say "sinister" because the consequence of this, for Revel, was that free societies had lost the ideological battle with the totalitarian world and could, in a not too distant future, also lose another battle that would deprive them of their most treasured possession: freedom.

If, put like this, in a very brief summary, Revel's theory might seem excessive, when readers immerse themselves in the boiling waters of *La Connaissance inutile*—a book in which the brio of the writing, the steeliness of the intelligence, the encyclopedic documentation, and the flashes of sarcastic humor come together to make the reading a hypnotic experience— and when they consider the concrete examples that support his theory, they will doubtless be shocked. Were *these* the great exponents of art, science, religion, journalism, and teaching in the so-called *free* world?

Revel showed how the desire to discredit and malign their own governments—especially if they were "right wing," as was the case of Reagan, Thatcher, Kohl, or Chirac—led the large Western media outlets—newspapers, and radio and television channels—to manipulate information, and even at times legitimize, through the prestige they enjoyed, flagrant political lies. Disinformation, Revel argued, was particularly systematic in third world countries that were viewed as "progressive," because their endemic poverty, political obscurantism, institutional chaos, and repressive brutality were attributed, as a matter of principle—an act of faith, preceding and impermeable to objective knowledge—to the perfidious machinations of Western powers or of those who, within these countries, defended the democratic model and fought against collectivism, single parties, and the control of the economy and information by the state.

Revel's examples were chilling because the media that he

used to illustrate his argument seemed the freest and most professional news organizations in the world: newspapers like *The New York Times*, *Le Monde*, *The Guardian*, *Der Spiegel*, etc., and broadcasters like CBS in the United States and RTF in France. If these outlets, which have the largest and most professional resources to verify the truth and disseminate it, could hide or distort truth out of ideological bias, what could one expect from media that were openly aligned—in countries with censorship, for example—or which had at their disposal much more precarious material and intellectual working conditions? Those who live in underdeveloped societies know very well what to expect: that, in practice, the boundaries in the media between news and fiction—between truth and lies—tend to vanish, so that it is impossible to know, objectively, what is happening around us.

The most alarming pages in Revel's book show how ideological passion could lead, in the scientific field, to the falsification of truth with the same lack of scruples that could be found in journalism. The way in which, at a given moment, the truth about AIDS was distorted, with the aim of smearing the Pentagon—in a brilliant advertising campaign that was later revealed to have been orchestrated by the KGB—showed that there is literally no bastion of knowledge, not even in the exact sciences, that ideology, with its powers of distortion, cannot breach and into which lies useful to the cause cannot be implanted.

For Revel there was no doubt: if liberal society, which had won the battle for civilization through its actions, creating the most human—or least inhuman—forms of existence in the whole of history, were to crumble and the handful of countries that had espoused the values of freedom, rationality, tolerance, and legality were to return to the sea of political despotism, material poverty, brutality, obscurantism, and naked power that had been, and still continues to be, the lot of most of humanity, then the main responsibility for this would lie within. It would be because this society—and the cultural and political vanguards above all—had yielded to the totalitarian siren song and its free citizens had accepted this form of suicide without reacting.

Not every form of fraudulent behavior outlined in *La Connaissance inutile* was political. Some affected cultural activity, eroding it from within. When many nonspecialist readers like myself have read in recent decades certain supposedly eminent intellectuals of the day, like Lacan, Althusser, Teilhard de Chardin, or Jacques Derrida, have we not suspected that we are dealing with a fraud, that is, laborious rhetorical works whose hermeticism masks their banality and emptiness? There are certain disciplines—linguistics, philosophy, and literary and art criticism, for example—that seem particularly suited to performing the con of converting the pretentious verbiage of certain modish arrivistes into fashionable human science. To confront this type of deception requires not only the courage to dare to swim against the tide but also having a solid cultural background in many areas of knowledge. The genuine humanist tradition, which Revel represented so well, is the only thing that can stop, or at least temper, the harmful effects on the cultural life of a country of these deformations—lack of science, pseudo-knowledge, artifice that passes itself off as creative thought—that are the unequivocal signs of its decline.

In the chapter significantly titled "The Failure of Culture," Revel summed up his autopsy in the following terms: "The great disgrace of the twentieth century was that the ideal of freedom was placed in the service of tyranny, the ideal of equality in the service of privilege and that all the aspirations, all the social forces originally grouped under the term 'the left' were reined in and placed in the service of impoverishment and slavery. This immense deception has falsified the entire century, in part through the fault of its greatest intellectuals. It has corrupted, even to the smallest details, political language and action, inverting the meaning of morality and enlisting lies in the service of thought."

I read Revel's book with a fascination that I had not felt for a long time for any novel or essay. This was because of the intellectual talent and moral courage of its author and also because I shared many of his fears and his anger about the culpability of so many intellectuals—sometimes the most prominent intellectuals—in the political disasters of our time: the violence and poverty that always accompany the destruction of freedom.

If the "*trahison des clercs*" could reach the dimensions denounced by Revel in the world of developed democracies, imagine what happens in poor and uneducated countries where social norms have yet to be established. Here we find the readiest allies, the most cowardly accomplices, and the most abject propagandists of the enemies of freedom, to the extent that the very notion of "intellectual," for us, seems at times something of a caricature, to be deplored. The worst of all is that in underdeveloped countries, this "*trahison des clercs*" is not often based on ideological conviction but, in the majority of cases, on pure opportunism: because being "progressive" is the only way to move up in the cultural world—since the academic or artistic establishment is almost always left wing—or, simply, just to do well (winning prizes, getting invitations, and even grants from the Guggenheim Foundation). It is not by chance or by a perverse twist of fate that, in general, our most fierce "anti-imperialist" intellectuals end up as professors in North American universities.

And yet, despite everything, I am less pessimistic about the future of an open society and of freedom in the world than Jean-François Revel was in this book. My optimism is based on an anti-Gramscian conviction: it is not the intelligentsia that makes history. Usually the people themselves—those faceless and nameless men and women, the "common people" in Montaigne's terms—are better than the majority of their intellectuals: more sensible, more pragmatic, more free when it comes to deciding on social and political issues. The reflexes of "the man without qualities," when it comes to opting for the type of society where he or she might want to live, are usually rational and decent. Were this not the case, there would not be in Latin America the number of civilian governments that there are now, and so many dictatorships would not have fallen in the last decades. And so many democracies would not have survived despite the economic crises and the crimes of political violence. The advantage of democracy is that the wishes of those "common people" sooner or later prevail over those of the elites. And their example can gradually take hold and improve their surroundings. Was this not, at the time when *La Connaissance inutile* was published, what was being intimated when we saw, with perestroika, the first timid signs of openness in the totalitarian citadel?

In any event, all was not lost in open societies when they still had in their midst intellectuals capable of thinking and writing books like those of Jean-François Revel.

TERRORISM AND DEMOCRACY

In 1987 a compilation of articles by Revel covering ten years (from 1977 to 1987) was published with the title *Le Terrorisme contre la démocratie*. They all focused on the attacks, the kidnappings, the assassinations and hostage-takings that took place in different European countries, the work of small extremist groups that, it was thought, were disconnected from one another and which, despite their victims and the anxiety they caused, were considered a marginal phenomenon in European political life. It is interesting to read today the virulent attack that Revel directs in these newspaper articles at this naive, superficial, and, ultimately, cowardly outlook toward a threat that would continue to grow until, some years later, it would shake all of Western political life and turn the terrorist into the central protagonist of politics in our day and age.

Almost all the articles argue that, contrary to what was then held as incontrovertible fact—that the terrorist acts in Italy, Germany, France, and Belgium were not connected and were marginal—all these acts shared an unequivocal aim, to attack and weaken democratic societies, and the different terrorist groups and cells were coordinated at a deeper level, aided or operated by remote control by Iraq, Iran, Syria, and also the Soviet Union, through its satellite countries like Bulgaria, East Germany, and Czechoslovakia.

Revel strongly criticizes Western governments for not seeing terrorism as a planned strategy by states dedicated to crushing democratic countries, a way, through terrorism, of eliciting from these countries, help, concessions, and privileges. He also berates Western governments for refusing to work together and coordinate their fight against this devious enemy, in the stupid belief that, by showing themselves to be meek and ineffective in standing up to terrorist acts, this would somehow deflect them onto other countries, thus safeguarding their own. Revel offers many examples of this flagrant lack of solidarity among Western nations, highlighting, for example, the storm of criticism in European countries that greeted the bombing attack on

Gaddhafi ordered by Reagan, who had tired of the terrorist acts committed by Libya against U.S. citizens and institutions in the Middle East. The clearest demonstration that one does not placate terrorism by making concessions, Revel insists in these texts, is that, despite having refused to extradite terrorists captured on its soil to the countries requesting extradition, France had been hit again and again by attacks and killings. From the perspective that we now have on this issue and the horrors that terrorism has inflicted on France in recent times, Revel's words can be seen as prophetic. Revel was one of the few political analysts to sense, from the first attacks committed in Europe by the Baader-Meinhof group, the Red Brigades, Action Directe, and ETA, that this was an antidemocratic and totalitarian offensive against free societies which—due to their inertia, their lack of reflection, and their lack of convictions, which downplayed and disallowed the perspective of the victims— would keep growing until it led, across Europe, to new outbreaks of the most antidemocratic forms of nationalism, and to the anxiety and confusion that have severe consequences for the survival of free societies.

THE THIEF IN THE EMPTY HOUSE

All Jean-François Revel's books were interesting and polemical but his memoirs, which appeared in 1997 under the enigmatic title *Le Voleur dans la maison vide* ("The Thief in the Empty House"), were also good-humored, offering an uninhibited confession of peccadilloes, passions, ambitions, and frustrations written in a light and sometimes hilarious tone by this Marseilles-born writer who found himself, due to the vagaries of life, having to give up the university career he had dreamed of in his youth and become an essayist and political journalist.

He seems saddened, as he looked back, by his change of career. However, as far as his readers are concerned, it was not a misfortune but rather a stroke of luck that, because of Sartre and a beautiful journalist whom Revel made pregnant when he was very young, he had to give up his teaching plans and head to Mexico and then to Italy to teach French language and culture. Dozens of philosophy teachers of his generation languished in university lecture halls teaching a discipline that, with very few exceptions (one of which is Raymond Aron, whom Revel describes in this memoir with affectionate perversity), has become so specialized that it now seems to have little to do with life. In his books and articles, written in newsrooms or at home, spurred on by history in the making, Revel never stopped writing about philosophy but, in the style of Diderot or Voltaire, he based it on a current problem, and his brave and lucid contributions to contemporary debates have shown—like those of José Ortega y Gasset in the Spanish language—that journalism could be highly creative, a genre that could combine intellectual originality with stylistic elegance.

In its depiction of key events and characters, the book shows us an intense and varied life, where important moments—the resistance to the Nazis during the Second World War, the vicissitudes of French journalism in the second half of the twentieth century—mix with rather more bizarre ones, like the joyful description that Revel gives of a famous guru, Gurdjieff, whose circle he frequented in his early years. Sketched with the broad brushstrokes of a deft caricaturist, the celebrated visionary, who dazzled a great number of gullible people and snobs in his Paris exile, appears in these pages as an irresistible drunken bloodsucker, draining the pockets and souls of his followers. These followers included—however surprising it might seem—not just gullible people who could be easily duped but also a number of intellectual and well-read people who saw Gurdjieff's confusing verbiage as a doctrine that could lead them to rational knowledge and spiritual peace.

It is a devastating portrait, but, as with several other people described in the book, the severity of the criticism is softened by the good-humored, understanding nature of the narrator, whose benevolent smile rescues, at the last moment, characters who are about to be crushed under the weight of their own cunning, vileness, cynicism, or stupidity. Some of the portraits of these friends, teachers, enemies, or simply colleagues of the same age and profession are affectionate and unexpected, like his depiction of Louis Althusser, Revel's teacher at the École Normale, who appears as a much more human and attractive person than one might expect from the Talmudic and asphyxiating commentator of *Capital*, or of Raymond Aron, who, despite occasional disputes and misunderstandings with the author when they were both star contributors to *L'Express*, is always treated with respect, even when Revel became exasperated at his inability to maintain a coherent position in conflicts that he often caused.

On other occasions, the portraits are ferocious and the humor cannot counterbalance the vitriol. Take the brief appearance of the French socialist minister during the Gulf War, Jean-Pierre Chevènement ("a provincial and devout Lenin, belonging to the category of idiots who look intelligent, that are more lethal and dangerous than intelligent people who look like idiots"), or the portrait of François Mitterand himself, who Revel was very close to before Mitterand's rise to power, and who vies with Jimmy Goldsmith for the title of the most unusual and deplorable person in the great parade of characters in these memoirs.

Revel depicts Mitterand as a man fatally uninterested in

politics (and also in morality and in ideas), who resigned himself to politics because it was a prerequisite for the only thing that mattered to him: to get to power and to keep hold of it. It is a memorable portrait, like an identikit picture of a certain type of successful politician: outwardly friendly, professionally charming, superficially cultured, relying on actions and phrases committed to memory, a glacial mind bordering on genius together with an uncommon ability to manipulate human beings, values, words, theories, and programs as the situation demanded. It is not just the leading figures of the left who are treated with jocular irreverence in the memoir. Many rightwing dignitaries, beginning with Valéry Giscard d'Estaing, also appear as models of demagogy and irresponsibility, capable of endangering democratic institutions or the future of their country out of petty vanity and a small-minded, shortterm vision of politics.

The most exquisite (and also the most cruel) portrait of all, a small masterpiece within the book, is that of the Anglo-French Jimmy Goldsmith, the owner of *L'Express* at the time when Revel was the editor of the magazine, a time when, incidentally, the magazine achieved a quality that it did not have before and has not had since. Scott Fitzgerald thought that "the very rich are different," and the brilliant, handsome, and successful Jimmy (who in 1997 kept boredom at bay by squandering twenty million pounds in the United Kingdom general election campaign of that year on a Referendum Party that would defend British interests against the colonial aspirations of Brussels and Chancellor Kohl) seems to prove him right. A human being can have an exceptional talent for finance and be, at the same time, a pathetic megalomaniac, self-destructive and awkward in every other respect. The account that Revel gives of the delirious political, social, and newspaper projects that Goldsmith dreamed up and then forgot almost at the same moment, the intrigues that he stirred up, against himself, in a constant sabotage of a company that, despite this, kept providing him with benefits and prestige, is hilarious, with laugh-out-loud scenes and stories that seem to come straight from a Balzac novel.

Of all the many careers and adventures in Revel's life—he was a teacher, an art critic, a philosopher, an editor, a gourmet, a political analyst, a writer, and a journalist—it was as a writer and a journalist that he found the greatest fulfillment and in which he made his most lasting contributions. Every journalist should read his account of the highs and lows of this vocation to realize how passionate it can be and, also, how distorted and havoc-making it can become. Revel refers to some key moments in which French journalism has uncovered a truth hidden until that moment by the "deceptive fog of conformity and complicity." For example, when a gimlet-eyed journalist made an incredible find, among the rubbish piled up outside a bank during a garbagemen's strike in Paris: evidence of a financial racket by the U.S.S.R. in France to bribe the Communist Party.

Another important story was the clarification of the mysterious comings and goings of Georges Marchais, the secretary-general of the Communist Party, during the Second World War: he was a voluntary worker in Nazi German factories. This second scoop did not, however, have the repercussions that might have been expected because, at that political moment, it was not just the left that was anxious to keep the revelation quiet. The right-wing press also kept it secret, because they were afraid that the presidential candidacy of Marchais would be damaged by the revelation of the Nazi sympathies of the Communist leader in his youth, and that his potential votes would switch to Mitterand, which would have damaged Giscard. In this way, rejected by the left and by the right, the truth about Marchais's past was minimized and denied until the matter faded away and Marchais could continue his political career without hindrance, right up to his comfortable retirement.

These memoirs show Revel in top form: ardent, troublesome, and dynamic, passionate about ideas and pleasure, insatiably curious, and condemned, because of his unhealthy intellectual integrity and his polemical stance, to live in perpetual conflict with almost everyone around him. The lucid way he detected the deceit and self-justification of his colleagues, the courageous manner in which he denounced the opportunism and cowardice of intellectuals who served the powerful out of fanaticism or for personal gain, made him a modern *maudit*, heir to the great tradition of French nonconformists, the tradition that caused revolutions and incited free spirits to question everything from laws, systems, institutions, and ethical and aesthetic principles to style and cookery recipes. This tradition is in its death throes today and, however much I scan the horizon, I cannot see who might continue it among the new batch of scribes, with the exception, perhaps, of someone like André Glucksmann, who unfortunately died a few years back. I fear, therefore, that it will disappear with Revel. But it will disappear with the finest honors.

The death of Jean-François Revel in 2006, after a painful illness, opened up an intellectual vacuum in France that no one has filled to date. His death deprived liberal culture of one of its most talented and battle-hardened combatants and left us, his admirers and friends, with an overwhelming feeling of destitution.